Unquenchable Spirit

Unquenchable Spirit

Twenty-Five Years in Pursuit of Adventure

by

Rob Shatzko

Safari Press Inc.

UNQUENCHABLE SPIRIT © 2014 by Rob Shatzko. All rights reserved. No part of this publication may be used or reproduced in any form or by any means without permission from the publisher.

The trademark Safari Press ® is registered with the U.S. Patent and Trademark Office and with government trademark and patent offices in other countries.

Shatzko, Rob

First edition

Safari Press

2014, Long Beach, California

ISBN 978-1-57157-438-1

Library of Congress Catalog Card Number: 2013932766

10 9 8 7 6 5 4 3 2 1

Printed in China

Readers wishing to receive the Safari Press catalog, featuring many fine books on big-game hunting, wingshooting, and sporting firearms, should write to Safari Press Inc., 15621 Chemical Lane, Huntington Beach, CA, 92649-1506, USA. Tel: (714) 894-9080 or visit our Web site at www.safaripress.com.

Dedication

*To my wife and best friend, Collette.
I am deeply grateful for her love, her patience,
and her acceptance of my obsession.*

Table of Contents

Foreword viii
Preface xi
Acknowledgments xv
Introduction xviii

Chapter 1:   The Beginning of the Quest 1

Chapter 2:   Stone: The Start of an Addiction 10

Chapter 3:   Blasting Bullwinkle... 23

Chapter 4:   Upping the Anti-Lope.. 31

Chapter 5:   In the Jaws of the Rockies.. 40

Chapter 6:   My Twobit's Worth 49

Chapter 7:   Ice Age: In Search of the Bearded One 61

Chapter 8:   "Ware" in the World Are We?................................. 71

Chapter 9:   A No Bull-S--- Caribou Hunt..................................... 87

Chapter 10: Another Moose on a Sheep Hunt............................ 99

Chapter 11: The Good, the Bad, and the Billy by Cassidy Caron 109

Chapter 12: Yukon Guide, Part I:
              The Call of the Wild 116

Chapter 13: Yukon Guide, Part II:
              A Sheep, a 'Bou, and an Underwear Bear 127

Chapter 14: Yukon Guide, Part III:
              No Bull Moose Hunting..142

Chapter 15: Yukon Guide, Part IV:
Trouble at Porter Puddle 153

Chapter 16: Dream Dall..168

Chapter 17: Full Moon at Tombstone 178

Chapter 18: California Dreamin'...187

Chapter 19: Introduction by Fred Webb 195
Quest for Nanook, Part I 196
Quest for Nanook, Part II 207

Chapter 20: The Forty-Four Ram:
Opportunity Meets Destiny 215

Chapter 21: Sheepish: A Horse-Hunting Adventure 222

Chapter 22: Fifteen Seconds by Cassidy Caron 237

Chapter 23: A Buck or Two 244

Chapter 24: Sheep against a Wall..250

Chapter 25: Russian Unorthodox by Cassidy Caron..................262

Chapter 26: Into Asia..273

Chapter 27: The Holy Grail 290

Foreword

Martin and I were manning a booth in the old FNAWS show in Vegas or Reno, sometime around 1990 when we first met Rob. Forgive me if I am a bit vague on dates. In those "good old days" we did shows all over the United States and ran hunts all over northern Canada, and just about 100 percent of our clients came from south of the border. In fact, as I recall, we had a policy that until the last American hunter died, or the U.S. dollar came to par, we would stick with our traditional market.

Rob and a couple of friends from British Columbia had dropped by to get some details on a muskox hunt we had donated to FNAWS for their auction. It is not easy to sell muskox hunts in a show mostly dedicated to sheep hunting, so we had lots of time to get acquainted.

As the guys walked away, Martin remarked, "You know, it only cost us a couple of ten-cent brochures, and those boys looked like they could survive one of our Arctic hunts. I hope one of them gets a good deal on that donated hunt."

"Yes," I replied, "that Rob guy especially, the one who let the others do the talking, would fit right in with our guides. I hope he has the money as I know he would have a good time!"

As things turned out, one of the guys bought the hunt on the auction and two others, one of them Rob, put down deposits before the show ended. This first muskox hunt turned out to be a success and started a personal and professional friendship that continues to this day.

Rob Shatzko, in his business life, is a top-notch building contractor from southern British Columbia. He is an expert in all phases of building, from planning to finishing. Whether building an apartment complex in BC or dog kennels for our polar bear team in Kugluktuk, Rob has the strength, the stamina, and the skills to make it all come together.

Somehow he has found the time to become a super sheep hunter, an accomplished horse trainer, an expert packer, and a guide in a Yukon mountain hunting camp; his other hunting activities are too numerous to list here. And he's still a whole lot younger and for damn sure in a lot better shape than I am.

When Rob said he wanted to write a book, I had no doubt that he had lots of ammunition; I just didn't know how in hell he had the time! Now, a few months later, the book is in the finishing stages. I have read it and enjoyed it and am honored to provide this foreword.

If, like myself, you appreciate down-to-earth stories of hunters and guides, horse wranglers and pilots, then you will feel at home with this book. If you are one of those people who wants to glass the other side of the ridge when you're ten miles from the tent and half an hour before dark on a dismal November evening, then you may notice Rob and me back in the shadows.

When we used to run fall hunts in the spruce woods of northern New Brunswick, I used to hate it when some dude started digging out maps and compasses. In my "Welcome to Camp Gentlemen" speech I would say something like this: "Boys, you are going out with an experienced guide from this area. LISTEN TO HIM! You can keep the map if you have forgotten your toilet paper, BUT THROW AWAY THAT GOD#@#N COMPASS! Dark comes early in this area, especially on a rainy day in the fall, be with your guide by dark. If you think you are lost, you are NOT because Coleman or Martin or one of the boys knows where you are. MOST IMPORTANT . . . If you are sitting up there, under a spruce top, with the rain running down the back of your neck . . . if you see someone coming with a flashlight, do not say 'Hello Fred,' because it will GOD#@*N WELL NOT BE ME!"

All hunting clients have stories about their guides and all guides have fond memories of their clients. Rob has seen both sides of the deal. As the disclaimer you see on TV a thousand times a day says: "The following may contain nude scenes and/or coarse language." Enjoy it!

Fred A. Webb
Chase, British Columbia
April 22, 2012

Preface

A preface is usually written by the acknowledged author of the book, but I have taken the liberty to write this one because, as you will see, I had great impact on the final version of Rob's adventures. The first thing I noticed when I sat down to help him is that the title of this book, *Unquenchable Spirit,* forms the acronym US. I discovered this quite by accident, and, I think it quite clever of Rob because, really, this is a story of us, three people brought together by fate or destiny or love to share this great adventure that is life.

"What?" you may say as you read this collection of stories, "three? I only see two, Rob and Cassidy."

But to illustrate how I am a part of this story, I will tell another. Cassidy and Rob and I were riding our horses together on the hundreds of acres of riding trails that are close to our rural property in Canada. These rides are rare because I'm afraid they do not challenge the great hunter-warriors. I think it was Mother's Day, and we were having some "togetherness" time.

Rob was riding a green colt. Cassidy was riding Rocky, the horse she has had since she was a child, and that she and Rob trained together. Rocky can be a bit of a firecracker. I was riding my leopard-spotted Appaloosa, Dakota, who is what we like to call "dead broke."

In no time at all, Rob and Cassidy were way in front of me. Bored, they were soon leaning way off the horses to grab at and break off branches of trees. Then, these said branches were being used to snap the behinds of each other's horses. When that no longer could hold their attention, they started standing up on the rumps of their horses, circus style, to ride.

Dakota and I, meanwhile, were shuffling along in the distance, with me sitting straight up and planted very firmly in my saddle.

I was enjoying the way the light came through the trees, and the forest smells, and the steady clip-clop of hoofs and the shouts of laughter from the two of them. I suddenly felt as if the three of us had been transported back in time, and there they were in the front, warriors between battles. I, on the other hand, was in the back as befitted the scribe.

I have been a scribe for as long as I remember, telling stories before I was old enough to write them. I cannot separate myself from the writing, and my career path has always led me to words. I am a graduate of the journalism program at the Southern Alberta Institute of Technology. I have written government papers and freelanced for newspapers and magazines. I have even written sermons for a sermon service! Then I found what I was meant to do. For the past twenty-seven years, using first the pen names Quinn Wilder and then Cara Colter, I have penned more than sixty tales for the romance giants, Silhouette and Harlequin.

Riding behind my warriors that day, I was aware it is a symbiotic relationship. Without the scribe, the storyteller, the feats and bravery of the warrior are unknown, they fall into the pool of time unacknowledged and unheralded.

I had helped Rob write several of his hunting stories for magazines *(Wild Sheep Forever, Muley Crazy),* and when he mentioned putting together a book, I was all for it, but I didn't know how we would find the time, between his hunting schedule, building commitments, and my book deadlines.

Then we found ourselves with an opportunity to go to Hawaii for six weeks. To my horror, Rob decided this "vacation" would be the ideal time to work, to pen his twenty-five years of hunting stories. His attitude toward writing a book is the same one he has when building a house.

That is, to borrow a phrase from Larry, the Cable Guy, "Let's get 'er done." One thing about Rob? When everyone else is quitting—whether it is on a tough foundation or on a trek up the mountain through an unexpected snowstorm—he's just getting going!

And so I awake in paradise to the *clackety-clack* of Rob's fingers on his new laptop. I shuffle downstairs in my zombielike state, grab a coffee, shake my head at him hunched over the keyboard, his two index fingers poised over his keyboard, straight up and down, like twin sewing machine needles. I go sit on the deck and listen to the birds and watch the cruise ships come into the harbor. I walk and swim and enjoy the sun.

Way too soon, Rob announces he has finished another story.

Generally, the rough drafts of each of these stories run to two or three pages. They contain a great deal of "and then and then and then." They are littered with misspellings, and it is quickly apparent grammar is not one of Rob's many strengths.

And yet, as I read them, there was always a kernel of something wonderful there. The embracing of grand adventure, an enthusiasm

for life, a bold way of living that is largely absent from this day and age. I would take the story, and proceed to hound, harangue, coach, and cajole poor Rob. What did you mean by this? How did you feel about that? What did that look like? What is the point of this story?

Slowly, the heart of each story would emerge. Though we had been together for twenty-plus years at this point, I had a most amazing sense, through these stories, of seeing an evolution, a person becoming who he was meant to be through the relentless pursuit of his dream.

It is not always easy living with someone who has a grand obsession. I am alone for that long period each year that constitutes the hunting season. During that time, keeping the fire going at home and putting out the fires that inevitably flare up in the business when Rob is absent falls on my not very broad shoulders. Though I like to feel there is no neediness in me, occasionally, when the water lines are frozen or I am watching the departing rumps of ten horses who have just stampeded through a fence that you-know-who did not have the time to repair, I feel the faintest niggling of well, yes, resentment.

But a long time ago, when Rob and I were at his graduation from the outdoor recreation program at Selkirk College, one of his instructors took me aside, and this is what he said to me: "I have literally taught hundreds of young men here at the college over the years. If I had my back against the wall, and the enemy was coming at me with knives in their teeth, and I could choose just one of those young men to stand with me? That one would be Rob."

I feel the same way. I have chosen one to stand with me, one to love even when the fences are down. I hope you leave these pages with a sense of having walked awhile with the remarkable man with whom I have spent the last two decades.

Collette Caron
Kailua Kona, Hawaii
January 2012

Acknowledgments

My grandparents, Bill and Mary Payne, are both gone now, but are so much a part of the man and the hunter I became. They were trappers and prospectors in northern British Columbia, and I grew up listening to their amazing tales of how they hunted and lived off the land. I was in awe of their savvy for survival, and I yearned for the life of adventure and self-reliance that they described.

I am grateful to my dad, Nick Shatzko. Though I have developed a hunting philosophy that differs from his, he was still the first person to put a gun in my hands. I can remember being allowed to shoot grouse with him when I was seven years old. Our best times together have always been in the woods. It is also my dad who gave me a work ethic, a never-say-die attitude, that has made every other thing possible.

Every life has a turn in the road that changes everything, and that turn came for me when Tom Milne took me under wing. With his guidance I began to see the world of hunting in a completely different light. Though we never called it that, Tom mentored me. He passed on the torch. He unhesitatingly shared his secret hunting spots, his years of accumulated wisdom, and his passion for a great sport.

Another turn in the road came when I met Mac Blackmore. He scorned the term "horse whisperer," and yet he was the closest I have ever seen to being one. He took me, a complete greenhorn, and put me on the road to becoming a horseman. Every time I am in the mountains with my horses, who load quietly, give me everything they have got, and go about it all with great calm and willingness, I send a quiet thank you to the heavens. I like to think Mac is up there, galloping an endless plain, with his stallion, Dollar, and Dollar's son, Twobit, the best little horse I've ever owned.

Fred Webb opened a brand new world to me by making my transition into the world of guided hunts absolutely painless. Some of my best hunting experiences have happened with Webb Outfitting. Fred is a true professional hunter, one of the funniest people I have ever met, and a genuine friend.

One day, while scrambling around the rocks of the Spence's Bridge area looking for what I am always looking for, a monster ram, I met Bill Pastorek. Bill was a member of the Wild Sheep Society of British Columbia. Up until that point, I had been unaware that there was a brotherhood (and sisterhood) of like-minded people who love the hunt, and want to preserve it. Bill welcomed me into that fold, and we remain friends, hunting buddies, and champions for the cause of wildlife preservation and management.

The greatest privilege any hunter can have is the privilege of passing on their great love of the hunt to one who is worthy of carrying that torch. My daughter, Cassidy, has been that person for me. She not only has embraced the lifestyle, she seems determined to take it to levels I have never reached. At twenty-five, she has taken seven sheep. She has just finished her first season as a sheep guide. She has written for outdoor publications, and I am honored to include some of her stories here. I stand in awe of the strong, ethical, passionate, and independent outdoorswoman that she has become and am humbled by any part I played in that creation.

I also want to acknowledge my life partner, Collette. She is in the background of every story, whether her name is mentioned or not. She has supported me and encouraged me when a lesser woman surely would have folded. At this writing, we have been together for nearly twenty-three mostly laughter-filled years. I have two nicknames for her. I call her Scooter, (my faithful assistant) because as often as not she is dealing with all the "stuff" that comes with running a business and a household while I am pursuing my dreams in some faraway place. But I also call her Dances-with-Words. Without her generous sharing of her gift as a storyteller, this book would not have ever become a reality.

And my deepest gratitude to a man who always chose anonymity over glory, and for the legacy he left that has helped me to find sanity in an insane world, for giving me the tools to embrace the fullness of life, one day at a time.

And a special thanks to Doreen Cardwell for so generously sharing her time to help with the photos and the computer and technical aspects of this manuscript.

And finally, these acknowledgments would not be complete without recognizing the most profound and compelling force in my life: To the Creator of it all, thank you.

Introduction

*U*nquenchable Spirit: Twenty-five Years in Pursuit of Adventure is a story that spans a hunting career that has taken me from bear attacks in the Canadian Rockies, to being stranded on an ice floe in the high Arctic, to standing on the rooftop of the world in the Pamir Mountains of Tajikistan.

I have been both a guide and the guided (including six hunts with a man I am proud to call friend, and who has agreed to write the foreword for this book, the legendary Fred Webb). I have harvested eleven animals that qualify for the Boone and Crockett record book.

More than just a series of stories that recounts a lifetime of hunting adventures, this manuscript reflects a personal evolution. I started this journey as a young man, who hunted strictly for sustenance, and became a man who considers the challenge of hunting for trophy animals to be at the very core of who I am. This passion for the hunt is in every chapter.

I consider myself truly fortunate in having passed on this passion to the next generation, and three of the stories I've included are by my daughter, Cassidy Caron, a staff writer for the *Woman Hunter*.

Whether you are an experienced hunter, or have never hunted at all, I invite you to come enjoy these stories of true wilderness adventures.

CHAPTER 1

The Beginning of the Quest

The birth of a trophy hunter.

"Moose!"

It was an early morning in central British Columbia in the late nineteen seventies. The entire family—my mom, my dad, my two sisters, my brother, and I—was crammed into an old Pontiac Parisian. We had been in Wells, BC, which is close to the famous gold rush town of Barkerville. While my mom visited her sister, my dad had been on a meat hunt with his brother-in-law.

As we headed south, he was grousing about his lack of luck when we came around a bend in the road, and a large bull moose was standing in a swamp about two hundred yards below the highway. We came to a screeching halt, and my dad bailed out of the car, ran around the back, and frantically opened the trunk. Cursing loudly and liberally, he tossed the contents of the trunk out in his effort to find the magazine for his bolt-action rifle. He couldn't find the magazine, but he did find some loose bullets and fed one in.

KABOOM.

Another one shoved in.

KABOOM.

And another. . .

KABOOM.

For every one of the five shots he got off, he fumbled and dropped a live round or two on the ground around the car.

The moose finally collapsed. He had barely hit the ground when my dad started complaining that it was a bull.

"The meat," he muttered, "is going to be tough and probably stinky. I wanted a cow." (Back in those days, it was open season on anything with a heartbeat.)

While he complained, I was running toward the fallen bull. It turned out the moose wasn't quite finished yet because when he saw the tow-headed kid racing wildly toward him, he got up and heaved himself across a stream. He crossed twenty feet of deep, dead calm water, and then died on the other side.

Hours later, after borrowing a canoe, and recruiting my uncle, and two others, we finally were on the same side of the stream as the moose. We quartered it out and began ferrying the meat across the creek. When we were done, I stood staring at the bull's rack.

"Leave that, we can't eat antlers," my father said. But I couldn't. I picked them up.

"If you're going to carry something, carry some meat."

But I didn't. I insisted on taking the antlers, and somehow, in between the sacks of meat wrapped in bed sheets and our suitcases, I managed to get those in the trunk, too.

I was thirteen, and that day that had started so early and ended at midnight represented my family's relationship with hunting. It was for sustenance only. That meant shooting does or small bucks or basically anything that could be legally killed. Just the word trophy hunter used to send my father into a rant.

"Those *blankety-blank* wasteful bunch of *blanekty-blank* slobs killing only for the horns!"

But even at thirteen, by taking the antlers that he would have left, something separated my hunting philosophy from that of my father's.

A dozen or so years later, in 1990, I was now a young man, a seasoned "meat hunter" providing for a family of my own. I had purchased my hunting license and two deer tags, a mule deer and white-tailed deer tag, at least a month in advance of opening day, and I had experienced sleepless nights anticipating the coming hunting season. I lay awake in the darkness mapping out my strategy for the next months. On opening day of 1990, I was on the road well before dawn, filled with eager anticipation.

The Beginning of the Quest

My season was over by three o'clock that afternoon. Done. Finished. Tags filled. Over.

Living in the North Okanagan at the time, I had driven out to my favorite cut blocks in the Monashee Mountains east of Vernon, BC. I shot a spike white-tailed buck in the morning. After cleaning him and loading him in the back of my truck, I drove on for several more hours through more cut blocks until I saw a spike mule-deer buck. I bailed out and shot him. I had him cleaned, loaded, and was back to my home before suppertime. The hunting season I had laid awake planning for and anticipating was over.

This was the problem with hunting strictly for meat and shooting the first legal animal I happened upon. The hunting seasons got shorter and shorter each year. Lying awake, again, that night, I thought there had to be something beyond this to hunting. I yearned for more. It wasn't the kill I was after, or I would have been satisfied with the two little spike deer hanging in my garage.

No, it was the thrill, the intensity of the entire experience that I craved. It was the smells and scents and sights. It was the feeling I got when I was out there: connected, part of the ancient dance of man and nature.

There is a saying that when the student is ready, the teacher will come, and I was about to experience a life-changing encounter. Several doors down from me, a new neighbor moved in. It turned out I knew him as he used to work with my dad when I was a child. He was an avid hunter. That year I spent a lot of time at his house talking hunting and looking with awe at the mounts he displayed proudly on his walls. He had a nontypical mule deer with twenty-three points, a giant whitetail, four mountain sheep, and a mountain goat. When I showed him the fruits of my 1990 hunting season, he snorted.

"Robby," he said, "the only way you're going to kill a big deer is stop killing those Bambis."

Hiking into Tom's secret place deep in the Kootenays.

Nothing he killed ever went to waste. He was a trophy hunter, the type of hunter my father disdained, but one who actually used the meat. He also told me that he preferred backpack hunting over road hunting, and he packed his entire camp, food, clothes, and sleeping bag up the mountain and spent several days by himself in the elements. He talked with reverence about the wind, rain, snow, grizzly bears, challenges, and discomforts. His name was Tom Milne, and he remains one of the best hunters I have ever known.

Over that winter, he became my teacher, my mentor, sharing his wealth of stories and experience and knowledge with me. Through Tom, I was beginning to understand hunting as a sport, not simply as a source of meat, a form of harvest not much different from farming.

When Tom invited me to hunt elk with him in East Kootenay, I was beyond excited. I was the runner who had been chosen for the Olympic team, the actor nominated for an Oscar, the scientist about to discover the cure. I recognized it as a pivotal moment in my life.

Armed with Tom's list, I purchased an aluminum external frame backpack, a dome tent, small cook stove, sleeping bag, and some wool clothing. I bought a new Ruger 7mm magnum (which I still have to this day) and a Bushnell Spacemaster spotting scope.

Finally, the day before the 1991 hunting season, I found myself a passenger in Tom's diesel pickup. I was on my way. After an eight- or nine-hour drive, we arrived at the Bull River in the East Kootenays.

On an unmarked dirt road, we stopped at a widened place marked only by Tom's memory. We unloaded our backpacks, fully laden with gear and food, and stashed them in the bush so that no one passing by would see them. Tom then drove his truck about eight hundred yards up the road and parked it. He left no clue to how to access his top-secret spot.

Of all the lessons Tom taught me, this one ranks very high: NEVER reveal the spot. Secrecy is the guarantee of good hunting in the years to come. I was deeply aware of the honor Tom was bestowing

The Beginning of the Quest

on me by sharing his secret place with me. Once we found Tom's very well-hidden trailhead—via several hundred yards of bushwhacking—we began hiking up a steep incline. It more resembled a goat trail than a hiking path. As a greenhorn to backpack hunting, I found it excruciatingly difficult.

My pack weighed forty-five pounds. Though I had worked all my life in construction, was only twenty-five years old, and considered myself to be in fairly good shape, I could not believe the strength and stamina that was required of me. Within minutes, I was pouring sweat, my back was sore, and my knees were killing me. My breath was coming in ragged gasps.

Tom, then forty-nine and a smoker, was moseying along the upward trail nonchalantly. Not only was he in better shape than me, but his pack was about fifteen pounds heavier! Evil thoughts popped into my head: from "What a great guy, my mentor and teacher" . . . had become "That bastard." I would learn later that stamina is something that builds up as time goes on, not something you're born with.

We followed that ribbon of trail into a hidden little alpine basin in the heart of elk country. By the time I stumbled into camp dehydrated, drenched in sweat, and nearly hallucinating from exhaustion, Tom had set up the tent and was sitting back, cigarette in hand, with a tranquil look on his face as if he had just arrived home and was relaxing in his easy chair.

After too short a rest, Tom was ready to go. We headed up into the basin to glass for elk. For the first time I was experiencing wilderness. We were far enough from the road that I could not hear a single vehicle. The air had a crispness to it. There was a sense of knowing we were on our own, in the best possible sense. It was a feeling of coming home to myself, of being independent and self-reliant.

That evening I saw things my experience as a road hunter had never allowed me to see. We were in a bowl, surrounded by the craggy ledges of mountains. There were mountain goats on many of those ledges above us. (The hunting of goats in the Kootenays is on a draw system and we did not have draws, but just being able to see them was amazing to me.) I was intrigued by this larger hunting world, and a new yearning was born. One day, I would come after a goat.

That evening we also saw a herd of cow elk, but no bulls. Secretly, I hoped we would not see any legal bulls. I was aware I had barely been able to pack my own sorry self up the mountain. I was dreading the thought of trying to carry several hundred pounds of elk meat, on our backs, the five miles of wilderness trail back to the truck.

Opening day came and went. Over the next couple days we saw many more goats, as well as many legal mule deer, and elk. We never saw a legal bull elk, which had to be at least six points on one side.

On the fourth day we hiked back down the trail. Our packs were slightly lighter as we had eaten most of our food. Despite the fact we had not harvested an animal and despite the difficulty of backpack hunting, I was aware I had enjoyed this hunting season more than when I had collected two deer the previous year and had been done by 3 PM.

I liked carrying my food and my shelter on my back. I liked pushing myself to my physical limits. I liked living by my wits. I liked having a world open to me that few people would ever see because of the effort it took to get there. I was definitely hooked on this selective style of hunting that was so different from the "whack 'em and stack 'em method" that I had learned at my father's knee.

In mid-November, Tom and I were once again en route to the Kootenays, this time to hunt muleys in another of Tom's secret spots. We were heading into a major rutting area. Getting there involved two hours of hiking through two feet of snow straight up the heavily timbered side of a mountain.

If we got off a shot, it would be in close quarters, fifty yards at the most. That meant moving slowly, looking constantly for anything that looked out of place, and glassing. Tom's rule was we were to shoot at nothing smaller than a four by four.

The Beginning of the Quest

I saw many bucks that first day, including some nice four points. Unfortunately, none of them stood still long enough for me shoot at a range of less than fifty yards in heavy timber. Tom harvested a nice 150-inch-class four by four buck on the first day. We went back to his camper instead of a tent.

The next day I got close enough to a white-tailed buck without spooking him. He was a three by three, and as I had no meat in the freezer I decided to take him. I remembered Tom's rule about only shooting a four by four, and decided that it only applied to muleys. I took him.

Tom shook his head, and said, "I thought I told you to leave the Bambis alone."

I countered with, "Hey, I'm progressing."

I was proud of my deer. It was the biggest one I had ever shot, even if it didn't measure up to Tom's four-by-four rule.

Over the next two days I continued to see and spook many good four-by-four muley bucks. Though I saw up to ten good four-point bucks every day, I was finding out becoming good at this kind of hunting was hard work. Now, of course, I know it is a lifelong process of learning the virtues of patience and stealth.

The year 1991 proved not to be my most abundant hunting season as I harvested only that one whitetail, but when I look back, I mark it in my mind as my most successful hunting season ever. It was the turning point, for that season changed how I would hunt for the rest of my life. It was the year I had begun the metamorphosis from meat hunter to trophy hunter.

And in hindsight, I wouldn't change a thing.

CHAPTER 2

Stone: The Start of an Addiction

"A cliffhanger of a sheep hunt changes the course of a life forever."

Just another fifteen minutes up the mountain and I would be putting the cross hairs on my first full-curl Stone ram, I said to myself. The seeds for this hunt had been planted the year before during an elk hunt in East Kootenay.

My friend and mentor, Tom Milne, had been a longtime sheep hunter, and on that elk hunt, as we sat around the campfire lamenting the lack of game, Tom had begun to wax poetic about the abundance of sheep in the north. After our return, we had brightened long winter months in the "no-hunting" zone excitedly planning a trip.

Now, in mid-August of 1991, Tom and I were in Dease Lake, British Columbia. I was embarking on a series of firsts. I had never hunted a Stone sheep, never been on a fly-in hunt, and never been this far north. The truth is, that as we started out, getting a sheep was not my top priority. I was more interested in getting a caribou or a goat. In fact, it had been difficult for Tom to get me to part with the fifty dollars to buy a sheep tag!

We flew from Dease Lake on a clear sunny morning, destined for somewhere in the Cassiar Mountains. As the pilot loaded the plane with all our gear he said, "Are you sure you are not moose hunters? Usually two sheep hunters have two packs and a box of groceries. You guys have enough stuff to feed an army."

Tom grunted disdainfully. "Thanks, but no thanks. I've been on those kinds of trips. When I come out of the mountains, I want to have a base camp that is like a hotel."

During the flight Tom tried to pry it out of the pilot about whether or not there were sheep at the lake.

The pilot replied, "Don't know," unapologetically. In fact, after the comment on our gear, the pilot probably didn't say more than ten words the whole flight.

Rob preparing for his first fly-in hunt.

After landing, we set up our base camp, the Wilderness Hilton, as christened by Tom. We had a six-man, freestanding dome tent, cots and foamies, lawn chairs, and a folding kitchen table. It looked like a permanent camp, and it took most of the day to get everything set up. Overdone? Definitely. But later I would be more than grateful for all the effort expended that first day.

The next day we set out for the alpine. My pack felt like it outweighed me by ten pounds. Tom, who was close to fifty years old then, assured me our packs (his was an old Trapper Nelson) weighed less than fifty pounds.

There was no trail to follow, so we went straight up through alders and windfalls. Our progress was painfully slow and extremely difficult. I was still very much a greenhorn, not just at sheep hunting, but at backpack hunting.

This was only my second backpack hunt. I was a guy who had not wanted to spend fifty bucks on a tag, and I had been even less eager to spend good money on a pack. The pack I had purchased was so cheap the frame bent in and pushed on my back. Add lack of experience with organizing items within the pack meant I had hard stuff jabbing me and digging into the small of my back. The weight shifted and was unbalanced. The shoulder straps dug mercilessly into my shoulders. Moving was pure torture.

When we finally reached the subalpine, about four hours later, Tom had outdistanced me considerably, which was as embarrassing as it had been the year before on our elk hunt. I was more than twenty years younger that Tom. I considered myself to be in peak physical condition. I was a nonsmoker.

As I pulled myself up and over the final heap of rocks and lay there gasping in a defeated heap, I saw Tom. He was stretched out on his back, blowing contented smoke rings at the sky. "What took you, Robby?" he drawled, not the least winded.

So much for the theory about smokers being short-winded. At this point, I was seriously considering taking it up.

"Tom," I gasped, "You'd make a great ad for the Marlborough Man."

Without giving me a chance to catch my breath, Tom put out his smoke and was off again. Two hours later we reached the edge of the alpine and set up a spike camp.

During our first few days, we covered a lot of country. My pack was lighter, and I was getting better at balancing it. I was toughening up, too. I couldn't let an old man put me to shame!

The hunt consisted of about 75 percent glassing and about 25 percent walking. We saw neither sheep nor goats. There were caribou sightings aplenty, but Tom, who had hunted caribou before, told me that amongst the ones we were seeing there was none of trophy quality.

I was amazed at how curious the caribou were. We had caribou come right up to us with their funny slow-motion gait. They'd look us

Stone: The Start of an Addiction

over with wild-eyed curiosity and then bound off at full speed, only to stop and run back up to us for a second look.

On one occasion, a caribou even came into our campfire for a closer look. He hung around camp for about five minutes. He cocked his head, stared, and then shook his rack in bewilderment at these weird two-legged beasts that had invaded his territory. Finally, he seemed to arrive at the conclusion we weren't worth his time and left.

It was the fourth morning at our spike camp when we spotted our first goat. He was right on the skyline on the cliffs above our small dome tent. It was a lone goat, and his horns looked pretty good, so we decided to stalk it.

Tom was not interested in taking it, as he had taken five goats over the years. It took us six hours of arduous climbing up a grass and talus slope. Even with the lighter packs, Tom was well ahead of me. We lost sight of the goat as we made our way over and through a little dip right before the final climb.

We belly crawled the last twenty yards and peeked over a large rock. The goat was gone. He was nowhere to be found. In total exhaustion, I fell asleep on the side of the mountain. I awoke to Tom gently snoring beside me, and the goat feeding about four hundred yards above me. Although not a record book animal, it would be my first goat. It was also the first time I'd spotted an animal before Tom!

The billy fed its way along a ledge and then over onto a nice level grassy knoll. Tom, who was awake by now, whispered to me to wait until we were out of the goat's line of vision so that we could sneak up on him. This took another hour. I waited impatiently as the tension mounted.

Finally, the billy moved to a place where he would not be able to see us, and we were able to stalk to within a hundred and fifty yards. The goat spotted us, and as he turned to face us, I saw that every muscle in his body was tensed to bolt. I aimed for his chest and squeezed the trigger. Although the goat took the bullet straight in the lungs, it still had enough energy to leap off the cliff.

"Oh," Tom said, "I forgot to mention goats almost always make a suicide leap if they can. I should have told you to try for a spine shot."

I thanked Tom for the belated advice, all the while hoping that my goat had not fallen too far down. We walked over to where the goat had jumped. To my surprise, the goat lay stone cold dead, hung up on a small patch of snow, less than eight feet below the ledge. Just beyond that ledge was about a two-thousand-foot drop. I would have never been able to retrieve him had he not gotten caught.

Tom was nervous enough about retrieving the goat from where he was. "Robby, are you sure you want go down there?"

One thing I've never been troubled with is any kind of fear of heights. "Don't worry," I said.

Tom shook his head. "Remember you have a young family to think about."

"I'll be fine." My years of working in construction have often put me a long way off the ground with no net.

I came up with the bright idea of throwing a rope down and shimmying down it while Tom held the other end. Tom was sweating bullets—not just because of the physical effort, but with worry. He hated the thought of my being suspended over a two-thousand-foot drop and he being the only anchor. At that time I wasn't bothered in the least, but now looking back with the wisdom of a few years under my belt, I feel a certain level of what-the-hell-was-I-thinking?

When my feet touched the ledge, I quickly tied the rope around the goat's neck and then hoisted myself, arm over arm, back up the rope, which Tom had not even anchored around his waist. He was holding it with his hands. Tom's brute strength was all that kept me from death by stupidity.

Stone: The Start of an Addiction

Once I was back beside him, we both pulled the goat up onto level ground. Tom breathed a sigh of relief and then sat down and had a smoke to calm his nerves. I've since taken a mountaineering course, so I now know that every single thing we did with that rope that day was dangerously, stupidly wrong.

We caped out the goat, deboned the meat, and loaded up our packs. Tom paused before we headed to the spike camp, and squinted down a valley.

"Robby, that looks like sheep country."

But the remainder of that day was spent packing the goat back to our spike camp. That evening Tom taught me how to turn the lips, eyes, and ears and how to prepare the cape for salting. This was a skill that would prove invaluable to me for my entire hunting career.

The next morning, with supplies running low, we opted to head back to base camp for more provisions. Before we left the spike camp, though, that valley that had hinted at sheep proved irresistible. We decided to have a look.

It took about an hour to reach a vantage point where we were able to look into the valley. We had only been glassing for a few minutes before Tom exclaimed, "Robby, I've just found two rams." While they were not legal (full-curl rule), we knew there would probably be more. Within an hour, I had spotted a heavily broomed full curl ram on top of one of the most formidable pieces of real estate I had ever seen.

Tom said, "Good, we have found them. Now let's go get some more groceries and be back here before dark."

On the way down, we found an old guide's trail about two hundred yards to the right of the grueling route we had used to come up the mountain. To make our trip a lot quicker, we decided to travel light by leaving our rifles hanging in a tree in the alpine. It only took us an hour and a half to make it back to base camp. (Because of a few problems I would later have with grizzlies, I would never do this today.)

At base camp, we hung up the goat meat and salted the cape and put it in a sealed container. We were back in the alpine in record time. Being back early, we decided to move our spike camp closer to the little valley, just out of sight of the sheep.

It was just getting dark by the time we were finished settling into camp. We sat down to have tea, and Tom lit a cigarette. A nice bull caribou decided to join us for tea. He wasn't big enough, so we just let him watch us while we watched him.

The sixth day dawned clear, but it wasn't long before the day turned gray, cold, and windy. We could see storm clouds rolling over distant peaks. We climbed the small ridge to glass where the sheep had been the day before, but found none. Disappointed, we started heading back to the tent before it started to rain. We brewed up some tea on Tom's portable stove and sat behind the leeward side of the tent. I'd barely had a sip of hot tea and Tom had barely lit a smoke when he froze.

"Hold it, Robby, don't move a muscle."

On the ridge directly behind me was a ram whose horns curled about four inches above of his nose. He was lying on the ridge looking in the other direction. I had never seen Tom get too excited about anything, but he was shaking.

"In all my years of sheep hunting," he said, with a bit of stutter, "I have never seen a ram this big."

Since I had shot the first animal, it was Tom's turn to shoot. Even if it hadn't been his turn, I would have wanted him to have that ram. We set up the spotting scope, and I sat by the tent, watching Tom belly crawl through the open toward the sheep. Amazingly, that ram did not seem particularly perturbed by our presence even though he had almost certainly busted us by now.

When Tom was within two hundred yards, the ram got up and walked over the ridge away from us. Tom ascended the ridge and crawled up behind a rock in shooting position only to find the ram was gone.

Stone: The Start of an Addiction

Through Tom's spotting scope, I could see the look of disappointment on his face.

He followed the sheep for a little ways but soon gave up and came back to camp, disheartened with what had just transpired. Oh, the highs and lows of sheep hunting! Later, I would have many of my own in my own sheep-hunting career.

The storm that had been hovering all day finally made landing. Rain pounded us, and we retreated to the tent and our sleeping bags to wait it out. When I awoke, about five hours later, Tom was gone. It was still raining, but not heavily. I crawled out and tried to figure out in which direction he had gone. I took my rifle and headed over to the spot where the ram had been lying, and I sat down and looked over the edge. Suddenly, I heard a rifle shot from behind me, toward the tent. Then I heard Tom's voice echoing from somewhere in the basin behind me.

"Robby, I got the son-of-a-bee. I chased him all over the mountain, but I got him."

I still couldn't see Tom, but started heading back toward camp because I figured he was somewhere on the other side of the tent. I got to within one hundred yards of the tent when I heard him bellow again.

"Robby, grab the video camera and the other packboard."

Now, I was able to see Tom. He was no more than four hundred feet directly above camp on a steep talus slope. Through my binoculars, I could see the ram that Tom was standing beside. I left my rifle behind, figuring I didn't need the extra weight. It was a hell of a climb straight up to where Tom's prize lay. The ram had broken one side of his horn off during the fall, but it was still impressive.

We took pictures, set up the video camera and shot some footage, and then got into the job of caping and removing the meat. Tom's quest was now over, and he told me the whole story.

He'd crawled into the tent when the rain started, but couldn't sleep knowing that ram was out there. He told me that I had fallen asleep immediately while he tossed and turned. Addiction to sheep can be a powerful thing. So Tom went out into the rain and sleet and went back to where he had last seen the ram.

He started walking around the mountain and ended up spooking the ram. He chased that ram all the way around the mountain, but the ram was always one step ahead. Try as he might, he was unable to get a shot at him. When the sheep was directly above our tent, Tom finally caught up with him. At two hundred and fifty yards, he took a moving shot and hit the ram, knocking him off a cliff. The ram fell about three hundred yards straight down before hanging up on a large rock. It was amazing there was anything left of him at all.

Once we had the meat, horns, and cape secured to our packboards, Tom sat back to have a smoke. He was looking up at where he shot his ram from and was describing the ordeal when suddenly he froze again.

"Hold it, Robby. Don't move. There's something on the skyline. Pass me the binoculars."

It was another full-curl ram feeding over the skyline! We looked at the best route for a stalk and finally decided that I would have to climb up an almost vertical ravine. Then, I would have to scramble up a large rock knob and shoot from there. Suddenly, I remembered leaving my rifle back at the tent!

"Take mine," Tom said, without a moment's hesitation. "Oh, and be careful. It has a hair trigger."

I began climbing as if I were in some kind of marathon. I had forgotten about the tiring ordeal of the previous five days. I went so fast that I started rockslides. In my eagerness, I neglected to take any water and soon began to pay the price. My tongue felt like sandpaper. My throat burned. I didn't care. I wanted that ram more than I had ever wanted anything before. Just another fifteen minutes up the mountain and I would be putting my cross hairs on my first full-curl Stone ram.

A ptarmigan flew out of the rocks in front of me. It startled me so badly I nearly jumped off the mountain. I didn't even know if the

Stone: The Start of an Addiction

Tom poses with two fine Stone sheep rams.

Tom kills time while waiting for the plane.

Stone: The Start of an Addiction

ram would still be there with all the rockslides I had created and with this ptarmigan I had just flushed. I reached the rock knob and crawled up. Amazingly, he was not more than fifty feet away. At this range, he looked even bigger than I had initially thought!

In my haste, I didn't think to take any extra ammunition for Tom's rifle. I realized I had just the three rounds that were in the magazine. I slipped the scope covers off and slid the safety off. I was lining up to shoot when the gun went off.

KABOOM.

I had totally forgotten the hair trigger. Luckily, I hit the ram. He started tilting over as if in slow motion. I gave him another one. This sent him right off the cliff, which was exactly what I didn't want to happen. I was luckier than Tom, however, because my ram hung up on a rock directly below the small cliff and didn't sustain any damage to the horns or cape.

Standing looking at him, suddenly and without warning, I was immersed in a feeling that overwhelmed me. I knew what it felt like to be a sheep hunter. I knew I was utterly and hopelessly hooked. I knew I had stumbled onto something worth devoting the rest of my life to.

Now I knew why those other sheep hunters were so crazy, especially Tom. I knew that I would do this again someday, and that I would probably dream endlessly of it until that day came.

Although I have harvested bigger rams since, this hunt will always stand out as my most memorable. It was the day hunting changed for me. It was the day a sheep hunter was born. It was the day a quest began. It was the day everything changed.

The next day we climbed the mountain and found the broken tip from Tom's sheep. We packed our spike camp, meat, horns, and capes and headed for base camp. This was the heaviest pack I had carried to date, but for some reason, fueled by my elation, it seemed light.

At base camp we sat for a full eight days of solid, heavy rain. Even with the Hilton, it was a losing battle to stay dry and warm until our plane came. One day, during our wait, the wind blew so hard that it ripped the side of the tent out. We made repairs in the rain while all of our gear got soaked inside. I read every piece of reading material I could find. I even read a copy of the hunting regulations, several times, including all the ads in it. We *paid* our dues in those eight days of misery.

And that's one thing every sheep hunter learns. There are always dues, whether or not you take a sheep from the mountain . . . and the real sheep hunter never minds paying them.

CHAPTER 3

Blasting Bullwinkle

Frustration on a sheep hunt leads to poor impulse control.

The day had arrived. The envelope was there.

This was the day every trophy hunter waits for. Better than birthdays, paydays, Christmas. Better, actually, than winning the lottery if what is inside that envelope is what you have hoped for and dreamed of ever since the day you sent off the application. But just like Christmas, where you ask Santa for the gift that doesn't come, and just like the lottery where someone else walks away with the millions, there is the potential for grave disappointment inside that envelope.

Today you can check your results on the Internet, but back in 1993 the result of the L.E.H. (Limited Entry Hunting) system came in the mail in the first week of July.

With trembling fingers, I tore open the envelope to see if I had been lucky enough to draw in one of the coveted areas of British Columbia where trophy animals roam. Within seconds, the happy dance commenced. I had drawn a Tatshenshini Dall sheep tag.

I had thrown in with my hunting partner, Tom Milne, as a group hunt, so we had to hustle to line up a plane for our dates. This would be my second sheep hunt with Tom, but the first time for a Dall sheep. After weeks of preparation, purchasing tags, poring over maps, we were on our way to Whitehorse in the Yukon. After a two-day drive, we boarded a floatplane that took us to a lake just inside the British Columbia–Yukon border.

This was my second fly-in hunt, which, of course, made me feel like an old hand. There was no anxiety associated with watching the plane go, only a sense of profound anticipation, of life holding possibilities I would not have dared to dream even a few years ago. There is a momentary pause on arrival in a place like this: the inhale of a deep breath of startlingly pure air, the awareness of the rugged

Rob standing on a glacial salt flat.

beauty of virtually untouched wilderness, a sense of yourself being exactly where you are supposed to be.

It is only a pause, a millisecond, before the work of setting up camp begins. Once the camp is organized, there is the rush of locating spotting scopes, setting them up on tripods, and aiming them at the jagged walls and slopes of the surrounding mountains.

To the south, we found three rams right away. Using the full-curl rule, we determined that they were not legal, but it was still wildly exciting to see these magnificent animals so close to where we were camped. It was only the first day.

I swung my spotting scope away from them, and noticed some white spots to the north of us on a gentle alpine slope. Through the spotting scope we were able to confirm that they were all Dall rams, perhaps a dozen of them. Three stood out from the rest, all with tremendously large full-curl horns. Unfortunately, those rams were about five miles on the wrong side of the British Columbia–Yukon border.

The next day we loaded up our packs with enough food to last about four days and headed south. We saw numerous mountain goats,

Blasting Bullwinkle

a few moose, and a grizzly. These mountains were very rugged with evidence of glaciation. There was little vegetation but plenty of talus rocks and streams of milky glacier-melt water.

Over the next few days we saw four more rams, but they were all short of legal. The hopes of success that I had the first day began to diminish. We had covered about ten to fifteen miles per day while looking in every nook and cranny of the countryside. The only sheep we could find were ewes and lambs. We both had other tags, for moose and goat, but Tom, my mentor, was after a sheep. Unless he saw a monster goat, better than the ones he already had, the only thing he was interested in packing out was a full-curl ram.

Being still young and relatively inexperienced at backpack hunting and trophy hunting, I was getting itchy. Though it would be years before I would meet Fred Webb, the legendary Arctic outfitter, I recognized my younger self in his story about hunters arriving with high standards, and by day four having an "If-it's-brown-it's-down" mind-set.

As our food supply dwindled, we headed back to base camp to replenish. Once back at camp we looked south again in the direction of the three rams we had spotted on the first day. Were there more rams in the valley behind them?

Sadly, there was a glacier-fed river between the sheep and us. It was one of those unusually hot summers and the glaciers had melted. That meant the water was probably two feet higher than normal. That didn't stop us, though it should have.

We made two attempts. Fully loaded, we found ourselves up to our waists in powerfully rushing water and so cold it was painful. The water promised to get deeper. We backed off. We moved upriver a little farther and tried again. Fanatical sheep hunters, yes. Bordering on crazy, possibly. But not that crazy. The crossing was simply too dangerous. Mournfully, we backed off for the second time.

Lesson learned: bring an inflatable boat.

Overlooking the river that would prove impossible to cross.

Blasting Bullwinkle

The next three days were spent hunting out of base camp looking over the areas where we had previously hiked, hoping to find something that we might have overlooked. About five miles south of our camp, I kept seeing a fifty-inch-plus bull moose still in velvet. He was always high on a bench and in willows up to his neck. With three full days remaining before the plane was to pick us up, and getting really itchy, I suggested to Tom that maybe we should shoot him.

Tom seemed to consider this for all of half a second or so. Then he said, "Maybe you should."

I'm afraid I was now in the "If-it's-brown-it's-down" frame of mind. I totally missed the tone of his comment, the subtle shift from my suggested we to you. I took his comment as approval, instead of what it was: Son, I'm just going to let you make your own mistakes.

So, with Tom's perceived acquiescence giving me just the incentive I needed, I was ready to get me a moose. I had never shot a moose. The closest I had been to a moose hunt was that day when I was thirteen and my dad had taken the rifle out of the back of our old Pontiac Parisian and shot an old bull right beside the road. Moreover, I had purchased a moose tag before Tom and I left home . . . just in case. The next morning, I told Tom I was going to get that moose.

"Maybe," Tom said, the closest he was going to come to giving advice, "you should just take a picture of him."

A picture? Tom had a good sense of humor! That moose was the biggest animal I had ever seen. A picture simply was not going to slake my hunting fever.

With Tom electing to stay in camp, and only two full days remaining before the airplane came to pick us up, I set off after my moose. I may have even been congratulating myself for the foresight I had demonstrated in purchasing a moose tag.

After a two-hour hike, I saw the moose in the very same spot. He was lying down, sleeping. Something in me hesitated. Shooting a sleeping animal was hardly the picture I had of myself as a hunter.

Unquenchable Spirit

And yet he was big. And I liked moose meat. And I had nothing to show for this ten-day adventure in the wilderness.

I lined up on the moose with my Ruger 7mm Magnum and squeezed the trigger. He lifted his head, and put it back down, done. It was the only time I recall feeling guilty about shooting an animal. That feeling was shortlived when I walked up to him. He was absolutely massive, probably a fifteen-hundred-pound animal. For some reason, the work involved in getting this meat to our base camp had not occurred to me until just that second. In my mind I could hear Tom's laconic suggestion that maybe I should just take a picture.

I spent the next four hours cleaning, skinning, and cutting my moose into manageable-size portions. Finally, I was ready to pack the meat in my external frame backpack. I loaded approximately eighty pounds of meat in the first load and packed it down to the valley

Tom contemplating the river crossing.

Blasting Bullwinkle

floor where I unloaded it before heading back up for the next load. I was still about four miles from base camp, but the going would all be level walking along the valley floor.

Having made that first trip without a problem, I proceeded to pack about a hundred pounds of meat into my pack this time. I made the trip, again, to the valley bottom. On the third trip, I shoved about a hundred and fifty pounds of meat into the pack. I sat down, threaded my arms through the straps, and tried to lift it. Nothing. I threw my full weight into it. I heard a distinct snap. I slipped the straps of my pack off only to discover that I had snapped my pack in half. Again, a little voice seemed to whisper in my brain:

Maybe you should just take a picture.

Necessity is the mother of invention, or so the adage goes. I had gotten myself in this situation, so now I needed to repair my pack and fast. I removed all the meat and took inventory of the tools I had. These included duct tape, binder twine, a knife, and a folding game saw.

First, I cut some branches and carved them to fit inside the aluminum tubing of my now broken external packframe. Next, I cut two more branches and spliced them against both sides of each frame and secured them with binder twine. I wrapped most of the roll of duct around my makeshift pack splint and tried it on for size. After adding some padding (my wool sweater) between my shoulder blades, I was ready to try again.

I loaded my pack—back down to eighty pounds, quick study that I am—and headed down to the now growing meat pile. I met Tom at the site, and he had brought his empty pack and was now loading some meat in his pack. He didn't say a word. He didn't remind me he had suggested taking a picture. But his silence spoke volumes. While Tom ferried back and forth to our camp, I made trip after trip back to the moose carcass. Eight trips and I finally had all the meat on the valley floor. It was around ten o'clock that night. It was after

Bullwinkle and the doomed pack.

midnight before I staggered through the tangle of willows and alders to the base camp. I was too exhausted to go back, or even to eat any of the meat I had been so determined to have.

The next day, our final full day before the plane came for us, was a hellish day of grueling, backbreaking labor. But we got every bit of that meat back to our camp.

When the plane arrived, the pilot eyed my bags and bags of meat and said, "That's a funny looking sheep."

Every hunt gives you something, but as often as not, it's not what you expect. This one gave me two new lessons to add to my growing arsenal of trophy-hunter wisdom:

1) Don't forget an inflatable boat.
2) If you see a moose on a sheep hunt, take his picture. You'll both be happier!

CHAPTER 4

Upping the Anti-Lope

A trophy hunt in the still fairly Wild West.

Though only a few short years had passed, by the fall of 1993, I was pleased with the way my transformation into a trophy hunter was paying off. I had gone from that pitiful one-day season in 1990 to this: arriving home from my Dall sheep/moose hunt in northern British Columbia and finding a letter from the Montana Fish and Wildlife Department.

It was another *"Woo-hoo!"* moment. I had successfully drawn a Montana antelope! And again, I had my hunting partner and mentor, Tom Milne, to thank. He had suggested trying for an antelope in Montana, and being new to trophy hunting, I was game for any new hunting opportunity or challenge.

I took a short break from hunting during the month of September. I had to finance my new obsession with that ugly pastime known as work. Soon Tom and I were en route, in a truck with a camper on the back of it, to eastern Montana. Back then, pre-9/11, crossing the border between Canada and the U.S. was a casual affair.

"Purpose of your trip?"

"Hunting."

I detected the enthusiastic glint of a fellow hunter. "Do you have weapons?"

"Yes."

"Excellent. Have a good hunt."

Those were the days!

Thirteen hours later, we had traveled through thick forests, mountain valleys, and foothills before arriving finally in eastern Montana. It was unpopulated and treeless, the grasslands rolling and seemingly endless. And then, our destination rose up before us, a little oasis in the middle of this prairie desert. Nestled in a river valley, our first glimpse of Jordan was a sign that welcomed hunters and directed them to the community hall.

We found our way to the hall, and considering how unpopulated that whole section of Montana had seemed, the place was packed. Serving tables were groaning under the weight of food prepared by women who knew their way around traditional cooking. There was turkey, roast beef, ham. There were bowls big enough to bathe babies filled with mashed potatoes. There were tables devoted exclusively to mouthwatering homemade pies. The price to enter this all-you-could eat extravaganza was five bucks.

The cause for this celebration? It was the Opening Day Feast, and it celebrated the fact that hunting season was about to begin! Jordan, Montana, was my kind of place!

We ate dinner alongside many of the local ranchers. We were welcomed like long, lost friends; they were genuinely happy to share their corner of the world with us. The conversations centered on hunting, the price of beef, and a strong dislike for the antihunting community.

"I hate bird watchers," one fellow drawled. "I don't allow them folks on my property."

This was my kind of place!

Many of the ranchers that evening gave us permission to hunt on their land. The next day, as a formality, we would get written permission. The permission slips we were given showed which sections of land we were allowed to hunt. This system prevents overcrowding.

There were low fences to keep cattle in, and there were ten hunters for each five square miles to ensure a quality hunt for all. Vehicles were not permitted, which was exactly what Tom and I had hoped.

We were up and out of the camper before sunrise on opening morning, waiting at the gate with the other hunters. It was the guy's equivalent of waiting for Macy's to open on Black Friday. Tom and I, like those Macy's leaders of the pack, were through the gate as soon

Upping the Anti-Lope

as it opened, hustling to get some distance between us and other hopefuls before legal shooting light.

In the regulations, legal shooting time is given to the minute. However, it seemed the air was filling with lead a hair before the appointed time. And once that first shot was fired? It was as though the shootout at the OK Corral had moved to eastern Montana!

The antelope were plentiful, and now, with the air filling with the sound of gunfire, they were running all over the place in pure panic. Neither Tom nor I saw a shot we would be comfortable making.

The length of the shot did not seem to dampen anyone else's enthusiasm. We observed hunters taking ridiculously long shots, upward of five hundred yards, at running targets. In those years, long-range optics (rangefinders were nonexistent) were rare. I think most of the shooters were using the "hold-over-and-hope" method.

About 10 AM after watching the frenzied circus for some time, Tom and I decided to split up and claim a high spot in the landscape for each of us. That way we might have some chance of intercepting the now stampeding herds of antelope.

I was beginning to see a pattern emerging. First, I would hear from three to ten shots. Soon after, from about a mile away, twenty to thirty antelopes would come charging over the horizon. There would be two or three bucks in each herd. I would watch them run like hell to the next piece of high ground where they would stop for anywhere from five seconds to a minute, scouting for their next piece of high ground. Some of them, by now, had their tongues hanging out of their mouths.

Armed with this new piece of knowledge about their patterns, I set out to the closest piece of high ground. About halfway up the ridge, I heard a lone shot from the direction Tom had taken. Through my binoculars, I watched Tom approach his downed antelope. I was glad that our first day of antelope hunting was turning out to be successful.

Once on top of my own ridge, I settled behind a large rock. I heard what sounded like the soundtrack for an old spaghetti Western, someone holed up behind the water trough, repelling a dozen charging enemies. Within minutes of that barrage, I was surrounded by a large herd of antelope. The does, in the lead, stopped, unaware of my presence. They were less than a hundred yards from me.

I held my breath, trying to fade into the rock, as three bucks trotted up the ridge, following the does. By now, I was completely surrounded by does, frantically scanning the terrain for their next place to run.

I zeroed in on the bucks and picked out the largest one. I placed the cross hairs behind his front shoulder and gently squeezed the trigger. At the sound of this new threat, the herd exploded and blasted off, warp speed, for the next distant ridge. My buck ran about fifty yards before collapsing in his tracks.

I approached my fallen trophy with a sense of gratitude and achievement. This was my first hunting experience of this kind. The environment was completely foreign to anything I was used to, but I had read the terrain and the behavior of the animals correctly.

The antelope was beautiful. They are, possibly, the prettiest animal I have ever hunted, if not the most challenging.

I was about halfway done cleaning him when I heard heavy wheezing and breathing approaching from behind me. A gentleman, white-haired and portly, was struggling up the rise toward us. When he finally arrived, he looked at me and the antelope before exclaiming in a very strong, somewhat breathless, drawl, "Boy, am I ever glad he didn't get away. I'd hate the thought of my antelope getting away wounded."

His antelope? I slid the new arrival a look. He nodded, pleased with himself.

"I don't think it's this one," I said. "He looked pretty healthy when I saw him."

"Oh, no. He's mine. I hit him all right. I followed his blood trail right to here."

Upping the Anti-Lope

A happy hunter has figured out how to extend the hunting season.

The only blood trail I had seen was the one that started precisely at the place where I had shot the antelope. I closed my eyes. The day and the hunt were becoming more like Macy's Black Friday every second. Were we going to be like two women haggling over whom the coveted item really belonged to? Not in my world. This was not the way I hunted.

Like the polite Canadian boy that I am, I chose to ignore him, gritted my teeth, and kept on working on my animal. While I did this, he kept up a torrent of chatter. It was rapid fire, and I couldn't help but think it was like his shooting. His rapid-fire bombardment at this herd had managed to chase them over the ridge and right to me.

I made note of the fact there was only one bullet hole in the antelope, with no exit wound. I let him keep on babbling away, and focused on that area. Pretty quick, I discovered the mushroomed out bullet neatly lodged in the antelope's chest cavity. I pulled it out, and upon examination determined that it was a 7mm magnum (.284 caliber) bullet from my rifle.

I interrupted Chatty to ask what caliber he was shooting.

He replied, ".30-06."

"There's only one bullet hole in this animal, and the bullet I just found is a 7mm bullet." The truth is it is very difficult to tell the difference between a .30-caliber bullet (.30-06) and a .284-caliber bullet (7mm) without calipers, especially when the bullets have mushroomed. But I didn't bother to tell him that little tidbit of information, as I was fast becoming very annoyed with him.

Chatty rocked back on his heels, silent for a full three seconds or so. "Well," he conceded, "maybe I missed. My scope must be out." He shook his head sadly. "Boy, to miss that shot, my scope has to be out by at least four feet at a hundred yards."

More likely what he was really thinking was: With the amount of lead I sent in the general direction of all those antelopes, I had to have hit something!

Upping the Anti-Lope

I said nothing; I just kept skinning the cape. After a while, Chatty even decided to pitch in and help me. With meat deboned, cape removed, and everything loaded, I put the pack on my back and began the long trek back toward our truck.

Chatty had attached himself to me. He pretty much never stopped talking the whole trip back toward the truck. By the time I met Tom, my head hurt from all that talking. Tom had his own fully loaded pack, and we met up about halfway back to the truck.

Chatty made the mistake of confiding in Tom that his scope was out by four feet at one hundred yards. Diplomacy was never one of Tom's strong points.

"It sounds to me as if it's you, not the rifle, that's out by four feet at one hundred yards."

I thought it might be the end of Canadian–American relations, but the old guy mulled it over good-naturedly and conceded, "Maybe so, maybe so."

We met a few more Montana characters, including one dressed in buckskins and a cowboy hat that was doing its best to live up to the description ten-gallon. He had an honest-to-God handgun in a holster on his hip.

"This here is my snake gun," he said with an affectionate pat.

As we headed home the next day, we mulled over the hunt. Though it had been different from any kind of hunting we had ever done before and though it wasn't the most challenging hunt, it had been fun. A new experience always has a way of waking up the senses. Both Tom and I agreed we would do a similar hunt again.

When we pulled up to the border to cross back over into Canada, it was late and we were exhausted. I live quite close to the border, so I know many of the officials who work there as they are my neighbors and friends. But this lady was brand new and very officious.

When we declared our unusual cargo, she eyed the skinned-out antelopes in meat bags in the back of the camper and said, "I'll have

Unquenchable Spirit

Rob, future hunter Cassidy, and Tom at home after the hunt.

to inspect them." Tom and I exchanged a look, trying not to look too gleeful.

I opened the camper door, and she went up the stairs and stepped inside. Antelope are not the loveliest smelling of animals, and these two had gotten particularly rank, but she seemed undeterred by that. I pointed to a bag. I was going to mount my trophy, so I had the antelope head, and I told her that was what was in the bag.

OK, so I might have neglected to tell her the head was skinned out. It was a skull with protruding glazed eyeballs and a tongue poking out between clenched teeth. Freddy Kruger would have trouble coming up with something so hideous looking.

I fired my third shot. This time the bullet went right into her head. She fell, killed instantly.

She was five feet away from me.

Were my troubles over? No. I could now see there were two cubs, not one, most likely two-year-olds. One was above me and one was below me. They came at me. They stopped, a synchronized and deadly dance. Both stood up and roared.

I realized that I hadn't even removed my scope cover from my rifle, so I yanked it off now. I had one bullet left. I tried to figure out which cub was going to get my last shot.

I started yelling, and the cub below me turned and ran a wide berth around me, heading up the mountain. The one above me kept coming. He would march in a step or two, stand up on his hind legs, and roar. Then he'd repeat the whole process, getting closer each time. He did this three times, maybe four. Finally, my yelling—or perhaps my choice of words—convinced him to disappear over the mountain with his sibling.

The entire episode unfolded in seconds. It happened so fast, in fact, that if I had even been looking in the wrong direction when I crested that mountain, I probably wouldn't be here today to be telling this story.

I inspected the sow briefly—I knew she was dead, and yet I had to make sure she was dead. I then moved away from the fallen bear and sat down. I was shaking uncontrollably. I dug some more shells from my pack and with my shaking hands making the task unbelievably difficult, I loaded up my rifle in case the cubs came back.

It wasn't long before the other hunter—the one whose pickup truck I had seen at the bottom of the mountain—came down from the ridge above. He called out to me. For once I was glad to see another human being. He had seen the entire thing, but from way too far away to be of any assistance. He said he felt my scent had been carried directly to the bears all the way up the mountain.

"This may sound crazy, but it almost seemed like those bears were waiting for you."

That year there were seven grizzly-bear attacks in that rugged region of the Rocky Mountains. Of those seven, two were fatal. Four were maulings. I was the only one who walked away from my bear encounter unscathed.

The other hunter and I hiked down the mountain. I reported the kill to the local game warden, wrote a statement, and signed it.

"Could it possibly have been a bluff charge?" he asked me.

"I don't know. But I sure as hell wasn't going to wait until she was on top of me to find out."

"Good answer. I think you did the right thing."

"Even if you doubted whether or not I did the right thing, I would rather take my chances in front of a judge than with that bear."

At that point, a normal person would have packed up his tent along with his dreams and headed for home. But it seems sheep hunters are a different breed, some would even say brain damaged, though I can only speak for myself. Brain-damaged as it may be, the next day I went up a different drainage, one I hadn't been up before.

I got most of the way up—I could taste the top of the mountain—when I fell down a rockslide. I twisted my ankle. Within minutes it was so swollen and painful that it felt as if someone was twisting a red-hot blade in it.

The mountains themselves had become an obstacle, as if I was in their jaws, being shaken, being shown how puny I was in the face of the sheer might of nature. At this point, I got the message: Go home. I hobbled and hopped my way off the mountainside.

I rested for a few days, but as soon as my foot started feeling better, the itch was back. This was the year. I had a goal. The mountain had shaken me, but I refused to back off.

My wife, Collette, had been planning on coming with me on one of my forays into the mountains, but after my encounter with the bear she lost interest in accompanying me anywhere but to a condo in Hawaii.

Still, having seen what the mountain could throw at a lone hunter, I asked my friend, Len Smith, if he would like to join me. He had already filled a sheep tag that year with a British Columbia Stone ram, but he was into chasing an elk while I chased my dream.

By the time we got back to the mountains, the weather had soured considerably. There had been snow or rain every day for a week. I suspected the full force of winter was nibbling at the mountain; I knew this would be my last crack at getting a bighorn for this year.

I hunted hard, climbing the mountains while Len focused in the valley below for elk. On the fourth day, I spotted a ram on top of a slide, at snow line. I lay down and set up my spotting scope. After ten minutes, another ram appeared. From my vantage point, they both looked legal. Suddenly, the first ram froze and looked right at me. I also froze and lay perfectly still. It seemed like an eternity.

Then the ram turned his head and resumed feeding. I rolled out of his sight line behind an alder bush. I sucked in a deep breath knowing how close I had come to blowing it. I knew the stalk was going to be difficult because I would have to keep myself concealed in the thick brush all the way up the mountain. About a thousand yards of thick alders separated me from the sheep.

It took two grueling hours of bushwhacking through those alders to reach the top of a cliff overlooking the slide. The sheep were gone. Setting my rifle aside, first I glassed carefully over the top of the slide until I was convinced that there was nothing there. Then, like an idiot, I half stood up to get a better look over the edge of the cliff.

I looked right in front of me. I thought I had glassed thoroughly, but with my naked eye, I spotted the two rams about three hundred yards away. They were both standing up and looking right at me!

Unquenchable Spirit

My heart was pounding nearly as badly as it had during the bear charge! I had to crawl back about ten feet to get my rifle. I looked carefully at the upper ram and felt that he wasn't legal by about an inch.

I waited a good ten minutes for the lower ram to turn his head to one side. He finally did, briefly, but I wasn't convinced that he was legal. It took another thirty-five minutes before he turned his head the other way. At this point I knew he was legal.

Now I needed a good rest for my rifle. I crawled back to a fallen log, aimed carefully behind the front shoulder, and squeezed.

KABOOM.

At first I thought I had missed because both sheep were running up the hill. I held my cross hairs on the neck of the running sheep, figuring my bullet might catch him in the body, and squeezed another one off.

Rob's Rocky Mountain bighorn.

In the Jaws of the Rockies

The ram slowed to a walk as I was getting ready for a third shot. He made it to the top of a small knoll and was wobbling as I aimed at him. The third shot was never necessary. He fell over into the ravine opposite of me. I lost sight of him, but a full three seconds later I heard a loud crash, knew he had hit bottom, and knew it was all over.

It took me a half-hour to get to him and when I found him he was horribly banged up. The horn that I knew was legal had broken off, his nose was ripped, and all his front teeth were smashed out. I was able to determine that both my shots had hit him. The second shot had not caught his body, but hit right where I aimed, in his throat. The bullet had literally cut his throat.

I carefully checked the side that was close and was able to confirm that it was legal by a quarter inch. Now I sat, finally still, admiring the ultimate trophy. This was what had kept me pushing myself beyond my limits. There was a sense of it finally happening: I had arrived as a sheep hunter.

The caping and deboning of the meat took about two hours, and that was followed by a long trip with a heavy pack down the mountain. When I reached the road at dark, I saw a six-by-six bull elk on the other side. I could have taken him with a short stalk, but I was too tired . . . as well as completely satisfied with what I had.

When I arrived at our camp, Len was already there. He was very excited for me. We sat by the fire late into the night basking in the light and glory of past, present, and future sheep hunts.

The next day I climbed back up to the kill site to retrieve the rest of the sheep meat, while Len went after the elk I had seen the night before. On the way back down with the remainder of the meat, I walked into another small grizzly. I had the rifle off my shoulder in a flash. Thankfully, the bear gave way after a short shouting match and ambled off the trail, allowing me to pass. But once again, I was on red alert, for I felt he was stalking me—and my backpack full of meat—as I hiked down the mountain.

When I arrived at camp in the early afternoon, Len was already there. He had been unable to find the elk but was ready to head for home. When I took my ram in for inspection, the local game wardens debated whether he was legal. They finally agreed he was and put the numbered plug in his horn. A week later, they phoned me and asked if I would bring the ram in as they wanted to have a second look at him. This is every sheep hunter's nightmare. The thought that I might lose my hard-earned trophy kept me awake at night. Thinking about it, I lost nearly as much weight as I had during the bighorn hunt.

For the second inspection, the head was put in a jig. Finally, it was declared legal, by—surprise—a quarter inch! Ironically, after a 60-day drying period, the barely legal ram officially scored at 170 4/8 net inches, which puts him in the British Columbia record book.

I've said this before, but it bears saying again: All sheep extract a price. This one had been particularly high: a sense of being shaken in the jaws of the mountain, a bear killed in self-defense, shouting matches with three other bears, a fall down a rockslide and a painful ankle. Finally, I'd been subjected to the worse stress of all. Nothing the mountain threw at me even compared to those sleepless nights of wondering if my sheep would be found legal.

But of course, the question always is, if you knew the price in advance, the toll that this particular hunt would take, would you do it again? As the kids say, "Well, *duh*."

CHAPTER 6

My Twobit's Worth

A little horse opens up a big world of hunting possibilities.

A herd of horses was galloping toward us, kicking up puffs of snow behind them. It was like something out of a movie. The horse in the lead was absolutely majestic, black on the front, spotted on the back.

I was here to make good on a promise to my wife, Collette. She loves horses the way I love hunting. She'd had a horse briefly when she had finished high school, and then she sold it to go to college. She had been dreaming about horses ever since.

And since Collette is that rarest of women—she supports my dream of hunting and doesn't complain about the time, effort, or money I spend on it—I wanted to support her dreams, too. For her birthday I had given her a stick drawing of a horse.

"What's this?" she had asked, squinting at the drawing. So, an artist I'm not.

"It's the horse we are getting for you."

OK, so maybe in the back of my mind I had the thought, *Maybe he will prove useful for hunting, too.*

That decision to get a horse led us to Mac Blackmore, known as kind of a wily old horse trader in our community. And it led to this moment when that magnificent herd of horses, led by the fiery black, was racing toward us.

But it was not the fiery black that Mac caught. No, the horse Mac caught was somewhere near the back of the herd. He was a scrawny looking little fellow, with a mane that stuck straight up in places, and flopped over in different directions in others. He had small, almost slanted eyes that looked distinctly beady to me. He was a dirty-looking white color, with a few faint speckles of dark sprinkled across his body.

"Name's Twobit," Mac told us. "Comes out of stud named Dollar. Quarter-horse stud, Appaloosa mare. He misses being a pony by a hand."

I had no idea a hand was a measurement for horses, but I could tell this horse was small by any standard. But, at barely five-foot-two, so was my wife.

After the horse was saddled, Collette got on and began putting him through his paces: walk, trot, and gallop. At the time I was a total novice. I had no idea which end of the horse to get on, let alone horse terminology such as gaits, tack, or breeds. My earliest horse experiences involved being kicked, bitten, and bucked.

After about ten minutes, I could tell by the smile on Collette's face as she loped that little guy by me that we would be taking this horse home.

"How much do you folks know about horses?" Mac asked, sliding me a look.

"Absolutely nothing," I said.

Mac smiled for the first time. "It's refreshing to hear that. I can't tell you how many people I sell a horse to who consider themselves bona fide experts after watching three episodes of *Bonanza*."

Though Mac scorned the whole concept of horse whispering, he is one of the only true horse whisperers I have met in my now over eighteen years of owning horses. And that day when I admitted I knew nothing, and bought our first horse for a thousand dollars, was one of the luckiest days of my life. Because that day the horse I got was Twobit, though I had yet to discover Twobit's worth.

It was also a lucky day for me because Mac took a shine to us. He delivered the horse (we had no horse trailer), shared stories, dispensed advice, and answered a million questions. Mac Blackmore made the difference between owning a horse being the nightmare it is for so many people, and the dream it became for us.

My Twobit's Worth

I very quickly found out this simple truth: buying a horse is the cheap part of the equation. I had no horse trailer, no barn, no corral, no tack, and no fencing of any kind on our ten-acre property.

The learning curve was huge for me that year. I invested several thousand in a corral and barn and fences. Collette spent hundreds more on tack (saddle blankets, halters, a bridle, etc.) Then, according to Mac, our new horse needed shoes, worm medicine, vaccinations, and his teeth floated.

Collette was riding from the first day, at first around our property, and then around the block, and then exploring the hundreds of acres of trails around our house.

I began to be intrigued, even though I was thinking of Twobit's potential for packing more than anything else. Within a couple of weeks of having him, I was sure I was missing out on the fun, so I decided to give riding a try.

Collette wanted me to try riding bareback first as a way of developing good balance and feeling in tune with the horse. I began to develop confidence as I moved back and forth between a walk and a trot. Twobit was very responsive to every command he was given. Unfortunately, I didn't know which command to give him. In other words, if I leaned forward that meant speed up, pressure from my knees meant turn, and if I leaned back that meant slow down.

Since I had been watching Collette go effortlessly between a walk and a gallop, I felt I should be able to do that, no problem. My wife is a bit of a bookworm, not the great athlete I am. So out in front of our house, riding bareback, I urged Twobit from walk to gallop.

His response was instantaneous. He reacted as though he'd been shot out of a cannon. My response? I lurched forward onto his neck. He thought I wanted more speed! He complied. I could feel myself slipping sideways. For a millisecond I thought I could correct it, but with that sideways slip there is a point of no return.

Unquenchable Spirit

The next thing I knew, great athlete that I am, I was on the ground. Did I mention the road in front of our house is gravel? Full of scrapes, I watched the horse gallop down the road.

After a second or two, Twobit seemed to realize he was now without a rider. He stopped, turned around, came back, and gave me a puzzled look as if to say, "What happened, you klutz?"

After determining that the only thing seriously hurt was my pride and a 16x16 square inch of road rash on my back, Collette suggested I get back on the horse and finish the ride. Frankly, I could have just as easily given up my future with horses right there. But I felt compelled to do the manly thing and try again.

Throughout that spring and summer I actually did learn to ride, even to gallop, and not get unloaded. Twobit had a way of adjusting himself to every rider and his abilities. My daughter, Cassidy, then six, was soon jumping on and off that horse as if she'd been born

Cassidy horsin' around.

My Twobit's Worth

to ride. She and Twobit were soon a formidable team at the local gymkhanas.

I remember one particular gymkhana when two girls on their shiny, muscled up, expensive quarter horses rode over to Cass and said disparagingly, "Your horse is sure funny looking. Can he run?"

Cassidy hunkered down in her saddle, and said, "Oh, yeah, he can run."

Twobit always gave everything he had, but that day it was as if he had swallowed lightning. That scruffy little horse won every first place ribbon that was to be had. With his short, stocky legs, he shut out those girls on their long-legged, fancy-pants horses, and I swear he knew it, too.

In those first weeks and months of having him, Twobit let us know he was lonely. Horses are herd animals. They hate being alone. Every time someone rode by our place on a horse he would whinny frantically and run along the fence lines.

At that point, I had to make a reservation if I wanted to go for a ride. I told Mac what we needed, and pretty soon our horsy family expanded. Our second horse showed up later that summer, a beautiful bay quarter horse named Latigo. We noticed how he soon became Twobit's shadow, and that became his name.

Even though we now had two horses, I still did not have the confidence to use a horse for packing. That fall all my hunts were conducted with a backpack. As a result, I focused most of my efforts on manageable animals that included deer, mountain sheep, and mountain goats. These animals, once deboned, could be packed out in one trip. But if I could figure out how to use my horses, I could go far into the mountains, where few other people could go, after moose and elk.

That winter, I had a few months off, so I approached Mac to ask him if he minded if I came and watched him and his boys train horses. He was delighted by my interest. Thus, at age thirty, my career as a horseman really began.

Unquenchable Spirit

That winter, I became Mac's right-hand man as he trained six green colts. I was there from dawn until dusk every day. We did endless groundwork, halter breaking, and driving. Pretty soon, the guy who had fallen off a horse on his first ride—that would be me—was riding green colts. With Mac's tutorship, soon I had those young horses reining, stopping, backing up, and standing still for mounting and dismounting. And as a bonus? Mac taught me how to load and unload packhorses.

By the end of that winter, Mac no longer considered me a greenhorn. I had a few hours on the clock of what has become a lifelong learning process. My confidence around horses had begun to build.

The spring of 1995 rolled around with new hopes of the upcoming hunting season. In the corral behind my house, I worked with horses, and practiced the packing techniques that Mac had taught me. Still, working in the corral and taking horses into the

Rob with Doug Kepke the day Twobit proved his worth.

My Twobit's Worth

wilderness were two different things. That fall would find me again backpack hunting solo.

That year, I shot a mountain muley early in the season, and packed him out of an absolute hellhole. Then, finally, after three weeks of nonstop mountain climbing, I harvested my Rocky Mountain bighorn. It took me two trips with my backpack to get him out. With each backpack trip, I felt a growing awareness. There was a different way to do this. There were horses at home in my corral.

That year, I also had drawn a goat for the same area where I had harvested my sheep. I had seen several good billies during that time. I found myself on the backside of the mountain where I had shot the sheep, looking at four billies.

I was halfway up a slide when the fog rolled in, and I lost all track of where I was. After several hours in the fog, I had to go down because it would be dark soon. When I was only about two hundred yards above the trail, a bull elk stood up right in front of me. Now my rule, hard learned, with backpack hunting is never to shoot anything I can't get out in one load.

However, the bull was so close to the trail that I figured he would be easy to get out if I went home and got my horses. I quickly aimed, squeezed, and dropped him before I could change my mind. The moment I saw those 380 pounds of meat on the ground was the moment I committed to horseback hunting. I cleaned and quartered him and placed the meat in game bags, but left it there.

I went home, recruited my friend Doug Kepke, a more experienced horseman than me, to come back with me. Hours before dawn the next day we were ready to go. Twobit just jumped in the trailer, eager to be off on his next adventure. Shadow was another story, however, and it took us almost a half-hour to get him in the trailer in the dark.

Lesson: Do not wait until you need your horse to realize loading in the dark is not the same as loading in the daylight.

Unquenchable Spirit

We drove three hours in the dark and arrived at first light at the trailhead. We rode the horses in to where I had left the elk. Already, I was feeling spoiled. *Damn, this was easy.*

Luckily, no grizzlies had found the elk.

Another two hours and we had the two horses packed, the meat tied onto saddles any way we could manage it. We were ready to begin the long walk out. The feeling of being spoiled remained. The horses were really doing all the work.

In fact, Twobit was so enthusiastic that he literally ran me over trying to pack out his half of the elk. It was like he had something to prove to the other much-larger horse.

About halfway out, the trail winds up a steep hill that goes for about two miles out of the valley and into a basin. This is a killer hill for both man and beast. Twobit was such a trooper that he literally pushed me up that hill, nudging me with his nose when I slowed. If I took a break and sat down, he would pull impatiently at the lead rope. I could almost imagine him thinking, *Let's go.*

In fact, that was his attitude the whole time we had him. *Bring it on. Let's go.* He really was a wonder horse, that ugly little appaloosa. Only two years earlier, I would not have spared a horse like him a second look. But now, he was demonstrating his worth in a brand new way. He was the little horse that could. And in those hours when he carried that elk out for me, he was, unknown to both of us, changing the way I would hunt forever.

We arrived at the horse trailer right at dark, and unloaded the meat from the horses. Once again, Twobit just jumped into the trailer without even being led in. He just loved to please his owners. Shadow, on the other hand, was a different story. We had to fight him into the trailer. It only took fifteen minutes this time.

We arrived home that night at 10 PM, a long day, but pivotal. Hours and hours of wear and tear on my back had been saved. The

My Twobit's Worth

ride in with the horses had been relaxing and fun. The pack out had been strenuous, but the horses had carried the load.

By the next year, I was experimenting more with taking the horses. Each year it became an easier decision to make. Now I don't even hesitate to load a half-dozen horses in a trailer and head out. Truth be told, I can barely imagine hunting without them.

As the years rolled by, I acquired more horses. I purchase only four-month-old colts, just weaned from their mothers. I take great pleasure in training them myself. This way any bad training or bad habits are my own fault. I have slowly moved to Fjords, and Fjord crosses. They are small, tough horses made for the mountains. They have a work ethic and an easygoing temperament that makes them a dream to train and a wonder to take on trips.

But there was always something about Twobit. His spirit was mightier than his size. I can remember once wanting to get into an area where spring runoff had made it impossible to cross a river with horses. There was a rickety footbridge, made for people, not horses. It had no railings and it was missing slats. The water was boiling up about three feet beneath it.

I led Twobit across. He moseyed along behind me as if he were following me up from the pasture to the barn. He followed me over that bridge with 100 percent trust. When we got to the other side, he gave his head a shake and yawned. Unfortunately, I was with three other people who could not (or would not) get their horses to cross the bridge.

Cowboys have this word they use rarely. It means an extra amount of try, a never-say-die spirit. They'll say of a man, "He's got heart." My wife's thousand-dollar horse had that. He had heart.

Twobit continued to win ribbons for my daughter. He excelled at every gymkhana event, though sometimes he got a little too steamed up doing the poles and would start knocking them down as if that was part of the game. He loved obstacles: When it came to stepping

57

onto makeshift bridges and over tires, not a horse could touch him. He continued to pack elk out for me and take me into places I never would have attempted to hunt on foot. Collette, as well as riding the trails, was taking English riding lessons on him and learning to jump.

The change happened so slowly that at first we didn't really notice it. Our fearless little horse began to spook at odd things. At first it was just a little jump sideways now and then. Then it was a bigger jump, followed by a 180-degree spin. Finally, it was pure panic—startling, spinning, bolting. He dumped Collette. Once. Twice. Three times. It was becoming a regular occurrence. She was sure she was doing something wrong.

When we first got Twobit, Mac had said to her, "Every single time you get on this horse, you will learn something and you will teach something. Make sure it's always something good."

Now, Collette became convinced there was something wrong with the way she was riding him, something she was doing that was

Cassidy, Jeff, and Richard using Twobit to pull their sleds.

My Twobit's Worth

making this brave little horse so fearful. It was her English riding instructor who suggested we get his eyes checked.

I came home from work the afternoon after Collette had driven Twobit in a trailer over two hundred miles to see a horsy eye doctor. She was crying inconsolably. Twobit had macular degeneration. His vision was already seriously impaired, eventually he would be totally blind.

"You'll have to put him down in due course. You'll know when it's time," the doctor had said to her.

"When it's time?" Collette said, with shocked disbelief. "It can't be. I just had him in a jumping clinic last weekend."

"Then you are one lucky lady." By lucky, he meant that she hadn't been killed.

But it wasn't really luck. It was that heart thing—that quality of giving it his all. It's a quality that you can't train into an animal. Some animals are simply born with it. And so, while he was going blind, he'd still been giving his utmost, trying his hardest. Nearly totally blind, Collette's cues, not his vision, had allowed him to jump. Nearly totally blind, he had taken to the roads and trails, never letting on anything was wrong, until some noise, or a car passing, or a flash of light, or a smell, triggered his panic.

Twobit was retired the day he saw the eye doctor. We never rode him again. We got him a little companion horse, and put them out in a field together, and the other horse acted as Twobit's eyes, allowing us to have him for a while longer. As long as that other horse was close by, where Twobit could hear him and smell him and stick close to him, he was content. But eventually, even that was not enough.

One day I caught him to change pastures. His steps were tiny and tentative, I had to keep ducking from how he was swinging his head nervously, trying valiantly to see. We knew it was time.

I've owned and trained and traded and bought and sold nearly twenty horses since then. Some of them are worth their weight in

Unquenchable Spirit

Cassidy taking the barrels at a local gymkhana.

gold. I still have Shadow. My daughter has an amazing Appaloosa named Rocky. Collette has a quiet, good-natured, and solid Appy named Dakota. I have a little Fjord named Chance who is an amazing packhorse. But of all of them, one remains set apart in my mind.

Way in the back of our ten acres, there is a now nearly flattened mound of earth between two white pines that used to be small and now are reaching for the sky. For a while you could see first-place ribbons, bright blue and shiny, covering the top of that mound. But eventually they faded and tattered, and then blew away.

Some places are meant to be marked, not on the soil, but in the soul. And in that place, a little horse whose spirit was way too big for his body, never knocks over a single pole. He packs out the biggest elk. He jumps the highest jumps. And he runs, forever, at the very front of the herd.

CHAPTER 7

Ice Age:
In Search of the Bearded One

An adventure in the high Arctic.

I stared out the window of the turbo-prop airplane. Beneath me was an endless frozen wasteland of small lakes interspersed with bits and pieces of land. It looked like Swiss cheese that had been riddled with bullets, giving it an appearance of having more holes than cheese. This was my first glimpse of the Arctic.

I felt both excited and apprehensive. It was 15 March 1996, an inhospitable time of year in the high Arctic barren lands of northern Canada. Temperatures can dip to well below minus forty degrees Fahrenheit. The wind chill factor can double that. And I was going to be sleeping in a tent? My obsession with hunting has led me to many different places, but I suspected this was going to be my most brutal test.

My adventure began a year earlier when I contacted Fred Webb Outfitters and booked this trip to hunt the only animal I know that has survived the Ice Age. The Inuit call him *omingmak,* the bearded one. He is the mighty muskox.

A mature male muskox can exceed six hundred pounds. Perfectly evolved to survive the harshest weather conditions on the face of the earth, muskoxen have thick black wool that is eight times warmer than that of a sheep. Even wolves regard them with wary respect because the muskox is both savage and smart.

When under attack they form a tight circle of defense with the calves in the middle and the massive bulls forming the outer perimeter. As they face outward, their huge hooked horns resemble those of Cape buffalo. Unaccustomed to being challenged, they have been known to become enraged at hunters and will charge.

Unquenchable Spirit

Fred Webb's exact words to me when I first inquired about this hunt were: "This is not a hunt for wimps." When it was put to me in those terms, I found myself irresistibly attracted to the element of danger, and after all, I was no wimp!

Getting to Kugluktuk, formerly known as Coppermine, a small Inuit village that is located on an isolated bay on the shores of the Arctic Ocean, is an adventure in itself. It involves a series of airplane flights, an overnight stay in Yellowknife, NWT, and a final flight aboard a 748 turbo-prop Hawker—a midsize plane that nonetheless seems far

A first glimpse of the Arctic landscape.

Ice Age: In Search of the Bearded One

too small for the vastness of the land. An hour later, we landed on a runway barely discernible from the ice and snowscape around it.

We were on a flat plain, surrounded by windswept rock ridges to the south. To the north was the Arctic Ocean, a chilling vision of fractured waves, preserved in ice. I had casually used the expression "going to the ends of the earth" many times. But that day, I was aware of having arrived.

I stepped out of the plane and was immediately encompassed by cold. I could feel the intensity of the air freeze my nose hairs instantly. My lungs felt like they had vice-grips closing around them. I hurried across the frozen runaway, a typical tourist in my blue jeans and jeans jacket, my winter clothes packed safely away in my suitcase. I raced into the Kugluktuk Airport terminal, which consists of several portable trailers bolted together.

Fred and Martin Webb greeted me and the other four brave souls who had come to hunt the *omingmak*. Hardly was Fred finished saying hello when one of the other hunters began pressing for a guarantee that he was going to be killing a big muskox.

Fred gave him a wintery look that matched the conditions outside the terminal and responded, "I ain't guaranteeing nothin'. I'm not even going to guarantee you will come back alive. The only guarantee I will give you is that we will hunt your ass off trying to get you a muskox."

Even though I am no wimp, I was scared to ask Fred any questions after that.

The next hour consisted of getting acquainted with our guides, picking up our licenses and tags, and getting outfitted in winter clothing, including the traditional Inuit caribou skin parkas. The parkas dispelled any romantic illusions I had remaining about the north. They were made of untanned hides. They were untanned because the tanning process uses salt, salt sucks moisture out of the snow, and can make the garments absorb moisture. Still, practical as they may have been, the parkas smelled distinctly of rotten feet.

In the renewable resources office, there was a large muskox skull on display. At that time it went number eight in the world. Fred, sending a sidelong look at the hunter who had been looking for a guarantee, growled, "Don't plan on killing anything that big, just hope for a good, respectable trophy."

Another hunter and I were bundled into separate *komatik* (Inuit sleds). A *komatik* consists of two wooden runners lashed together with wooden struts, and a makeshift box on top. The sides of the box consisted of a canvas tarp folded over the top to block the intense wind from blasting the hunter in the face.

Inside the box, I was wrapped with more untanned caribou hides, and the relief from the biting cold was almost instant. The whole assembly (which looks somewhat like an outhouse turned over on its side) was attached to a snowmobile by a rope. My guide, Henry Kaituk, would drive the snow machine.

We set out across the pack ice following the Arctic coast for about an hour. Being inside the *komatik* is a bit like riding the salt-and-pepper-shaker at the local amusement park, though after a while, I adjusted to the constant jolting and felt quite comfortable. Considering the extreme cold outside, I was amazed by how warm I stayed. Only my feet got cold, and then only after a very long time. We turned inland on a frozen river, and that was a much smoother ride than the pack ice had been.

I could see out the sides of the *komatik*, and I would peek out at my Inuit guide who wore only a ball cap and sunglasses on his head. It looked like he had on a light ski jacket. At our first break, I asked Henry why he wasn't wearing a caribou parka like the one I had been provided.

"Too warm out," he told me. Apparently the Inuit save the caribou parkas for the dead of winter, when temperatures routinely go to minus sixty degrees Fahrenheit.

Ice Age: In Search of the Bearded One

We traveled all day, stopping several times to glass for muskox and to eat frozen bannock, which was akin to chewing on a piece of plywood. The tea, thankfully, was in a thermos, and hot. Munching bannock, I became acutely aware of how unforgiving this land was. There was not a stick of wood for a fire, not a place to seek shelter, not even a landmark to note your position.

As darkness was falling I began to worry that we were not going to get to the camp before dark. When we next stopped, I asked Henry where the camp was.

"Right here," he said. "We camp anywhere."

My admiration for the Inuit people, and how they have adapted to the land, was just beginning. By the time our hunt ended, it would be boundless.

Henry and the other Inuit guide, Charlie Bolt, began dismantling the sled. Within minutes, our *komatiks* were rearranged into makeshift tents with caribou hides on the ground to insulate us from the snow and ice. Our sleeping bags went on top, with more caribou skins on top of them. In the next twenty minutes, my guides prepared supper: bannock, canned beans, and canned fruit. It all had to be thawed out on the stove.

The lantern served as a heater as well as for light, and it was amazingly cozy inside the fragile structure in the middle of the Arctic plain. It was minus forty degrees F, according to our thermometer. I had yet to learn the hardest part of winter camping in the Arctic-bathroom break. I was soon to discover it is comparable to getting a root canal with no anesthetic.

The next day was cold and windy. We packed the *komatik* and went searching farther into the frozen wasteland. After crossing several large lakes, we caught our first glimpse of the *omingmak* and before lunch we had seen several herds of the majestic woolly beasts.

Around lunchtime, we finally came to a herd of muskoxen that had a good bull. Through a coin toss it was agreed Charlie's hunter would shoot first. While he got ready, Henry left on his snowmobile.

Charlie's hunter made a good shot and harvested a huge bull that would go well into the Boone and Crockett record book. I looked at the great beast in awe.

When Henry came back, I asked, "Do you think I'll get one as good as that?"

He looked it over, and said, "A little better."

Henry was a man of few words. We headed off to the east while Charlie and his hunter stayed to dress out their muskox.

Far off in the distance, Henry spotted seven bulls together. He was looking at them with his naked eye, and he could tell that there were several good ones in the group. I—with my fancy binoculars—could barely make them out.

We parked the sled and walked to the top of the nearest ridge. Battling wind and cold and wearing the arctic boots that white people call *mukluks* and the guides called moon boots made this hike seem longer and harder than some sheep stalks I had been on.

Then, suddenly here they were. *Omingmak,* the bearded one, was two hundred yards away, looking back at us, mildly curious. They were all huge, primitive beasts, straight out of the Ice Age.

Though I would like to say I was in awe of being in the presence of such a perfectly adapted animal, the terrible truth was I was so cold that I just wanted to shoot and be gone. I asked which one was the biggest and Henry told me the one on the right. I looked them over some more, and thought maybe the one in the middle was bigger.

Henry insisted it was the one on the right.

I took his word for it. I fired my 7mm magnum, and to my amazement the muskox neither flinched nor staggered. He just stood there. I fired several more times, aiming for behind the front shoulder, and the result was the same. The only way I could tell

Ice Age: In Search of the Bearded One

Rob with his "bearded one."

Unquenchable Spirit

I was hitting him was from the solid *thunk* sound a bullet makes on impact.

Finally, Henry said, "I think he's had enough."

It is very difficult to tell exactly where to shoot on a muskox because there is so much hair on them. The big bull began to wobble, and it was suddenly apparent he was dead on his feet. A few seconds later, he fell over and was still. Despite the cold, I felt enormous respect for the toughness and perseverance of these great prehistoric beasts.

When I walked up to my fallen prey, he seemed to grow larger and even more massive. He was like a fallen warrior, a creature who had successfully battled twenty years or more in this land of inconceivable cold and barrenness. Later, he measured at 116 6/8 Boone and Crockett points. To this day, I still don't know if I shot the largest bull in that group. There were at least two other bulls with him that would have easily made the Boone and Crockett book.

In the brutal cold, we worked diligently to get this great woolly beast dressed out. By the time we had the meat, head, and hide loaded, it had really begun to blow. I was face to face with my worst fear, whiteout conditions in the Arctic.

I thought the cost of harvesting the great beast was going to be my life. However, if Henry shared my anxiety, he did not show it. He nonchalantly headed off into the blizzard and his instincts and his intelligence—his amazing ability to know this land—brought us safely back to the other guide, hunter, and camp. I was amazed at his incredible sense of direction in a land where compasses do not work and everything looks the same.

The next day the storm had blown over and we headed back to Kugluktuk, bouncing all the way. Shortly after we arrived, the other hunters also arrived with their muskoxen. Both of theirs were also well into the book. One ended up being number four in the book, and mine ended up being number thirteen. (Both have long

Our komatik packed up and ready to go to town.

since been beaten back, mostly by hunters who also hunted with Webb Outfitting.)

Fred met us upon our arrival back in Kugluktuk, gave our beasts a cursory glance, and said, "Those are nice muskoxen, boys."

Fred refers to his outfits as No BS hunting, and from what I saw, he delivered exactly that. No BS, but a quality hunt where safety comes first.

I feel deeply privileged to have been able to experience the Arctic landscape in all its cruel magnificence. The people, so resilient, adaptable, and courageous, made me wonder if I wasn't a bit of a wimp after all.

They say the Arctic casts a spell and that once you go there, you are forever under its lure and you will always go back. I believe this to be true.

CHAPTER 8

"Ware" in the World Are We?

A wilderness adventure turns bad . . . very bad.

The canoe rocketed through the churning white water. It was taking all my strength to avoid the sharp rocks protruding from the river. I thought it was about as bad as it could get. And then we rounded the next bend.

Ahead loomed a logjam as big as a house. Even more terrifying was the huge whirlpool that swirled and sucked in front of it. It looked big enough to swallow a herd of buffalo, and we were just two guys in a small canoe.

Rob hiking in the high country to no avail.

Though my whole life didn't flash before my eyes, I did think back to the beginning. Somehow when Rick Green and I were planning this trip, we never imagined it turning into an escapade like this. Even the canoe was not part of the original plan.

Our hunting trip into the wilderness of northern British Columbia started out as a backpack trip. Rick had heard a rumor of monster Stone rams near the headwaters of the Gataga River. Rick and I were recent acquaintances, having met at British Columbia's Wild Sheep Society's fundraising convention. It's interesting how quickly friendships can blossom with a shared enthusiasm (fanaticism) for sheep hunting! Within weeks of our first telephone conversation, we were flying north from Prince George in a Beaver floatplane with enough gear to last us a month.

Two-and-a-half hours later, we landed on a remote lake near the headwaters of Weissener Creek. The area looked like good sheep country and we were very enthused about the next two-and-a-half weeks of hunting, which is a long time to spend in one spot if there are no sheep in the area.

We spent the next five days intensively scrutinizing every square inch of our new surroundings with our spotting scopes. We crossed a low pass into the south Gataga watershed. We even crossed a glacier in hopes of finding a hidden basin that might contain a small band of rams. It was to no avail. We found it sheep-less. A more horrible scenario would be hard to imagine.

There were, however, a few goats, a couple moose, and lots of grizzlies. In fact, we were plagued with G-bears. Everywhere we looked, we saw grizzlies. We saw them feeding, we walked into them, and we even had one follow us up a slide. I had to take a shot over his head to get him to leave.

Though our spirits were high, we knew when we were beat. As time is always a factor, I didn't want to waste mine in a nonproductive

"Ware" in the World Are We?

area. Rick agreed. So we came up with plan to get ourselves moved to a spot where we knew sheep existed.

After studying the map, we came up with the hair-brained plan of hiking out to a cabin at nearby Weissener Lake. This was long before the days when satellite phones were so common, so we hoped to find a radio there so that we could contact our pilot and have him move us.

If there was nobody at the cabin, we would continue on to Fort Ware and contact him from there. Estimated time: two days walking if we had to travel all the way to Fort Ware. We packed a five-day supply of food, Rick's tent, both sleeping bags, and one rifle. Our packs weighed about twenty pounds each, which meant we would make good time. We were prepared for the worst, or so we thought.

Now this is where our real adventure began.

We started hiking around the north side of our little lake early on the morning of the sixth day. There was a good trail all the way to the end. At Weissener Creek we had anticipated finding a well-used guide trail, but instead we found the trail grown over and crisscrossed with game trails. We made the first of a series of creek crossings. In the beginning, we removed our boots, but after half a dozen crossings we decided to leave them on. After all, we were going to make Weissener Lake cabin before dark!

After three hours, we completely lost any evidence of the trail and began bushwhacking through swamps and windfalls while following the meandering creek toward Weissener Lake. Our walk that first day took thirteen hours and by comparing the terrain we had traversed to the map, we were only halfway to Weissener Lake.

Rick's feet were blistered from walking with wet boots. The bugs were bad. When we pitched the tent at the end of the first day, we found ourselves in the middle of an old forest fire burn that was choked with windfalls. We were exhausted.

The next morning we fought our way out of the burn and into a huge swamp that the map indicated went all the way to Weissener

Our adventure begins when we were left at a wilderness lake.

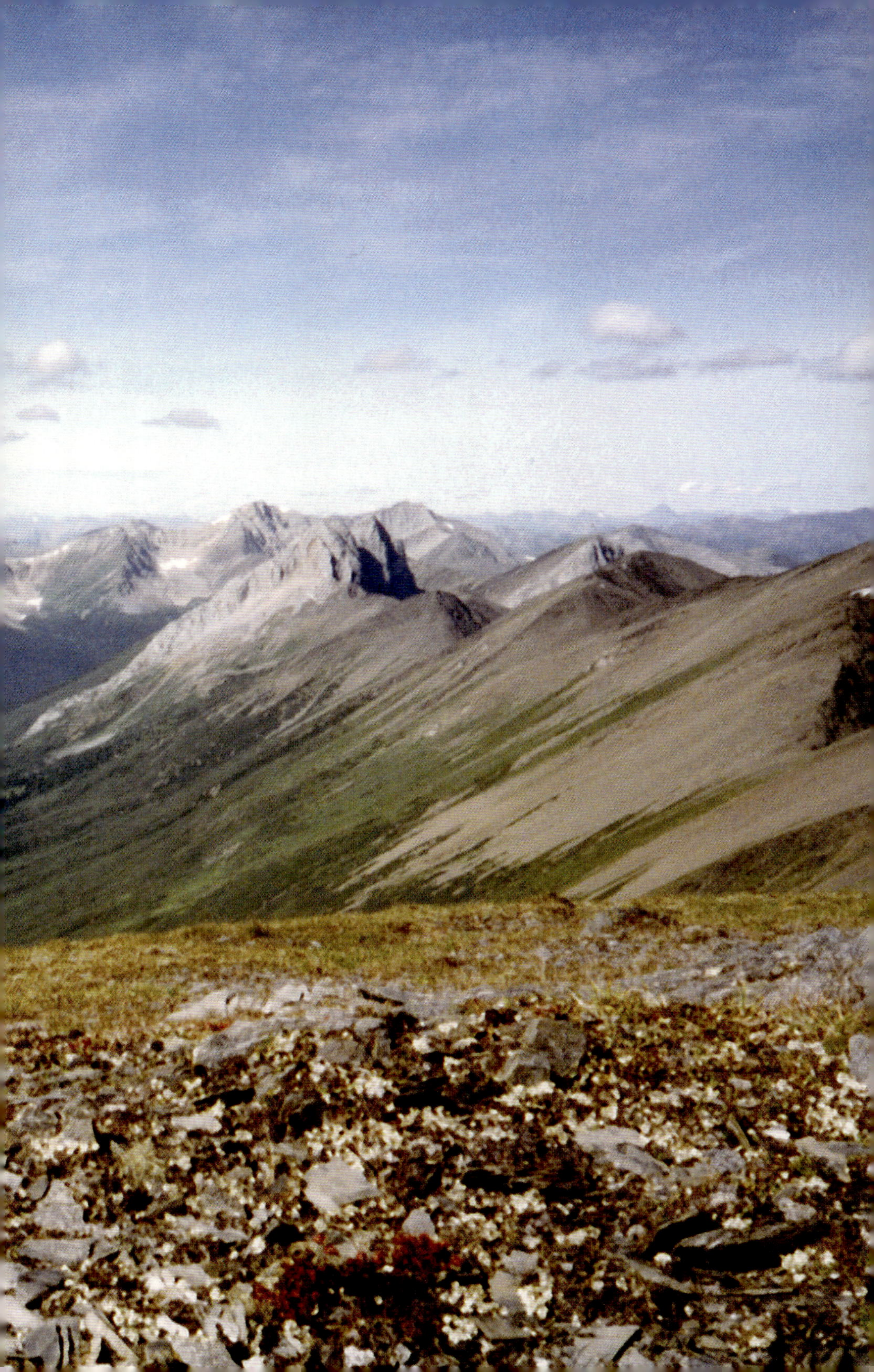

Lake. Our progress was painfully slow at this point. We ended up slogging through water up to our knees, our boots being sucked down into mud and sludge. The mosquitoes plagued us. We wiped handfuls of them off our faces, but there was no relief from the onslaught.

According to the map, the swamp went for another six miles. We were facing the ugly prospect that we might have to spend another night out, possibly even in the swamp, and then I spotted an old oil barrel. It was the first evidence of people that we had seen since leaving our base camp. Never have I been so glad to see trash in the wilderness!

From there we found a trail wide enough to drive an ATV. We followed it an easy eight miles, and it led us directly to the cabin. The empty cabin. We were dejected to find the cabin uninhabited. There was no way we could go back, and we were not feeling great about going forward, either. A calendar inside the cabin indicated the inhabitants had left only three days before we arrived.

There was no two-way radio either. We now realized that we were going to have to continue our trip to Fort Ware, like it or not, and we didn't like it one bit. We had walked for eleven hours that day and had traveled forty miles total, the hard way. This was double what we had estimated. Could the rest of the way be just as full of pitfalls?

The next morning it rained hard. We decided to stay in the cabin for a day and dry out our clothes and give Rick's blistered feet a rest.

I could see no trail along the north side of Weissener Lake. We figured that whoever owned the cabin was using a boat to access it. There was a canoe behind the cabin, so we decided to borrow it to canoe down the lake. In normal circumstances we would not have been borrowing items that did not belong to us, but because Rick's feet were in such bad shape, we felt it would be worth the extra expense of having the plane return the canoe to the cabin. We figured that there had to be a trail from the end of the lake directly to Fort Ware. We also used their chainsaw to build some paddles out of a couple of planks as there were none to be found.

"Ware" in the World Are We?

Early the next morning we set out paddling six miles toward the west end of the lake along the north shore. Rick informed me that he had had very little canoeing experience.

"Don't worry," I responded, "We'll be fine. I have lots of experience with canoes."

We found no trail leading from the end of the lake toward Fort Ware. In fact, we found out later that we had completely missed the trail that went along the south side of the lake and then up over a low mountain pass away from the lake directly to Fort Ware.

With no trail to follow, I was convinced that these people were accessing their cabin by riverboat. If riverboats could come up it, we could canoe down it. As well as growing up around water and canoes on the Shuswap River, I had taken a white water canoe course several years prior to this trip and knew how to run mild rapids if we should encounter any.

We entered Weissener Creek within an hour of leaving the cabin. It was shallow and easy going at first. I gave Rick a few last-minute instructions on paddling. He was in the bow paddling while I was in the stern calling changes and steering the canoe.

We hadn't gone very far when we encountered our first riffle. We made it through with ease. This was followed by several miles of small rapids that were easy to navigate. They helped to build both Rick's and my confidence levels. The water became quite fast-moving and we made good time.

Then it calmed and we came around a bend to a large logjam. We pulled the canoe ashore and inspected the logjam more closely. It was at this point that we realized that the owners of that cabin could not have been using riverboats to access it.

We now considered our options. Disheartening as it was, we could use the towrope on the canoe to pull it back up the river and look for a different way out.

I decided to have a look at the logjam. At the beginning of the day, I had traded in my wet hiking boots for a pair of soft-soled water shoes.

I climbed up on a log, and finding it slippery, I deliberately stepped on a knot to get some grip. I'd forgotten just how soft-soled those water shoes were. The knot punctured through the bottom of my shoe and penetrated into my foot about an inch.

Pain shot up my entire leg. I pulled my foot off the knot and looked at the blood gushing from the gaping wound. Rick's feet were both severely blistered, and now I could barely walk. Our options had just become very limited. Luckily, Rick had brought painkillers with him. I took four pills, bandaged my foot, and put my hiking boots back on.

Now we couldn't turn back. Hiking out was no longer an option. Besides, there was no trail on either side of the creek. We were stuck. But again we had no choice. We had to get unstuck. We finally managed to find a route over the logjam, but it was no fun dragging the canoe over. I tried not to think about what would happen if one of us slipped and fell between the logs into the raging torrent beneath them.

Back on open water, I optimistically informed Rick that that should be the last of the logjams. Within minutes, we rounded a corner and were faced with another one. It was not as bad as the first one and we were able to drag the canoe over it easily. We had to cross over eleven more logjams before we were clear of them in that section of the creek. None of them were as bad as the first one, however.

The creek joined up with the McCook River and became slow moving and winding. We cruised along lazily for several miles into the wide-open valley of the Rocky Mountain Trench. Just when we had been lulled into thinking the worst was behind us, the river began to pick up speed. We encountered our first set of large rapids.

Rick yelled that he hoped I knew what I was doing. I hoped I did, too. Trying not to show my own fear, I called to him to just paddle and I would steer.

All the instruction I had taken came back to me. I remembered the sculling draw, the pry, and the sweep. We battled a hundred yards of white water, and braced ourselves for the "standing" waves that appear at the end of most rapids. They soaked Rick up to his waist. Still, we had made it, and we congratulated each other heartily.

The river began to narrow between large cutbanks on either side. This made me nervous because I thought we might be going into a large canyon. We stopped several times, got out of the canoe and limped up the banks to scout out what lay ahead. Finally, we had to decide to stay on the river because climbing the banks was becoming too difficult for me with my injury.

At each bend and twist, we would steer into the back eddy to try to read the river ahead of us. (A back eddy is a place that is found on a bend in the river where the current reverses flow, and it provides a small pocket of calm.) Now we were encountering rapids more frequently, but they did not have the fierceness of the first one. We would run them, pull out into the back eddy, rest, read the river, and charge ahead.

I have had many close encounters in the wilderness. I have been charged by a sow grizzly with cubs, I have almost been hit by lightning, I have nearly stumbled off cliffs, I was pinned inside a flipped Zodiac in the Pacific Ocean, but I have never once felt so close to death, as I then felt. I did not share with Rick my growing sense we would not be coming out of there alive.

There were too many unknowns ahead. These narrow cutbanks (about forty feet high) on either side of the river could take us into a box canyon or over a waterfall. The river had become a raging torrent of whirlpools, standing waves, and rapids. The canyon continued for what I estimated to be ten miles, the rapids unrelenting.

It occurred to me if we ran into rapids we could not handle, if the canoe flipped, if we drowned, no one would come looking for us. The plane was not even due back to our original drop-off point for ten days. We had left a note saying we were hiking out. Not canoeing. If we went missing, we were going to end up on *Unsolved Mysteries*. No one would ever find us. Or maybe our bodies would eventually float into Fort Ware.

I thought of my wife, Collette, and our three kids—Richard, Jeff, and Cassidy. And I knew I might be going down, but I wasn't going down without one hell of a fight.

After what seemed like an eternity of navigating this watery trench from a nightmare, I noticed the slope of the cutbanks gradually fading. The river calmed. The last time it had calmed, we had come to a logjam. I braced myself for the worst. Sure enough, around the next bend we came face to face with the biggest logjam yet. We immediately pulled out of the main current. The river was very swollen and wide at this point, flooded beyond its banks, and up into the grass and trees.

I knew the dangers of getting sucked under a logjam. Many people have drowned this way, and I didn't want to add my name, or Rick's, to that list. We beached the canoe (a figure of speech, since there was no beach) and took our map out of its Ziploc bag.

We discovered that we were at the confluence of the McCook and Fox Rivers. The logjam went as far as the eye could see. There was no safe way to drag the canoe over this one. Then we looked to our left up on the hill. A trail. Finally, a trail. It was about eight feet wide. According to the map, this was the Davy trail.

Rick grabbed his pack and announced, "I'm never getting back in that canoe. Not even maybe."

Right about then that sounded good to me, too, though with my foot being so bad I was not sure it was going to be an option for me.

"What are we going to do about the canoe?" I asked.

"We'll buy them a new one."

Now that I had decided I was going to live, it seemed to me this trip was getting more expensive by the minute. As it turned out, my feeling I was out of the danger zone was also premature.

I grabbed my pack and rifle and we both limped down the trail. When we had gone about a mile Rick said, "Rob, there's some people over there."

"Ware" in the World Are We?

"No way," I said gently, taking into account he had been under tremendous strain.

"No, really!"

I caught up to him. There was a cabin. And people. A group of five natives were milling around, and were now watching us with interest, and mild surprise.

After exchanging greetings, Rick asked them how far it was to Fort Ware. One young man replied about eighteen miles by trail. We thanked them, I downed another handful of painkillers, and we headed off.

The young man caught up with us a few minutes later and invited us to spend the night with them at their cabin. He noticed I was limping badly. He had probably also noticed me taking the painkillers.

Suddenly nothing seemed more inviting than to sit down, eat warm food, and enjoy solid ground. We accepted their generosity and went back to the camp. Introductions were made all around. The young man's name was Aaron Charlie.

We told our story of where we had come from and what had happened. Antoine, Aaron's father, who had been in this valley his entire life, was impressed. He knew the kind of country we had crossed, the challenges we had conquered.

Antoine told us he had been hunting and trapping all his life. He would leave town sometimes for two months at a time and eat just about anything that got in his rifle sights. He had eaten beaver and moose and caribou and porcupine. He told us they were heading out on a hunting trip to Fox Lake, another thirty miles up the valley. He said they needed to get away from the hustle-bustle of town life in Fort Ware (population less than two hundred). They had a string of pack dogs to carry their gear.

I realized this old man, and his children, lived my greatest adventure on a daily basis. A country he thought of as his backyard had nearly killed me. He was as much at home here as I was in my living room.

The natives knew the people who owned the canoe and the cabin at Weissener Lake, and Aaron and a friend went for the canoe. Aaron carried it much of the way by himself. As a carpenter, I consider myself to be in excellent physical condition, and I have seen many strong men. But I have never seen anyone in such good physical condition as Aaron.

Sending a cautious look at Rick, I asked what the river would be like to canoe into Fort Ware. Antoine said the river was pretty good all the way to Fort Ware, that there were only a few bad rapids and logjams. And there was one spot, about a mile from the town, where there was a drop in the river of about four feet. He said that we might have to portage that one.

I think Antoine knew I wasn't going to be able to walk eighteen miles. I was also thinking we had an obligation to return the canoe, and that a plane was not going to be able to pick it up from here. I know Rick thought we should just buy a new canoe, but now that I was going to live, I was adding the costs up inside my head. By the time we bought a new canoe and flew it up to Weissener Lake we would probably be out two thousand dollars.

At that point, Rick made it clear that there was no way he was getting back in that canoe. I didn't blame him, really. I asked Aaron if he would canoe down the river with me since he was also an experienced canoeist and knew the river. He agreed readily.

Antoine took a look at our crude homemade paddles. Rick's, in particular, was much worse for the wear. He had broken it, and by the last set of rapids was paddling with the blade only. Antoine and Aaron quickly made new ones with their chainsaw. Theirs were quite a bit better looking than ours had been—and lighter, too.

Early the next morning, Rick set out for town with a light pack and my rifle. Aaron and I set out on the river shortly after. Aaron said the river was quite a bit higher than normal for this time of year. It was running very fast as soon as we entered the current.

"Ware" in the World Are We?

We came to the first set of rapids within minutes of entering the river. We handled them with ease. I was in the front now with Aaron, the more experienced canoeist, in the stern. During the next two hours, we ran a lot of rapids and covered about thirty miles of winding river.

Some of the standing waves were so large that they dumped several gallons of water over me and my gear. Still, it was a beautiful day for canoeing. Not a cloud in the sky. For the first time since we had set our sights on Fort Ware I was enjoying this endurance test. Or was it an adventure?

The river wound from one side of the Rocky Mountain Trench to the other. It was about forty-five miles of snaking, winding water from the native camp to Fort Ware. During the last fifteen miles the river jumped its bank in places. We encountered some very large logjams. While none of them blocked the river, they looked very threatening as we shot past them at uncomfortably close range. We could see the incredible power they possessed as there were trees three feet in diameter pinned underneath the water alongside them. We knew that if we capsized here, or got too close to the jams, there would be no escaping death.

Aaron told me of a friend of his that had drowned a few years before on this river. The haunting thought of not making it back alive crept once again into my mind.

We shot forward down this raging torrent. Aaron informed me that we weren't far from the little chute that we would have to portage around. He said that some people he knew had run it a few times in gentler conditions. Ahead was whitewater as far I could see. The canoe rocketed through the churning water. It was taking all my strength to avoid the sharp rocks protruding from the river. I thought it was about as bad as it could get.

And then we rounded the next bend. Ahead loomed a logjam of monstrous proportions. It was as big as a house. Even more terrifying was the huge whirlpool that swirled and sucked in front of it. It looked big enough to swallow a herd of buffalo, and we were just two guys in a small canoe.

There was a large gravel bar sticking out to the left. On the right loomed the logjam. The huge whirlpool swirled in between them as we paddled hard to stay on the left side of the river. There was only a four-foot width of safe water between the gravel bar and the whirlpool. I paddled hard to get the front of the canoe into the safe zone.

Suddenly, I could feel the stern of the canoe swinging into the whirlpool. I gave one last tremendous heave, hurling the front of the canoe into the edge of the gravel bar and then leaping from the canoe with the bow rope in hand. The powerful current sucked the canoe back into the whirlpool with Aaron still in it. I yanked the canoe onto the gravel bar. It held. We paused to catch our breath.

We then launched the canoe on the lower side of the gravel bar. With my heart still pounding from the excitement, we continued on the raging river from hell. Within minutes of the logjam episode, Aaron yelled the chute was ahead. We paddled frantically toward the left side of the river, which is where the portage trail was. The river was so swollen and fast that we missed the pull-out and were swept toward the chute. I grabbed some branches from an overhanging tree, and Aaron did, too, but the current was too strong. The branches broke.

"We have got to take it on the right!" yelled Aaron.

I paddled with all my might, but the current sucked us to the left and over a huge rounded rock about the length of the canoe. We slid over the rock and dropped four feet back into the main stream of the foaming, wild river. All this seemed to be happening in freeze frame. It was like a bad dream come to life: stuck, powerless to move in the right direction.

My senses were heightened, and I could feel and hear the rock scraping the bottom of the canoe. Then the bow went right under water with me still in it. It emerged from the boiling foam still upright. I was stunned that we hadn't capsized.

A rare, peaceful moment.

I turned to look at Aaron, who was visibly shaken. I noticed he had his rifle slung over his shoulder. Sheepishly, he told me he had thought we were going to flip and he had hoped to save his rifle.

The next ten minutes I used a large cup to bail the canoe while Aaron paddled. Ahead I could see that we would be entering a very large river. It was the Finlay. Aaron said he had never seen it so high at this time of year. He told me that it was at least twenty feet higher than normal. Another ten minutes went by, and then we were in view of Fort Ware.

We landed the canoe, and I found a phone and immediately contacted our pilot who was very surprised to hear from me. He promptly left Prince George to come to our rescue. Rick came limping along two hours later, and we waited for the plane. Aaron headed back for his camp later that afternoon.

The plane came droning in and landed by our canoe. We told him our story while we loaded our gear and tied the canoe to the side of the floatplane. Once airborne, we were back on the route we had come. I couldn't believe how bad the river looked from the air.

Twenty minutes later we landed at the Weissener Lake cabin and unloaded the canoe. We left a thank-you note at the cabin and were airborne again. Another twenty minutes found us back at our original base camp. We were no longer interested in moving camp to another lake.

Rick said, "Get us as far away from here as possible."

We spent that night in the Mackenzie hotel in Mackenzie, British Columbia. I cleaned my wounded and now infected foot. We estimated that we had traveled over one hundred miles by water and land.

I have told this story many times, and have become used to the reactions. The most common is that I'm a fool, that I took impossible chances with my life, and that I'm lucky to have survived. All these things are quite possibly true. And of course, from this trip, I have learned things to share with others: Do your homework, prepare for the worst, and expect the unexpected.

But along the line another thought has crept into my thinking, and it has only grown stronger over time. We live in an age that worships safety. An age that has tamed man's spirit of adventure. We no longer go anywhere without our seat belts and our bicycle helmets. Our lives are predictable from morning until night. But for a few days, in some of the only country left in North America that is truly wild, I lived moment by moment, by my wits and by my strength, and finally, perhaps by the grace of a good God.

And I discovered something within myself, and that is the essence of who I am. Adventurer. Hunter. Survivor. I live secure in the knowledge that whatever my faults, and they are many, I have been given an unquenchable spirit.

CHAPTER 9

A No Bull-S--- Caribou Hunt

*More great hunting with
my most unforgettable character, Fred Webb.*

I take pride in the fact that the majority of trophies I have harvested have been through my own ingenuity, knowledge, and toughness. For my first seven years of trophy hunting I guided myself or mentored by my friend, Tom. Sometimes with him, sometimes alone, I explored and discovered most places worth hunting in my home province of British Columbia.

But there were animals calling my name and areas I needed to explore that were not in my native province. In 1996 I embarked on my first guided hunt with Fred Webb in Kugluktuk (formerly Coppermine), and harvested a magnificent world-class muskox.

But, aside from the success of the hunt, Fred, like that series they used to have in *Reader's Digest,* became one of my most unforgettable characters. How can you not like a guy who has the company slogan "NO BULL S--- HUNTING" and who lives up to it, besides?

Fred is crusty, foul-mouthed, and has a razor-edged sense of humor. His ability to tell a story is unparalleled. He is a straight-shooter who never hesitates to call it as it really is. And in the far North, a landscape so harsh and unforgiving that it can kill a man as hard and as fast as any place on Earth, Fred is the man you want to have your back. So, in September of 1997, I embarked on my second hunt with Fred Webb and Son, this time to Courageous Lake, in the barren lands of the Northwest Territories. I was after a Canada central barren ground caribou.

In Canada, those of us who want to fly into the North have limited options, an extra gauntlet to run, if you will, and that is our national airline. Kept running with almost nonstop government bailouts, this airline shows its gratitude to the Canadian taxpayer by being absolutely disdainful of the flying public.

I boarded my flight in Calgary, switched planes in Edmonton, and landed in Yellowknife the same day. One by one people picked up their bags, until there was just one person left standing there, and not a single bag left on the carousel. That person, naturally, was me.

After several phone calls, the clerk at the Air Canada counter, without a trace of apology, informed me that he had no idea where my luggage was—possibly Edmonton—but that it should show up early next morning. As we had to spend the night in Yellowknife before flying out the next day, I was not too concerned. The next morning, when a trip to the airport proved my luggage was still AWOL, I became very concerned.

The expeditor took us all to the renewable resources office to get our licenses and tags. Months before, Fred had strongly recommended getting two caribou tags. They were five dollars each, and Fred would claim an extra five-hundred-dollar fee only if the hunter chose to take a second caribou. I was happy to part with that ten dollars, my only happy moment in the morning, as a return trip to the airport confirmed the worst possibility: still no luggage.

I had the clothes I was wearing: jeans, jacket, sneakers. It was bad enough heading into the north without proper clothing, but I also had no rifle.

"Mr. Shatzko? We have to go."

The expeditor's tone was urgent. The other hunters were waiting, the floatplane dock was ten miles from the main airport, and my Air Tindi flight to Courageous Lake could not wait any longer. I could either head for that plane or stay in Yellowknife. I headed for the plane, though I wondered how this hunt for caribou was even going to take place with no rifle and no clothes.

The Air Tindi flight had ten passengers, all hunters going to Courageous Lake. The two-hour flight took us over Great Slave Lake, a massive body of water that looks like an ocean, then over the North's boreal forest, and finally we were in the barren lands. We landed on

A No Bull-S--- Caribou Hunt

Courageous Lake, a thirty-mile-long stretch of water. The camp, right on the edge of the lake, wasn't exactly pretty. In fact, it looked like a haphazard assembly of tin cans cut in half.

The barren lands had intrigued me since I was a kid. They look much like the alpine, except flat. Except for the occasional willow in a creek draw that might come up to your chest, there is no growth higher than a foot. There are six-inch-high blueberry bushes, and lichens, but mostly it is rocky, barren country, aptly named.

Fred greeted everyone as they got off the plane. I felt like an old friend as Fred introduced me to his buddy, a guest at the camp, Dan Herring. I told him what had happened to my luggage. Fred had some choice words for our national airline. Few people are as skilled with choice words as Fred, and he had my full admiration as he strung together six, four-letter words in a combination I had never heard before. I prize ingenuity.

Without a moment's hesitation, Dan stepped in and offered me the use of his rifle and clothes for my hunt. To this day I feel grateful for the unexpected generosity of a man who would also become a good friend over the years. Once settled into our sleeping arrangements—those cut-in-half tin cans were the bunkhouses—we started to get to know each other a bit.

The diversity of hunters is always amazing to me. Some of these guys were extremely wealthy, others, like me, saved their pennies for an adventure like this. One guy had been sending money in hundred dollar installments for a number of years. There were a few women, one a dentist, her quarters divided from ours by a curtain.

After everybody (but me) had stowed his luggage, we headed to the main tin can, the cookhouse. There we were treated to one of Fred's famous briefings. If memory serves me, it went something like this:

> I'm not going to guarantee you that you will shoot anything. That depends if the caribou have read the script or not. It depends on the weather:

If there's too much wind, we cannot launch the f!#%$&g boats. If there is too much fog, we cannot launch the f!#%$&g boats. And mostly, it depends on whether or not you can shoot worth a f!#%.

Of course, I already knew this about Fred: He likes to deflate high expectations immediately. Then if you get anything, you're happy. I've been on guided hunts since then, and usually the exact opposite is true: The outfitter always claims he has the biggest animals on earth and he is always determined to make you believe you are going to be the one to get them.

We were divided up into groups of two hunters per guide. The hunts were to be conducted using aluminum motorboats to scour the shorelines of the huge lake for caribou. We then met at the shooting range where Fred gave us his next speech. If memory serves me correctly it went something like this:

"I don't give a f!#% whether you can cover a three-inch group with a dime at three hundred yards. All I want to know is this: Can you hit a f!#%$&g empty case of beer at one hundred yards?"

I've always liked Fred's no-nonsense, redneck approach to everything. I'm not sure everyone does. I think the dentist may have been religious, which is not something you would brag about in Fred's camp. She looked pretty wide-eyed by the end of his second speech. The next day, after a hearty breakfast, we headed out to our designated part of the lake.

To protect the innocent, I am going to call the other hunter whom I shared a boat and a guide with Buddy. Buddy, for reasons known only to him, had only purchased one caribou tag. Because of that, Fred gave him specific instructions.

"Buddy, let Rob shoot the first one. That will give you a measuring tape to field judge the size when your turn comes."

But I think Buddy must have got stuck on the "I'm not going to guarantee you that you are going to shoot anything" part of Fred's

Colin Havioyak heading to the hunting area.

welcoming speech because when we saw caribou on a distant ridge, and beached the boat, Buddy was beside himself.

"Nothing worth shooting," our Inuit guide, Colin Havioyak, said.

This may have only been my second guided hunt, but I knew these guys did this for a living for a reason. They loved it. They knew these animals. They knew this country. I knew I could trust Colin's judgment and his instincts.

Buddy took off running toward the bulls.

"I think he is going to shoot one of those small bulls," Colin observed. "Weren't you supposed to shoot first?"

"Yes, but," I watched Buddy run, "I don't think there's going to be any holding Buddy back."

Colin shifted his focus from Buddy's mad dash across the barren lands to some bulls wandering near where we had beached the boat. "Nothing big enough," he said again. Maybe not, but there was one a lot bigger than the one Buddy was chasing up the ridge.

We started walking toward the bigger caribou and got within one hundred fifty yards when I saw Buddy stop. He looked back at us, saw the bigger caribou, and began to run back toward us, waving his hands madly to let us know it was his.

Colin watched him approach and gave his head a sad shake. "I think he is going to want to shoot that bull. Do you think I will be able to talk him out of it?"

Buddy was close enough now that I could see the look on his face. It was the fevered look of a gold miner who had just spotted a nugget, and who had totally convinced himself it was the real thing, not fool's gold.

"I doubt it," I said.

Buddy arrived. Completely ignoring our native guide, his breathing labored, he asked me, "Do you think that he's a big caribou?"

This was my first time up close and personal with a caribou. How would I know? So, I answered his question with the same question. "Do you think he's big?"

A No Bull-S--- Caribou Hunt

Apparently that's all he needed. With Fred's no guarantees ringing in his head, in the first fifteen minutes of the first day of our hunt, Buddy flopped down on the ground, used a rock as a rest, and aimed at the caribou.

Colin looked at me and shrugged.

Buddy squeezed the trigger. At the report of his rifle, the largest of that group of small bulls fell in his tracks. Buddy was ecstatic. For about two seconds.

Maybe he noticed Colin and I were not sharing his enthusiasm. By the time he was at the downed caribou he was already having second thoughts. "I don't think he's very big," he said nervously, his eyes darting from the caribou, to me, to Colin.

I responded, "Oh yeah, he's a nice one."

Colin remained silent.

Buddy turned to Colin, and with a mixture of hand signals and Tonto language, he said, "Me want the heart."

Any sympathy our guide, who spoke excellent English, had for Buddy visibly evaporated at that precise moment.

I waited to see what Buddy wanted the heart for, wondering if he was going to bite into it raw a la Dances with Wolves, but Buddy was failing to entertain in any way.

"I'm taking all my meat home with me," he announced.

After pictures and butchering, we loaded the caribou in the boat and continued to hunt. About noon, after looking at many caribou, Colin took us back to base camp to unload the caribou and have some lunch. Fred, diplomatic as always, eyed Buddy's prize. "I told you to let Rob shoot first so you could f!#%$&g field judge it better."

Actually, for Fred, that was diplomatic. He showed remarkable restraint of tongue. His facial expression was a whole other story. After Fred's ringing endorsement, Buddy hung out watching other hunters arrive back in camp with caribou. All of them bigger than the one he had shot. The slow sulk was beginning.

93

Unquenchable Spirit

Since Buddy's hunt was over, Fred wanted him to stay in camp for the afternoon, but Buddy was not, as we had already seen, a great listener. When we went back out that afternoon, Buddy was firmly planted in the boat, waiting for us. We saw plenty of caribou, but nothing big enough to satisfy Colin.

The next day we headed in a different direction on the lake, still with Buddy aboard. Fred told him in no uncertain terms his hunt was over, but I took pity on him and let him come along to watch. Fred managed to confiscate his rifle, though.

When you see a truly large animal, no matter what species, you know instantly, and that morning turned out to be no exception. Luckily Fred, being the amazing, if somewhat cynical, judge of human character that he is, had insisted Buddy leave his rifle in camp. Had Buddy had his rifle, I doubt if he could have restrained himself.

We saw four or five caribou trotting on a bridge of land between two bays of the lake. Even to my untrained eye, one was an absolute giant. His antlers looked as big as his body. Colin crashed the boat into shore and we bailed out.

Up until this point, Colin had been the epitome of calm. Now his calm was gone, his voice burning with urgency. "Shoot, Shoot!"

Fresh out of the boat, I had nothing to rest my rifle on . . . and the little herd of bulls was doing its best to exit stage right. The shot was about two hundred yards. With no time to look around for a rest, I had to attempt an offhand shot. Could I hit the side of a beer case at this distance?

Apparently not.

I squeezed off, but the bull showed no sign of being hit. The bulls were now really moving, thundering across a small peninsula. I raced to higher ground where I found some rocks for a rest. When the monster caribou paused for a brief second, I squeezed off again.

A No Bull-S--- Caribou Hunt

A side view of a magnificent rack.

This time the magnificent bull broke from the herd and went straight into the water. He got out about three feet deep, and keeled over. Colin was excited. I was ecstatic. Buddy was not happy.

It took nearly half an hour to get the boat around the small peninsula through the shallow water to my trophy. We threw a rope around his antlers and towed him into shore to take pictures.

"I think it's way bigger than mine," Buddy whined.

"No, no," I said, wishing I'd let Fred keep him in camp so he couldn't rain on my parade, "I think they are nearly the same size."

Buddy was not fooled.

Buddy's sulk was deepening by the second, and not improved by the fact he had managed to get his feet wet. We gutted the caribou, and I saw both my shots had hit. We loaded the animal in the boat, and headed back to the main camp.

Buddy was having his revenge: He desecrated the antlers he was so envious of by using them as a drying rack for his socks. Finally I got tired of the silent sulking and said to Buddy, "This one could have been yours if you would not have shot that one yesterday." Buddy's answer was to send an accusing look at Colin.

When we arrived back, Fred met the boat. His eyes lit up when he saw my caribou. Fred is not easily impressed, so I knew then that I had shot a truly magnificent animal.

"Rob," he said gruffly, master of the understatement, as always, "you've just got to stop shooting these small ones."

He congratulated me as everyone else in camp came down to admire that caribou, the biggest taken so far. As it would turn out, that caribou was the biggest one taken that year out of Courageous Lake. He gross scored 375-inches-plus, which was well past the 330-inch minimum for the Boone and Crockett all-time record book.

As more and more people milled around my caribou, Buddy took Fred aside. The next thing I heard was Fred's elevated voice.

"I don't give a f!#%. Do you see a corner store here where you can just waltz over and get yourself another tag? I told you to buy two tags, and you were too f!#%$&g cheap, so tough s---."

Boy, if Buddy was too cheap to spring for two tags, I wondered how he was going to feel when he found out Air Canada would charge him a dollar a pound for all that meat he wanted to bring home.

Many more caribou came in at the end of day, none as big as mine, but all were still bigger than Buddy's.

Day three, with Buddy stuck in camp on Fred's orders, Colin and I, and several other hunters who hadn't yet tagged their second caribou headed out. We looked at many good caribou, but with the pressure off, we could be really selective and just enjoy the hunt.

A No Bull-S--- Caribou Hunt

Colin, the legendary Fred Webb, and Rob.

Toward the end of the day, I saw a unique-looking caribou with double shovels. I decided to take him, not so much for size, but because of his uniqueness.

When we arrived back at camp, I learned that Fred had called Air Tindi to come early to fly all the tagged-out hunters with their trophies. He also had started dismantling the camp, which would be shipped out, as this was the last hunt of the season.

He took me aside and said, "I really just want to get that whiny son-of–a-b@&%# out of camp."

Being one of the tagged-out hunters, I would also be on that plane with Buddy. The next day, with Dan's clothes and rifle returned to him, I left Courageous Lake. I sat as far away from Buddy as was possible. I didn't want to be around that whiny son-of-a-b@&%#,

either. Every hunt teaches lessons, and this one had several: One, listen to your guide; two, there is no whining on a hunt.

At the Air Tindi floatplane dock, I was informed that my luggage and rifle had arrived in Yellowknife. The next day I was on my way home. I had to pay extra baggage fees for the caribou antlers. Air Canada acted as if, by even loading them, they were doing me a big favor. You'd think they might have wanted to compensate me for my lost luggage and for the fact they could have ruined my hunt for me. You'd think that maybe, just maybe they would go out of their way to make my trip home as pleasant as possible, but no. That is not their way.

As I finished wrangling with them, I turned just in time to see Buddy dragging his meat and luggage across the airport. I turned back to the clerk at the counter.

"Are you guys hiring? I know someone who would be perfect for you."

Footnote: After sixty days' drying time, my caribou scored just over 365 inches net.

CHAPTER 10

Another Moose on a Sheep Hunt

(Or when will they ever learn?)

One thing I have learned over my years of hunting is that while many people claim a love of the sport, few are truly fanatical. I, however, definitely fall into the latter category. I arrange my life around hunting; I don't arrange hunting around my life.

And so I was disgusted when three people who claimed equal dedication to their sport as I, one by one cancelled on a fly-in hunt we had been planning for ten months.

I've changed their names to protect the guilty, but it went something like this: Mike said he couldn't afford it; Bill said he couldn't get time off work; Joe, a whole two weeks before we were scheduled to leave, said his wife would not let him go. (Now that last one is a really poor excuse.)

My deposit was on the line. The pilot had already penciled in our dates. I tried to get someone else to go. No luck on such short notice. (Thanks, Joe.) Even though I would now be paying the entire flying costs, I decided to be a true fanatic. I was going.

And then I heard a little voice.

"Dad, I sure want to go."

"Huh?"

I looked at my eleven-year-old daughter, Cassidy. At first, I was the responsible dad. I dismissed the idea as impossible. What kind of dad traipses into the wilderness on an extreme backpacking excursion for two weeks with his eleven-year-old daughter?

But then that fanatical side took over. The thing was, even at eleven, she had that fanatical side, too. Cass and I had been shooting grouse and gophers since she could pick up a .22 rifle. The local farmers lined up to keep us supplied in bullets.

Unquenchable Spirit

That year, Cass had taken her hunter-safety training course. It was as soon as the law allowed. She was the youngest in her class, and she aced the test. In no time, she had a hunting license, and I had taken her on a successful black bear hunt in the spring.

I began to think, what better way to pass the torch than have her accompany me on the ultimate mountain hunt?

As for being tough enough for the often extreme conditions of sheep hunting, I wasn't worried about that; Cass was not your normal eleven-year-old girl. At four, Cass had hiked to a famous landmark with us, five miles, each way. There was no quit in her. If the adults could do it, she could do it. At five, on an outing with neighbors, a little boy pulled her hair. She unceremoniously clocked him. When he went sobbing to his aunt, the aunt cast Cassidy a glance and said, "You picked on the wrong girl." At eight, she saved her own money, bought a colt, and we trained him together. No matter how many times she came off that horse, she dusted herself off and hopped right back on. She rides her Rocky to this day. She had a well-honed sense of justice and was still taking on those boys who picked on girls. As far as I know, she never lost one of those schoolyard altercations.

So, maybe it was reckless, or maybe it was recognition of someone with a spirit that matched my own, but whatever the reason, I found myself at the sporting goods store loading a cart with extra small camo clothes, a woman's backpack, and the smallest hiking boots they could dig out of the back room.

Once outfitted with all the gear, I had to figure out how she was going to carry it. Even with most of the gear on my back, she was going to have to pack a little over thirty pounds.

I dusted off my battered old Parker-Hale .30-06 and squinted through the four-power Weaver scope. What's a first hunt if you don't get to pack your own gun? With that and numerous assurances to my wife that I would bring her daughter home safely, we were set to go.

My daughter's first excursion into sheep country.

Cass had never flown in a small plane before, and her eyes got pretty big at the sight of our tiny plane sitting on the tarmac near Dawson Creek, British Columbia. As our pilot adjusted the shoulder straps on her seat belt, I saw her visibly pale. Here he was assuring Cass that the seat belt would keep her safe when we flew upside-down!

It was a fairly routine flight over vast northern muskeg. I was happy to see that Cass had settled in. After a while she no longer looked as if she was going to throw up all over the precious gear piled up beside her. After about two hours of jostling around to the loud drone of the engine, our airstrip was in sight. The airstrip was a gravel bar, haphazardly leveled out. It was complete with a ragged Canadian flag serving as a windsock.

"We're landing there?" Cassidy's eyes had grown big again.

The pilot turned and grinned at her. "We're going to try."

The plane tires bumped over the old river rocks, finally jostling to a halt. As we unloaded, the pilot turned to me.

"Are you sure you want to wander off in the wilderness with your young daughter? There are grizzlies out there."

He was probably considering phoning Child Find or Social Services. I glanced at Cass who was already dragging gear off the airstrip. She looked about as happy as I'd ever seen a kid look, and I don't think it was just because we'd survived the flight.

She was as excited about this hunt as I was. Probably even more because this wasn't my first rodeo, but it sure was hers.

"I'm sure," I said.

Moments later, our pilot was taxiing up the runway ready for takeoff. I surveyed our provisions one last time before he took off to make sure we had not forgotten anything. I gave a casual wave as he raced by us and became airborne seconds later.

I found a good place to camp about fifty feet off the landing strip and we set up the big tent. This was to be our main base camp for the next ten days. I also had a small dome tent that we would use for spike camping for three to four days at a time.

That evening we hiked up the open hill above our camp. We were surrounded by wildlife. We saw a large group of ewes and lambs on a grassy open hillside. Below them were several bull elk. In the valley bottom directly behind camp were three young bull moose, all still in velvet, feeding in a large swamp.

I felt that sensation I often feel when I hunt like this: a sensation of homecoming, of being where I most want to be. I glanced at my young daughter, watching those three moose, and I'm pretty sure she felt that way, too. Cass looked as if this was the grandest adventure of her life, and nothing could keep her from it.

"Are we going to shoot them, Dad?" she asked eagerly.

"This is a Stone sheep hunt," I told Cassidy. "Sheep hunting is as tough as it gets, and you have to stay focused on sheep. Forget about shooting a moose or an elk."

Another Moose on a Sheep Hunt

I had learned this lesson the hard way, but I didn't pass that on to her.

Early the next morning we set out with full packs to the south. It did not take long to find a well-used horse trail. We climbed rapidly out of the forested valley into an open alpine valley that split two smaller valleys. There was evidence that other hunters had recently hunted here as horseshoe tracks and horse droppings were scattered along the trail.

We camped for two days at the junction of the two smaller valleys. Unlike our original camp, we were unable to find any sign of life hiking out from the spike camp. Cassidy, however, handled carrying her pack surprisingly well for a young girl, and a small one at that. Even though she had a pack that probably weighed nearly half as much as she did, she did not complain. I have seen grown men who whined a whole lot more.

I think part of her motivation was worrying that I wouldn't let her come again if she was a sniveler. Baptism by fire.

After two days coming up sheep-less, we headed back to base camp. We spent the night there, topped up our supplies, and headed out early next morning in the other direction from camp. We saw lots of game that day, but it was all the wrong kind. There were mountain goats, moose, elk, caribou, and ewe sheep, but no rams.

We passed several horse camps on this new horse trail and some of them had hunters on them. One guy, a hunting guide, informed me that there was a grizzly on a kill just up the trail. I called his bluff and ignored his warning and continued down the trail. There was no grizzly or any sign of a dead animal on the trail. I think he was just trying to scare us off what he regarded as his territory.

We passed several more hunters with a string of six packhorses. They all stared long and hard at Cassidy, and then gave me looks I interpreted as witheringly judgmental of the dad in the remote wilderness with his daughter.

We spent several days wandering farther and farther northeast of our base camp, but, again, we were unable to find any legal rams.

Unquenchable Spirit

As we trudged the twenty-plus miles back to camp, I was utterly exhausted, and poor Cass was worse . . . and we had miles and miles yet to go.

Right then, I wrote off the idea of killing a sheep. We'd been hiking and scouting for days. I felt we had left no rock unturned. There were no legal rams here. I decided now was the time to relax my stand on a moose or an elk. I didn't want Cass to end her first serious hunt with the bad taste in her mouth of being skunked. So, I told Cass if we made it to camp that night, we might have time to shoot a moose the next day and then fly out earlier than the time we had scheduled with the pilot.

With that new motivation, we finally made camp. That evening, even though I could see she was played out, Cass was restless with excitement over the chance at a moose in the morning. Even though I was bone tired, I couldn't help but feel a bit of her raw enthusiasm. I was so proud of her for her perseverance and determination. She was no quitter.

The next day, searching for a moose, Cass stopped short. "Dad, what's that?"

I turned toward the swamp where she was pointing. A lone gray animal was moving quickly along a moose trail. I raised my binos and was surprised to see that it was a ram making his way across the valley floor.

We quickly shed our packs and crept through the brush. I had never seen a ram in such a strange place before, but then again, I had never had an eleven-year-old girl as my hunting partner either, and that seemed to be working out OK.

We intercepted the ram as he paused beside a murky pond, dipping his head to drink. We crouched directly across the water, only about a hundred yards away. Cass gripped the old .30-06 with nervous determination, but as the ram turned his head I could see that his horns fell just short of being legal.

Another Moose on a Sheep Hunt

I watched my daughter's face fall as she experienced another one of the many letdowns of sheep hunting. As I have learned over the years, hunting sheep is as much a mental game as it is a physical one.

The next morning, we decided to give moose one last try. We awoke early and walked back to the swamp behind camp. There were five bull moose and several cows and calves feeding in the swamp. I know how much work a bull moose can be, so I quickly surveyed the situation and determined the closest bull was only about four hundred yards from the landing strip.

I turned to Cassidy and said "We will shoot that one."

She quickly protested, "But Dad, that one over there is much bigger."

Of course I knew that, but I also knew that bigger meant more meat to carry. He was also about eight hundred yards away. I turned to her and tried to convince her that the smaller one was better.

"He's the biggest one you've ever shot," I teased her (because she had never shot a moose).

But she wasn't about to be teased out of it. She stuck to her guns: "I want that one."

Take away my father-of-the-year award, but then I just out and out lied. "The wind is blowing in the wrong direction over there, and if we go after him he will spook before we are in shooting range."

That sounded reasonable to her. "OK."

With the decision made, we stalked to within fifty yards and set up to shoot using my backpack as a rest.

"Dad, I can't see over the willow bushes."

Sometimes you can forget when you are hunting with someone who is four-foot-six that they have special challenges. So, I had her rest the .30-06 on my shoulder and aim at the unsuspecting moose.

"Dad I can't find him in the scope."

"Just take your time."

She finally found him in that old 4X Weaver scope and squeezed the trigger. Although I was deafened by the muzzle blast right by my

105

Cassidy is all smiles after shooting her first moose.

ear, I could see that he was hit hard. He ran about fifty yards and collapsed head over heels.

I gave her a hug and congratulated her on her second big-game animal. After picture taking we began butchering the moose.

Six hours later, we had all the meat at base camp. I made a hike over to the outfitter's camp and asked if I could borrow his satellite phone as I wanted to fly out early with our moose meat. He gladly loaned it to us, relieved, I think, to have us out of his hair.

Another Moose on a Sheep Hunt

I phoned our pilot and informed him that we were unable to find any legal rams but that Cassidy had shot a moose and we would like him to come and take us out early. He arranged to arrive the next morning, but he left me with a caution:

"I hope that this does not put me overweight for takeoff. That is a short air strip."

That evening after feasting on moose tenderloin, we burned everything that we did not need including my leaky leather boots and an old tarp. We were trying desperately to lighten up the load, and that was in the days before I had any kind of environmental conscience.

The next morning, with our camp dismantled, we waited for our flight out. Shortly after 10 AM the plane landed and taxied over to our pile of gear and moose meat. The pilot surveyed the pile of meat nervously. Then he told us the wind conditions weren't favorable, either. We loaded our meat and our gear with a sense of urgency.

Finally, everything was on board. I was in the front, beside the pilot. Cass was in the back. The pilot taxied the small plane to the farthest extent of the runway and even pushed as far as he dared into the small willow bushes to get as much runway as possible. As he revved up the engine, I realized this was the most dangerous thing I had exposed my daughter to on this trip.

The plane lumbered along the gravel, picking up speed. But it felt to me as if the plane was groaning with the extra weight. It seemed like it was too heavy to get the speed it needed for takeoff. It just wasn't going fast enough. I could see the willows at the end of the runway looming larger. Beyond them was a line of spruce trees. And beyond that was a swamp.

The trees flew by in a blur to my right as I puckered up my behind to help the plane lift off. Finally, with what seemed like a hair to spare, the plane floated off the ground. I swear I felt branches scraping the belly of the plane. I'm sure I heard Tom Milne, my old hunting buddy, whisper in my ear, "A moose on a sheep hunt? When will they ever learn?"

Cass settled back in her seat, apparently unperturbed by the hair-raising takeoff. She sighed with utter contentment. "Dad," she called over the roar of the engine, "I got a moose."

Not a word about being skunked on a sheep. Not a single complaint about the hardships of hiking long distances and carrying huge weights. I could see it in her. That hunting was more than a passing interest.

And that's when I knew something way more important than a sheep hunt had happened. Way more important than a moose hunt. She was young and had a lot to learn, but there was still not a doubt in my mind. Cassidy was a true fanatic. My new hunting buddy was sitting in the seat right behind me.

The northern moose adventure was just a beginning. By the following season, it was clear my young daughter was going to be the family's next hunting fanatic. A lot of great seasons have since passed, but those first years of passing the torch were the rocks that formed the mountain.

I'm proud of the hunter Cassidy has become today. She is strong, confident, and fully independent, often braving the wilderness solo. Even so, we still have our best hunts together.

She is currently a staff writer for the Woman Hunter *magazine. The following story, about her first mountain goat hunt, was published in her Adventure Series, which appears in each issue of the* Woman Hunter *magazine.*

CHAPTER 11

The Good, the Bad, and the Billy

The tale of my first mountain goat.
by Cassidy Caron

From the very first minute of my first hunt I knew that this was something I was born to do. Even at such a young age I could feel something strong and primitive coursing in my veins, drawing me to the wilderness. But blood instinct alone played only a small part in the creation of the hard-core huntress that prowls the Canadian wild today. There is one person who can be solely blamed for this odd evolution: That would be my dad.

His passion for the sport, toughness, and ceaseless pursuit of adventure has rubbed off on me in our fifteen years of conquering mountains together. If there ever was an easy road, we avoided it.

Which brings me back a dozen years, to a wintery valley in British Columbia's Kootenay region. It was early November and snow blanketed the surrounding mountains like somebody had iced them with way too much Betty Crocker vanilla. I was thirteen, and even the cold couldn't dull my glow of excitement. This might be the hunt where I had a chance at my first mountain goat. Several earlier attempts had resulted in a lot of hard work and heartbreaking disappointment.

But that primitive fire in my soul was alive as we clambered out of the truck at the end of the road and eyed the distant icy cliffs. My cheap binoculars quickly iced over, but I pretended I was still diligently looking for prey. Dad announced that he had found some goats.

"They aren't in a very good spot. It's going to be really tough to get at them," he confided.

I already had my pack on. He looked at me, sighed, and off we went.

After four hours of battling through thick, untouched forest and up nearly vertical avalanche chutes choked with alder, we broke through the tree line and emerged onto a frozen, windswept ridge near where we had spotted the goats.

It was already midafternoon, so we made a hasty search for a flat camping spot, which resulted in an equally hastily pitched tent. The tent ended up at close to a forty-five-degree angle down the lumpy, bumpy hillside. It had been impossible to anchor it to the frozen mountain as attested by the many bent pegs and uttered curses. The rocks we used as hammers ended up piled inside our already tiny shelter to secure it to the earth. That done, we were ready to look for the goats.

I was sweaty from the hard hike and the hard work of setting up the tent, and the cold whipping wind hurling bits of powdered snow into my face felt awful as we crept around the ridge and glassed the area where we had last seen the goats. They were still there, and through the spotting scope we quickly found a nice billy bedded alone. Unfortunately for us, he was higher on the mountain than the rest of the herd. The only cover between him and us was a thin strip of trees that had miraculously prevailed on what could only be described as a cliff.

The going was so steep that I had to pass my rifle up to Dad so that I could pull myself up with both hands. My mom is reading this, so I shouldn't talk about the waterfall. It was twelve years ago, so I guess the statute of limitations must be up.

When we reached the end of the trees, we were at the same height as the billy. All we had to do was edge around the cliff and get a shot at him. What we had failed to notice before happened to be a large frozen waterfall between him and us.

It was as beautiful as it was deadly, the white cascading ice plummeting thousands of feet into the valley below. When my father shows fear, I know that something is genuinely not right. I could see and sense his trepidation as he tiptoed across the glassy ledge of flat ice just above the drop of doom.

I can still feel each step I took across that frozen pool; my eyes fixated on the place where the ice turned blue and plummeted off

The Good, the Bad, and the Billy

the mountain. One slip and it would all be over. When I reached the other side, rock never felt so good under my boots.

I had barely regained my breath when the billy was in my sights. Did he ever look small through my four-power Weaver scope! I had worked so hard, I couldn't possibly ruin it now . . . could I? I was shaking all over the place. Cross hairs on, cross hairs off. Dad's hand patted my shoulder.

"Take your time; he doesn't know we are here."

Deep breath.

BOOM.

The goat glanced around. Even to my thirteen-year-old eyes I had clearly missed.

Another round.

BOOM.

The billy faltered and went down over the edge of the cliff. I was so excited that I almost fell off the cliff, too! That is until I realized he hadn't landed yet. Countable seconds passed before we heard him crash back to earth.

I felt sick. Would there be anything left of my majestic billy goat? It took almost two hours for us to inch back down the icy cliff and find the billy at the bottom. By some miracle, he was mostly intact!

I was elated and at the same time sad that I had killed such a beautiful animal. I held the legs and ears for Dad as he dressed the goat, and all the while my mixed emotions so distracted me that I failed to notice how really cold it was and how dark it was becoming.

By the time we had the goat in our packs, darkness had fallen. That was when we discovered that we had one flashlight between the two of us. Although the light had been mine, Dad led the way with the light and I struggled to follow. All I could see was a thin halo barely squeaking by the frame of Dad's pack. I couldn't see where my feet were going at all, though my control over them was poor anyway, under the heavy, goat-laden pack. I was marching like a zombie, eyes

Unquenchable Spirit

Cassidy gets her goat!

straining at the pale light when suddenly it disappeared completely! I stopped fast, the toes of my boots hanging over an abyss.

A groan rose from somewhere below me. I searched the darkness, piecing together what happened. Dad was eight feet below me, straddling an alder that grew out of the sheer mountainside. With a full pack. *Ouch.*

I found my way around the outcrop Dad had fallen off of, and we continued down the mountain. We finally made it back to Camp Luxury. I desperately wanted that box of Kraft Dinner I had packed for supper, but with our lack of water and our state of exhaustion, it was all we could do to thaw out granola bars in our armpits for dinner.

Dad was in our downhill sloping tent first, and I'm pretty sure he was snoring before I figured out how to arrange myself between him,

The Good, the Bad, and the Billy

the piles of rocks, and the already frosty tent wall. I finally wedged myself in, only to discover that my Thermarest provided about as much traction for my sleeping bag as a slip n' slide. It didn't take long for me to be deposited in the narrow bottom of the cone-shaped tent.

Teeth gritted, I shifted from side to side in my mummy bag, propelling it upward. The maneuver had to look like a bad abs exercise in one of those awkward eighties fitness videos. All I wanted was sleep. *Sllllide*. Back to the bottom of the tent. The hard, uneven ground pressed into me in the most uncomfortable places. Dad continued to snore.

As I wiggled upslope yet once again, I felt the tent dislodge from its precarious roost. I held my breath. The tent slid ever so slightly atop the thin layer of snow, and then stopped. Whew, that was close.

Suddenly, the tent began to rocket down the mountain. I could hear it, in all its nylon glory, zipping along well-lubricated terrain.

"Dad."

Snore.

"DAD!!!"

Like a crazy carpet of doom, the tent was picking up speed.

"*Huh?*" Dad was awake.

Zzzzzsh. Zzzzzsh. Nylon over grass.

"*OOOWWW!*" In unison. Nylon over rock.

Finally, the tent piled into a small clump of trees. The roof above our heads was still sort of where it should be.

"*Uh? Huummm.*" Snore. Not much excites Dad. Actually, I think our new position may have been an improvement from the previous one in the comfort department because I did finally sleep.

I awoke to something wet and cold pressing into my face. It had snowed. What snow had survived the toboggan ride down the mountainside last night had now collapsed the tent and was right on top of me. Our body heat had melted the snow through the tent and we were lying in a puddle that had saturated our sleeping bags. Everything was soaked. The sun wasn't over the peaks yet and it was subzero. Twelve years later, I can say that I have never had a more unpleasant morning in the mountains.

We trudged fifty yards through snow following the drunken path of our toboggan tent and dug out our packs. Only the sight of my goat made me feel better. We didn't waste any time loading up, and I was only too happy to carry my hide and horns even though my soaked sleeping bag and uneaten box of KD were really heavy.

It didn't take me long to realize that something was wrong with my load. All of the weight seemed to be resting above my head. If I even leaned a tiny bit forward, it resulted in a somersault followed by a barrel roll down the steep mountain.

"DAD!"

He was way below me. Finally, somewhat impatiently, he stopped.

"There's something wrong with my pack!"

He was carrying all of the meat and most of the camp, so when he took off my pack and hefted it, I can maybe see why it didn't seem strange to him. Maybe he forgot I was like four-foot nothing.

"It's fine." Annoyance.

I was tough. I knew it. I guess this is what packing a mountain animal out is like. Two steps, lean forward. Flip. Roll. I was like a Jack-in-the-Box or, worse, a slinky going down the steps.

The windfalls when we got into the timber were particularly bad. My legs weren't really long enough to straddle them. Flip. Fall. Can't get up. All the weight above my head. I find a way.

Finally I emerged in the bottom of the cutblock where the truck was parked way above me. It was impossibly steep. There was no way I could climb that hill.

"DAD!"

The Good, the Bad, and the Billy

Already at the truck, he peered way down at me and made his way back down the slippery clear-cut. He shouldered my pack and got not ten yards up the steep slope before he turned and said, "Jeez, Cass, this pack is top heavy! There's something wrong here!"

Although it was twelve years ago, the tale of my first mountain goat never fades from memory. If anything, that adventure with my dad defined and shaped the hunter I am today: Impossible is nothing; go hard or go home!

CHAPTER 12

Yukon Guide, Part I: The Call of the Wild

Trailing in: This is no place for the faint of heart.

I think every man, and certainly every hunter, entertains the notion that maybe he was born in the wrong time. Hunting may even be about that primal desire to recapture a time when a man had to rely on his wits, his guts, his instincts, his strength, his courage just to survive.

Even though I had come a long way from that raw youth who hunted deer for sustenance, it seemed the more I hunted, the more I yearned for that mystical "something" a man feels in the wilderness that he feels nowhere else on earth. The Yukon is one such wilderness. It has called men with that yearning like no other place on the face of the earth. Those who have not heard that call may not understand the power and the pull of it, but in the year 2000, I felt the draw as surely as though I was being towed. Linked to the ghosts of those long-ago miners lured to the great unknown by the promise of gold and adventure, I yearned for the opportunity to find out who I was and what I was capable of doing.

Technically, at thirty-four, I was probably too young to be experiencing a midlife crisis. Still, there is no denying that to those around me, my personal "Call of the Wild" looked insane. I had a wife. Kids. A job. Responsibilities. But I also had this feeling. It's now or never.

And so when the construction industry that employs me slowed down, I didn't see my getaway as a problem. I saw it as an opportunity. I moved to the Yukon and worked as a carpenter there. Then one day, I phoned Yukon outfitter Chris Widrig.

"Have you ever guided before?" He sounded skeptical of my interest in trying the guiding life.

Yukon Guide, Part I: The Call of the Wild

"Just my kids."

"Have you ever worked with horses?"

Sometimes your ducks just line up. I hadn't imagined when I bought my first horse several years earlier that it would be a piece in the puzzle that would help me quench this thirst I had for adventure. Now I could tell Chris that I owned ten horses and that I had trained all but two of them myself. My experience with horses must have made up for my lack of experience in guiding because before I knew it I had arranged to meet Chris in Whitehorse on 10 July.

So, a few weeks from that phone call, I found myself beside Chris Widrig, driving to Mayo, in the Yukon. From there we would trail horses out to Chris' area, a four-thousand-square-mile piece of ruggedly isolated real estate snuggled up against the Mackenzie Mountains.

Indian guide Jimmy Johnny.

The next day I met the other guides I would be working with for the next two-and-a-half months. Jimmy Johnny was an Indian guide, humbly unaware of his own fame. He was one of those small wiry guys, a man of few words. John Sievers had a Viking look about him. Karl Thomas and Rick Mortimer both had that look of men who were throwbacks to another age: as at home with horses as most men are with cars, totally at ease in a land that does not suffer fools lightly.

I was the greenhorn, and I saw that same skepticism I had heard in Widrig's voice reflected now in the eyes of these veteran guides and wranglers. Was I tough enough? The truth was that they had all done this a hundred times before. And they'd seen guys like me a hundred times before, too. Most thought they could do it. And most failed. As we set out from the trailhead at McQuestion Lake to traverse some of the deepest wilderness remaining on earth, I was deeply aware that the law of averages was against me.

After a short briefing, horses were saddled and we were on the trail. We had four packhorses, five saddle horses, and twenty loose horses. Jimmy took up the lead, and he set off at a bone-jarring trot. Several loose horses followed, some packhorses joined the parade, and then one rider inserted himself into the middle of the melee. The remaining horses seemed to notice, with a touch of panic, that the train was leaving without them and galloped after it. The last three riders, including me, took up the rear.

This was not exactly what I had been picturing. Western art, hunting magazine photos, and my own ventures into the bush with equines had prepared me for an orderly packstring, horses tied together, nose to tail. Instead, we seemed to have a mobile and extremely disorderly three-ring circus heading up a well-beaten trail.

Whenever a horse broke out of the ranks, he was chased back into the frenzy by one of us in the rear, with lots of rope popping

Yukon Guide, Part I: The Call of the Wild

and profanity. Jimmy, who trotted in the lead, made sure that none of the loose horses passed him.

To me the method—or lack thereof—seemed chaotic. I thought at any minute one of those horses was going to take it into his head to turn around and run back to the trailhead. And I was experienced enough to know that what one horse does, they all do.

But, amazingly, the loose system worked. We covered a lot of ground that day, pounding through bogs and trees at a flat-out speedy trot. When we finally reached the camp spot for the day, I was exhausted. Ahead Jimmy and Karl were already putting hobbles (chain shackles) around the horses' ankles, bells around their necks, and turning them loose in the grass meadow beside the camp. As soon as the packhorses and saddle horses were untacked, they were hobbled and let go, too.

Twenty-nine horses on the loose. This was also new to me, and it seemed like an invitation to disaster . . . or at least desertion. I was used to tying my horses to trees when I camped for the night. But the horses seemed happy to be on grass. Their bells made a cacophony of sound as they hopped around seeking out the most succulent grass or threw their heads down to feed.

As I pitched in to set up tents and get a fire going, I kept my doubts to myself about the loyalty of horses to stick around. We were thirty miles from where we had started. I was living the way men had lived a hundred years ago: no phone, no electricity, no lock on the door, actually, no door to lock.

And just like those men—the part they forget to tell you about in the storybooks and movies—I tumbled into a sleeping bag that night too tired to take off my clothes. I slept effortlessly despite the constant clanging of the horse bells.

In the morning, I pulled my weary body out of my sleeping bag. The fire was already going and the coffee was on. I could hear distant bells, so the horses, to my amazement, had not headed back to the trailhead during the night. Two of the guides were already "wrangling"—bringing the horses back in from their night of wandering and grazing.

I cooked bacon and eggs, and over breakfast there was a bit of discussion about the geography we would be covering that day. The discussion seemed to be heavily weighted toward a crossing called the Swimming Hole. I was sure I noticed just a bit of trepidation in some of these old hands.

When Chris had conducted my job interview over the phone, he'd neglected to ask me if I'd ever swum a horse across a river. The answer would have been no. There is a quite a distance between sitting in your armchair at home, restless for adventure, and actually experiencing it. Somehow a place called the Swimming Hole had not really figured into my fanciful imaginings of a summer in the wilderness.

Soon we were on the trail again. Again there seemed to be a sense of urgency. We rode through bogs that sucked worse than a Hoover. Twice, we had packhorses stuck in that oozing black slime. Both times the saddles had to be removed to let the horses struggle themselves free, writhing and plunging and with rolling, panic-stricken eyes until they powered their way out of the mud.

And in boggy country like that? Your constant companion is bugs, also conveniently left out of storybook and movie accounts of great adventures. They had not played a part in my fantasy, either. But the reality was that hordes of humming, whining, stinging, and biting mosquitoes and black flies dogged my every move.

In the middle of the afternoon, when I was beginning to hope the Swimming Hole was nothing more than a hoax conjured up to frighten the newcomer, I heard splashing in the distance. Then silence. Then splashing. Cursing. I came around a bend in the trail that crested a hill. At the top of that hill, I found myself looking straight down into a huge, murky swamp of a pond. It was bordered on all sides by thick trees and thicker bog.

Yukon Guide, Part I: The Call of the Wild

The first of many river crossings.

There was one way across, and despite the old Western romance of watching the herd lunge into the water with great churning splashes, I could feel my stomach churning a bit, too. I watched as the splashing stopped as the horses lost the bottom and began to swim, noses held high.

I intended to stop and think for a minute about how best to get across this morass, but my horse barreled down the hill and launched himself into the water with such enthusiasm that I found myself up to my waist in freezing water before I could prepare myself properly. In an instant, all I could see was my horse's head sticking out of the water. I hung onto his mane and the saddle horn for dear life.

An eternity later, his front hoofs found solid footing under the water, and he propelled himself forward with such intensity that I was thrown up onto his neck. It all happened so fast that I barely had time to prepare for it. In hindsight, I don't know how you prepare for swimming anyway. You're going to get wet.

Once on the other side of the Swimming Hole, we all stopped and emptied our boots. I pulled my rifle from the scabbard and drained the water from it. I saw a few sidelong glances sent my way, faint grins. I had just passed a test of some sort. It was baptism by fire.

Actually getting across the Swimming Hole turned out to be the easy part. Riding for hours, soaking wet, was the hard part. Being swarmed by a million nasty biting, unrelenting swarms of bugs was the hard part.

That night, I again fell into my sleeping bag, too exhausted to even have the thought that adventure was not quite what it is cracked up to be. I buried my head in my sleeping bag to escape the mosquitoes that had swarmed into the tent with me and were starving for my blood.

I was now more than sixty miles away from the nearest car or medical station or telephone. I was a two-day ride away from mattresses, light switches, and hot showers. I could not order a pizza, walk down to the corner store for ice cream, or turn on the television or a radio to see what had happened in the world that day. In two short days, this had become my whole world: mosquitoes, horse bells, exhaustion.

But when I woke up the third day, I felt like a sailor who had found his legs. I looked around at my world, heard the distant clanging of bells, grabbed a halter, and went in search of horses. This had become my world, and I found I liked it.

That day, the trail gradually pulled away from the swampland. The bug presence lessened slightly. We were gaining in elevation. By midday we passed Bonnet Plume Outfitters camp. John Sievers told me that he had spent summers for his entire life at this camp. He had helped his father build the cabin. He said it was the only home he had ever known. No wonder he seemed as at home in

Yukon Guide, Part I: The Call of the Wild

A first glimpse of the mountains.

this country as most men would be in their easy chairs with their newspapers and cup of tea. We had followed a fast-flowing river that day, and when we made camp, I noted I was not as tired as I had been the night before.

Day four we followed the same river and camped that evening beside a large air strip near an abandoned mining exploration camp. There were expensive canvass-wall tents, collapsed and in various stages of decay. There was a kitchen tent complete with a large cook stove, tables, even some canned food just left to the elements. The tables and chairs were the only things holding up the mostly collapsed roof. There was a half-full, two-thousand-pound bottle of propane still attached to the stove.

Jimmy told me that this camp had been abandoned several years prior to our arrival. I guessed that it was not in the mining exploration company's budget to fly out all their garbage, and in those days no one gave much thought to the environment.

Day five we rode to the headwaters of the river that we had been following for the last seventy-five miles and crossed over a low pass. I finally saw the beginning of the mountains where we would be hunting. I caught my first glimpse of alpine. We passed into a new valley and continued east toward the border of the Northwest Territories. That evening we camped beside a new stream, a tributary of the Bonnet Plume River.

I felt excited. I was becoming more used to the daily demands that horse travel entailed. I now understood how it must have been for the early pioneers. I felt alive, at one with nature. I was thirty-four years old and had a sense of having missed something important by not being here sooner.

Our sixth day was long. We forded many, many streams before riding into the wide-open Bonnet Plume river valley that evening. We camped beside a small lake just off the river. I don't know whether it was a small lake or a large pond, but the guys referred to it as Porter Puddle, named after one of the guides from years gone by whose last name was Porter.

Later that evening, around 11 PM, Chris flew in and landed his SuperCub on the small lake. (This far north—about seventy miles south of the Arctic Circle—it never gets dark in July.) He was checking in to see how we were making out and had brought us some fresh food from the base camp. As he made ready to leave again, I noticed I was once again getting the sidelong looks.

Yukon Guide, Part I: The Call of the Wild

Rob's trusty 7mm in pieces after the long trail to camp.

Jimmy Johnny later told me why I was being watched: The guides were all waiting to see if I would get on that plane. Jimmy told me money was changing hands as they bet on whether I would stay.

"Not many men make it," he said. "They ride this far, the plane comes, they get on it, we never see them, never hear from them again." He spat. "The worst ones are the ones who call themselves cowboys."

Well, I was no cowboy. I was just a carpenter with an insatiable yen for adventure. And the truth was I was having the time of my life.

Day seven we crossed the mighty Bonnet Plume River. We rode up an unnamed creek through a narrow canyon for most of the day. We never left the creekbed, walking on gravel and sandbars and crossing the creek numerous times. Toward the end of that long day, we broke over a low pass and made our way toward a small lake about two miles long.

I could see a cluster of small buildings at the far end. It was the Goz Lake camp. We arrived about 8 PM. Chris had flown in the cook and her husband and one of the other guides. We arrived to a hot meal cooked for us.

We had ridden for seven days and covered over two hundred miles of trail. During the trip one of the horses broke my rifle. Settling into my cabin that night, I felt as if I was the luckiest man alive. I was living the dream. I had answered the call of the wild, and on that endless trail away from all that was familiar and civilized, I felt I had found myself.

CHAPTER 13

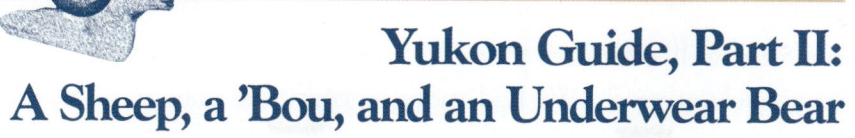

Yukon Guide, Part II:
A Sheep, a 'Bou, and an Underwear Bear

A doctor from the deep South gets a little more than he bargained for.

I had been in the Yukon with Widrig Outfitters for a month, including the week it had taken to trail in the horses. I was as far away from civilization as a man can get in this day and age. A huge percentage of my life now revolved around horses: finding them, catching them, saddling them, balancing pack boxes, and securing loads. Each day began with at least two hours of hard work getting ready for the day's hunt. When all went well, the camp functioned like a well-oiled machine. When it didn't, it was like a forty-car pile-up on the freeway.

I had been on horseback every day for the last thirty days. I'm confident if I had an opportunity to compare notes with a man who had lived a hundred years ago, our experiences would be very similar: depending on horses, cooking over open fires, washing in creeks. For me, this was heaven.

I had also guided my first hunters, and both had taken fine Dall sheep. The hunts were uneventful, which is what the outfitter wants: success with no excitement. My next hunt, however, was about to make up for that.

My new hunter stepped off the floatplane that had just landed at Goz Lake. I was introduced to Dr. Milstead, an orthopedic surgeon from Shreveport, Louisiana.

"Call me Sonny," he insisted in a drawl.

Gray-haired and bearded, he looked old, and I wondered if he would have what it took. Then again, at age thirty-four, I thought everybody with a gray hair was seriously over the hill.

At first I was a little intimidated by Sonny's title and accomplishments; I felt conspicuously rough around the edges and not very well educated. But in a very short time, Sonny put me completely at ease. We had more in common than not. Love of hunting is a powerful bond.

Sonny and his friend, Dr. Cliff Coffman, were to hunt together with Chris Widrig and me. We would pack up and head away from the base camp for ten days. Although our main target was sheep, the doctors also had caribou and grizzly tags. We would take a packstring consisting of four saddle horses and four packhorses. We had no horses to spare, so it was imperative that we pack our horses efficiently.

As is the case with most hunters coming into this kind of country, the two doctors had way too much stuff. It was not that they lacked knowledge of what to bring; they were over-prepared. This is far better than being under-prepared for the Canadian wilderness, as it can be incredibly unforgiving, but for the sake of the horses, I still had to pare down on the amount of gear they took with us.

For me to be away from base camp for ten days, I knew what I would need: two pairs of socks, the ones I had on, and a pair to change into; an extra pair of pants; one pair of long johns; one sweater; one spare T-shirt; a change of underwear; a hat; and rain gear. Because I could not expect the doctors to be quite as rough and tumble as I am, I generously allowed them twice that. We still left a mountain of their stuff behind, but they were good-natured about it, trusting me with the details of their adventure.

To our personal gear we added ten days' worth of food. All this was carefully weighed (using the left hand/right hand scale method) and divided into eight pack boxes. The rest of the gear, tents, and sleeping bags were stacked on top of the boxes, and everything was firmly lashed down under a tarp. By the time we were ready to go, the packhorses looked like little mini sporting-goods stores.

Rifles went into scabbards on the saddles, and spotting scopes into bags tied on behind the saddle for easy access. Rain gear was also tied onto the saddle within easy reach. A day's supply of sandwiches,

Yukon Guide, Part II: A Sheep, a 'Bou, and an Underwear Bear

chocolate bars, and drinks went into the saddlebags. I carried my empty pack behind the saddle, also.

By the time we were ready to go, the whole camp was on the move. We looked like a clan of gypsies breaking camp. There were five guides and all the clients, and all of us were mounted. All twenty-nine horses were in use.

For a while, we all shared the same trail, and then to the dismay of the horses, each party of hunters and guides began to move in different directions. Chris and I along with our two doctors and four packhorses headed north, down a river flowing toward the Arctic Ocean. The spike camp that was our destination was sixty miles away, a two-day journey.

Chris was at the front. He seemed to have a dislike for riding, and led his horse, choosing to walk. At that time, Chris was the only person I had ever seen who could keep up a pace that easily outdistanced a horse. Chris was followed by the four packhorses, who roamed loose, and then by Sonny and Cliff on horseback. I rode drag, pulling up last.

The packhorses protested leaving their herd, stubbornly turning around and doubling back in an effort to rejoin the herd, so the first hour kept me busy trying to keep them all moving in the right direction. After that, they sullenly settled in, with only the odd heartbroken and hopeful whinny sent out into the wilderness.

We followed a well-used horse trail along the banks of a very swollen river. There had been several days of torrential downpour, and the river was in full flood even though it was only the second week of August. Chris led the way, on foot, until we came to the first river crossing. The water in the river was murky and moving swiftly. These conditions always make it hard to determine the best place to cross.

Chris surveyed the banks for a moment, jumped on his horse, and over the strenuous balking of the animal, finally prevailed and forced him off the bank. *"Awwwwwwh"* screamed Chris as he plunged into the water up to his thighs and his horse up to its withers. Within seconds, all we could see were two heads bobbing down the river, one of them yelling expletives the whole way across. We followed their course until they emerged dripping, on the other side. The packhorses ignored where Chris had plunged off the bank, and meandered downstream.

"Follow them," I called to Sonny and Cliff.

Sure enough, the loose packhorses found a spot that was satisfactory to them. Even though they could not see the bottom of the river, the horses had unerringly chosen a route where they did not have to swim. Horses have memories like elephants. They knew exactly where the trail was even though they hadn't been on it since last year. Sonny, Cliff, and I got wet to our thighs, which is a whole lot better than cold water to our necks. The rifle scabbard stayed dry. If there is one thing I hate about crossings, it is getting my rifle wet.

Chris was back off his horse, walking, seemingly unaware he was dripping wet. A quarter of a mile later we were crossing the same river. Once again Chris mounted. Once again he ignored the cues of his horse. Once again he plunged into the water with a ceremonious war cry. Sonny, Cliff, and I followed the packhorses upstream to a different place. We didn't even get wet.

The third crossing came. I was beginning to suspect Chris liked swimming as much as walking, because I knew he had picked the wrong place even before I heard the shrieked expletive.

I turned to the doctors. "Just watch what Chris does, and don't do that."

That day we crossed the river eleven times. Out of those eleven times, the doctors and I ended up swimming with our horses three. Chris, eight. Soaked and nearly frozen after the last crossing, we stopped briefly to put on dry clothes and eat a sandwich. The sandwiches were soaked, but we didn't even hesitate to eat them. After draining the water out of the rifles, without so much as a hot cup of tea, we were back on the trail.

Yukon Guide, Part II: A Sheep, a 'Bou, and an Underwear Bear

Chris had a sense of urgency knowing we had hard miles to make and a limited time to make them. Sonny had been on many guided hunts, including African safaris, but this was his first sheep hunt. Though he was uncomplaining, he could not have been expecting this kind of discomfort. I think even Cliff, who had been on three previous Dall sheep hunts, seemed to be a bit dazed by the extreme conditions.

Around 4 PM that afternoon, we spotted five Dall rams on the other side of the river with one really good trophy in the group. Because Cliff had already harvested a Dall sheep, he wanted Sonny to be the shooter. Chris and Cliff carried on down the trail so that Sonny and I could hunt the ram.

Even though we had put in an exhausting day, I knew things can change in a hair with sheep hunting. You never put off until tomorrow what you can do today because by tomorrow it can be raining. Or snowing. Or fog can have moved in. Or the sheep have moved out. But one thing we didn't have to worry about was daylight. We were in the land of the midnight sun. This far north, less than a hundred miles from the Arctic Circle, even in August, it never really gets dark. The light dims briefly, the sun wallows on the horizon, and then it is daylight again.

Something about spotting the sheep had energized us. The exhaustion of a hard day of travel had evaporated, and we decided to make a move on the rams that evening. I tied the two packhorses to some trees, unpacked them, and set up the tent. Again, there was a sense of urgency. Supper was a chocolate bar. Eating is not a priority when you are hunting.

Within an hour, we crossed the river on horseback. I chose a place, and though the river was still rushing and murky, we got lucky and arrived on the other side dry. This was good since I had convinced Sonny to leave most of his clothing at the base camp, and by then he was down to his last set of dry duds.

We tied the horses to trees beside the river. Now, believe it or not, the work really began. With packs minimally loaded with chocolate

Unquenchable Spirit

bars and the spotting scope, we headed up a steep embankment. From the other side of the river, I had planned a route up the mountain to the rams, but it was a matter of physical endurance to get there.

The stalk was three hours through scrub brush that slowly gave way to bunches of grass and rock. It was always up, some places steeper than others. Mind you, this was on top of seven hours of hard, hard riding.

Any doubts I might have harbored about Sonny, "the old guy," had evaporated. I have to tell you, Sonny surprised me with how well he held his own. Tired, yes, he was, but an absolute trooper. To come from an office and operating room to this and to perform so well won my respect.

Once in position, Sonny handed me a fancy contraption I had never seen before. "It's a rangefinder," he told me.

Rob with Sonny's ram.

Yukon Guide, Part II: A Sheep, a 'Bou, and an Underwear Bear

I'd never heard of it. But after I ranged the ram at 330 yards, I was a total convert. I have rarely hunted without a rangefinder since. I asked Sonny if he was comfortable with making such a long shot as we could not get any closer without being seen. His response was, "No problem."

Before I could get my binos up, Sonny dropped to the ground, aimed his .300 Winchester Magnum, and fired, all in one movement. With the naked eye, I could see the ram rolling down the hill. My respect deepened even further. The doctor couldn't be spending all his time in the office and operating room. That man could shoot!

We made our way to the fallen ram, and Sonny was elated. The ram measured just over thirty-eight inches on both sides and was heavy around the bases.

The elation carried us both through the next few minutes of picture taking and backslapping, but weariness was really setting in as we loaded the packs. The trip down the mountain went faster than up, but it still took two hours. It was difficult to carry such heavily laden packs down such a steep incline. Sonny held his own again, taking his own cape and horns, while I packed the meat.

In fact, Sonny did better than me on the way out because I had a touchy knee. It locked up as we headed down, and then the knee dislocated. This was not a first-time thing, and Sonny watched, clearly astounded, as I shoved my knee back into place and kept going.

It was past midnight by the time we crossed the river. Just as my horse was climbing the far bank, Sonny's horse stepped into a hole in the river, plunging both of them over their heads in icy water. They emerged, and the horse found his feet and lunged forward so powerfully that Sonny somersaulted off the horse's back and into the water. Because he was still wearing his backpack full of meat, he was like a turtle on his back. In other words, stuck.

I quickly tied my horse to a tree and ran back and plunged into the water after Sonny. By now Sonny was as used to being wet as dry, and again I was struck by the fact that man had absolutely no whine in him. Once back in the saddles, we hurried the final ten minutes back to the tent. I took the saddles off the horses, hobbled them, and set them loose with bells.

There was no fire and no food. Sonny had no dry clothes. It was two o'clock in the morning, and a kind of twilight fell over the land as we crawled into our sleeping bags, dog-tired. Thus, Dr. Milstead's first day of the hunt had come to a close.

The next day, we slept in. In the morning we finally had some hot food, and then we used the fire to begin drying clothes. I spent half the day cleaning and salting the sheep cape.

Sonny wanted to have a look at my knee. By then, at age thirty-four, I was already paying for some pretty hard living and rough treatment of my poor body. I'd already had five knee operations, and one on my shoulder. Sonny inspected all my zippers and shook his head.

"Boy," he said in that slow Southern drawl, "you are a mother's nightmare and an orthopedic surgeon's dream."

By afternoon, with clothes dry and the sheep looked after, we were ready to move again. We headed up the trail that Chris and his hunter had traversed the day before. By evening we set up camp just below a pass leading into the next valley. I hobbled and turned the horses loose and set up camp.

There were lots of grizzly sign in the area. That, in itself, would make most people nervous. Having seen Chris's face, ruined in a grizzly bear attack, wouldn't have helped. So, Sonny had normal nervousness about all the bear sign, but he also had the hunter thing. He said he was interested in taking a bear.

I said, "Stick with me, Sonny. I am a grizzly magnet."

This is the absolute truth. Although it could be the amount of time I spend in places that grizzlies hang out, it seems to be more than that. I know other people who spend the same amount of time

Yukon Guide, Part II: A Sheep, a 'Bou, and an Underwear Bear

in wilderness areas like the ones I frequent, and they have rarely seen a grizzly. But, at the time I was guiding Sonny, I had experienced at least twenty pretty up-close and personal grizzly-bear encounters, from bluff charges to having to kill a bear in self-defense.

"Bear with me," I said, and Sonny laughed at my double entendre. I didn't know how true those words were going to prove to be.

That evening, I placed the sheep skull in the tent with us. Sonny looked at it, still with little pockets of meat and brain matter clinging to it, and said, "Do you think that's safe?"

"We'll be fine. I don't want something coming in and packing it off during the night."

Sonny looked troubled, probably thinking of the "something" that would do that, and wondering if the thin nylon wall would be much protection against "it." Against his better judgment, I'm sure, he bowed to my expertise without argument, and we both settled in to the tent for the night.

It was about 5 AM when I was awakened to the sound of a pack box moving outside of the tent. It sounded like a bowling ball rolling around inside a crate.

Half asleep, expecting to see a troublesome wolverine, I unzipped the tent and poked my head out.

I came face to face with a rather large grizzly.

From four feet away, his scent filled my nostrils. His head looked like a pumpkin. His beady little eyes locked on mine. Busy walloping the pack box with skillet-size paws when I interrupted him, he now stood frozen. I was, too, for half a second or so. It was one of those "Oh, @#%&" situations.

I slipped backward into the tent and shook Sonny urgently. "Sonny, wake up. Ginormous. Grizzly. Outside!"

Looking back, I am astonished by the workings of my own mind. Somehow, instead of grabbing my rifle and getting back outside, in defense of life and limb, I was thinking, *Sonny has a tag.*

Unquenchable Spirit

Sonny jerked awake, grabbed his .416 Rigby, and crawled outside. I grabbed his .300 Winchester Magnum and went out after him, prepared to do battle. The bear was gone. Seconds before, he was right outside the door of the tent. Now, nothing. Sonny, still half asleep, was probably wondering if it was that warped Canadian sense of humor again. We crept around the tent, side by side. I wasn't going first because much as I had come to like and trust Sonny, I didn't want to get shot up the backside if he got excited.

Which he did . . . because the bear was right behind the tent. He was less than thirty yards from us, on all fours, with his ears laid back and the hair on the thick hump of his neck standing straight up. A bear will snap his teeth if he wants to warn you. If he's going to charge the silence is deadly. That silence at that moment was lethal.

Sonny and I both brought up our guns to our shoulders. Standing beside Sonny's .416 Rigby when it went off was like standing beside a cannon. And, apparently for the bear, it was like standing in front of one, too. The bear dropped in his tracks. No finishing shot was necessary. That bear didn't even kick. He was deader than a doornail. I have never seen an animal die so quickly.

The whole thing happened so fast that I don't think either of us ever really felt frightened. The normal elation—that other emotion of a hunt—was missing, too, because there had been none of the elements of a normal hunt, like spotting an animal and stalking it. Still, as the shock wore off, Sonny was pleased with his bear. It was just over seven feet long, a good size for a Yukon grizzly.

We realized we were both in our underwear. I made Sonny pose with the dead bear, freezing, in his underwear so I could snap his picture. That photo was true to the story and how it unfolded.

Once things settled down, I took a closer look at the damage the bear had done to our camp supplies. He had obviously been quite busy for a long time before I heard him. The pack box containing all our bacon, eggs, and sheep meat had been dragged away from camp.

Yukon Guide, Part II: A Sheep, a 'Bou, and an Underwear Bear

I found it about fifty yards away, with the lid torn off and punctured with teeth marks. Every bit of food had been eaten. The inside of the box had practically been licked clean. Nearly a hundred pounds worth of food had gone down that grizzly's gullet.

That bear was an out and out pig, and I was glad we got the bastard before he'd managed to get into the pack box he was rolling beside the tent. It contained the salted sheep cape. Luckily he didn't get it open, as a sheep cape is pretty much irreplaceable. I was well aware we'd been blessed with luck that morning. Not only had he not gotten to the cape, but we also got him before he decided

Heading out to meet Chris with Sonny's ram and bear.

to rip open the tent, with us in it, in search of that skull with its tasty morsels still attached.

"I told you to bear with me," I said, "not that I would have wished this experience on anyone."

"Are you kidding? You just gave me the finest story of my hunting career."

The remainder of the day was spent preparing the bear for a life-size mount. After waking up with a bang, the rest of the day was pretty much uneventful. I have to admit, that night I slept a little uneasily wondering if we had camped on some kind of bear migration route.

We packed the next day and headed for the valley where Chris was camped. About two hours into the trip, we came through a low pass on a tundra plateau and found ourselves face to face with a sow grizzly and what looked to be a two-year-old cub. She began snapping her teeth at us. Then she began pacing back and forth across the trail about seventy-five yards in front of us.

Sonny, sitting on a dancing horse that was preparing to bolt, might have had the passing thought that the whole bear-with-me thing was getting old. We got off the horses because our chances of getting dumped were improving by each second the sow refused to back down. We grabbed rifles from scabbards. This time Sonny had the .300 Winchester Magnum and I had the .416 Rigby.

"Sonny, take a shot over her head to see if that spooks her. Just wait, I'll get a good hold on the . . . KABOOM. . . . horses."

The horses yanked free of my hold and bolted back in the direction we had just come. The sow rolled on the ground, roaring, and rubbing her head. At first, I thought Sonny had shot her.

"Nah," he said. "Just gave her a haircut."

It might have been the ringing in her ears making her roll around like that. She rolled around for a good two minutes, and then staggered to her feet and followed her cub across the tundra.

Yukon Guide, Part II: A Sheep, a 'Bou, and an Underwear Bear

Now, I was faced with the decision of chasing the horses or staying to see if she was well and truly going, which I thought she was. I left Sonny and chased the horses. I finally caught up with them feeding in a meadow about four miles back down the trail. They were utterly content, as if nothing had happened. Meanwhile, I had run so hard I felt as if my lungs were going to blow out. Horses being horses, they weren't nearly as eager to be caught as I was to catch them, and I had to do some more running before I had them all tail-tied together and was riding back along the trail toward where I had left Sonny. It was about an hour before I got back to him. He was sitting down, and he was as white as a sheet with beads of perspiration on his forehead.

"Boy am I ever glad to see you!"

I wondered if he was having a heart attack, but as it turned out, the bear had not gone on her way. She had come back and charged him again, and again. Sonny stood his ground and kept his rifle aimed at the bear. He drew an imaginary line, and if the bear crossed it he was going to kill her.

The bear repeated the process of bluff charging numerous times but would stop short of the imaginary line each time. Still, each time she also came a little closer than the time before. The charges went on for nearly half an hour until finally the cub grew bored with waiting and wandered off. The sow finally followed her cub.

I arrived about twenty minutes after she had left, but Sonny was still on full alert not knowing if she was going to try sneaking in on him from a different direction. To this day, I am in awe of the courage and discipline Sonny showed in not shooting that bear.

Once things settled down, and Sonny was able to catch his breath, we resumed our trip toward the valley where Chris and his hunter were camped.

"Man," Sonny said, not unhappily, "this is sure turning out to be a hunt I'll never forget."

Back at base camp with trophies from a very successful hunt.

    We arrived in the other valley later that evening to find Chris and his hunter with a ram that Cliff had harvested the day before. We told them about our misadventures with bears. Chris said that was very near to the place he had been mauled by a grizzly, with a yearling cub, the year before. It had been a brutal mauling where Chris had to be airlifted out by helicopter. I am certain, because of that sow's lack of fear and aggression toward people, and the age of the cub, it was probably the same bear.

    The next day we set out toward base camp in a different direction from the way we had come, a kind of a round trip, the scenic route. Two days in, we spotted a bachelor group of bull caribou high on a plateau. There was a shooter bull in the group and it was decided

Yukon Guide, Part II: A Sheep, a 'Bou, and an Underwear Bear

that Sonny would shoot the bull as Cliff was not as avidly interested in taking a caribou. All four of us hiked up to the plateau, and Sonny made another great one-shot kill. The caribou gross scored around 370 inches.

This turned out to be a dream hunt for Sonny. He had arrived with three tags, and he went home with three trophy animals, though I think he valued the lifetime's worth of hair-raising stories as much, or maybe even more, than those trophies. We had crossed raging rivers, had encounters with bears, and logged over a hundred and forty miles on horseback.

When Sonny had gotten off that airplane, I had wondered if he was tough enough for the trip. He was. In spades. Now, I watched as his plane left Goz Lake. He was on his way back to his life . . . and I was on my way back to mine.

After the plane was gone, I breathed in the silence, listened to the clanking of bells, and drank in the scenery. I turned to greet my new hunter. I wouldn't have traded places for anything.

CHAPTER 14

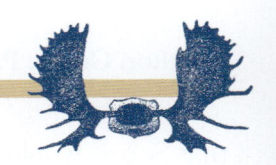

Yukon Guide, Part III: No Bull Moose Hunting

What do you do with a client who admits he's in bad shape and can't shoot, either?

It was late August as I was getting ready to welcome my third group of hunters. August in the Yukon is not like August anywhere else. Fall is in the air. We had already experienced a frost. Leaves were changing color. Days were getting shorter. Bugs were getting fewer.

"They're after moose," Chris told me. "They'd like a caribou, too, but mostly moose."

Moose. Great. I had been here more than six weeks. In that time I had seen sheep, grizzly bears, and caribou. I had not seen a single moose. So, as I watched the hunters walk the gangplank (come down the floatplane ramp) I thought, *Welcome to your very expensive horseback ride.*

"Hi Rob, I'm Mike." The new hunter looked me over, and then laid it out. "I'm here to have a good time. There are a few things I think you should know about me. First, I'm a lousy shot, so I need to get close to an animal if I'm going to kill it. Second, I'm out of shape. I smoke and I drink. Lots. Basically, I'm here to have a good time and get drunk."

Not a single mention of a moose as part of his expectation for his trip. This was a relief to me.

"Mike," I said, "I appreciate your honesty. I'm a little sick of hearing guys claim they can shoot the eye out of a fly at a hundred yards." In the back of my mind, I added, *and as long as you don't get your hopes up for a moose, we probably will get along fine and have a pretty good time.*

I went through the process of whittling Mike's two large duffel bags down to one by eliminating a lot of clothing. I actually was glad to see him show up with too much stuff because it was easier to leave

Yukon Guide, Part III: No Bull Moose Hunting

the extra in camp than to make some essential item magically appear. I let him keep the booze, thinking it might help him deal with the disappointment of no moose.

Mikes hunting partner's name was Jeff. His guide was to be Jimmy Johnny, the famous Indian guide from Mayo, Yukon. (Jimmy told me he didn't like being called Native American or First Nation. He held that this was the hubris of a younger generation.) Until this point, I had guided with Chris. No doubt he was checking me out to see if I knew what I was doing. After hitting a home run with the previous clients, I was being let loose with Jimmy.

The next day, we did the gypsy-caravan thing again, all twenty-nine horses, guides, and clients getting ready to leave the Goz Lake base camp. This time, as the rest of the gypsies headed south, Jimmy and I headed west, back along the trail in the direction we had just come. The only one left behind was Chris. Chris, a licensed pilot, would now be doing the flying that was required to get the moose meat out of the spike camps so it wouldn't spoil.

As we turned to leave, I took a quick glance back at the Goz Lake camp. I had no idea that that glimpse would be the last time I would ever see it.

Given Chris' talent with river crossings, and the colder weather, I was just as happy to be with Jimmy. Jimmy took the lead, and I again took up the rear to keep an eye on our hunters and to make sure the loose packhorses kept in line with the lead horses.

We rode that entire day, until we arrived back at Porter Puddle and set up camp for the night. Mike and Jeff kept up a fairly steady stream of wisecracks and good humor, especially once they cracked one of the bottles. They were fun guys to be with. I was pretty sure they would take the no-moose thing pretty well.

The next day we packed up again and headed for an unnamed lake that Chris had shown us on the map. He told us that ten years ago a guide and hunter had taken a big moose there. He didn't say that in front of the clients, and though I said nothing, I felt a ten-year gap was not exactly a hopeful sign. There was no real horse trail, so we followed game trails along an unnamed creek, over an unnamed pass into the open valley that contained the unnamed lake.

I was delighted to see some fresh moose sign. Things might be looking up for Mike. But eight hours later when we arrived at the lake, I still had not seen an actual real live moose.

We set up camp at the unnamed lake and settled in for the night. Mike and Jeff were jovial, constantly laughing, joking, and poking fun at each other. They were a bit like two ten-year-old boys in a boring class, basically not focusing on the task at hand—hunting. But in a way, I saw that as a good thing. They had no idea we were not seeing moose. They probably thought we would eventually arrive at some magical valley, where, *ta-da,* moose would suddenly appear, and that they would be close enough for even the worst shot to get one.

That night Jimmy made his famous bannock. The recipe had been passed down to him from his grandparents, people who never spoke a word of English. These hunters liked Jimmy's bannock so much that we decided to name the unnamed lake Bannock Lake. (The name, it seems, stuck). Mike and Jeff produced a video camera to record Jimmy's recipe.

This is it exactly: "This many flour," Jimmy said, scooping up four large handfuls of flour and putting them in his bowl. "This many baking soda." Two small fistfuls were dropped into the bowl. "This much salt." He showed a scattering in the bottom of his palm. He added water until it was sticky then threw it in a frying pan sizzling with lard so we could all have seconds.

"That's a ten-thousand-dollar bannock recipe," I told the hunters as I munched on the best bannock ever made.

"How do you figure?" Mike asked.

"That's what you paid for your hunt, and that might be all you get."

Yukon Guide, Part III: No Bull Moose Hunting

They both laughed. It was a good thing that they were OK about being teased about their foolishness with their money. It was a bad thing that they thought I was kidding. I still wasn't sure about the moose. The drinks came out and the guys toasted the beauty, the ride, the bannock, their friendship, and their guides, even though we had not as yet produced anything but a bannock recipe that I use to this day, and maybe they do, too.

The next day we split up, Jimmy took Jeff to the west, and I took Mike north over a plateau. When we reached the highest point of the land, to my great relief, I saw my first moose in the valley below. There was a cow and calf and at the other end of the meadow was a small bull. A small bull was better than no bull, so we moved in closer.

As we closed the distance, I spotted a movement about five hundred yards below us. Upon further investigation, I determined that the animals were a small bachelor group of caribou bulls. There was one real good one in the group. *Hmmm.* Maybe we'd arrived at the magic valley after all.

I pointed out the big bull to Mike, who had not seen him at all. I was fairly certain the bull would make the Boone and Crockett record book, not that that is something you ever share with a client, just in case you're wrong. And, of course, there was always the chance Mike might not make the shot. He had been more than honest about his abilities.

"Are you interested in him?"

"Hell, yeah," Mike said, "Just look at the size of him."

"Are you sure? I understand you want a moose more, and if you take this one, it will take up at least two hunting days, and possibly three to cape him, look after the meat, and get him out of here."

"I'm sure. That is the biggest caribou I've ever seen."

"Mike," I reminded him, "That is the only caribou you've ever seen."

"I want him."

Rob with Mike's Boone and Crockett caribou.

Yukon Guide, Part III: No Bull Moose Hunting

And so the stalk began. With it foremost in my mind that Mike had made it abundantly clear he was a lousy shot, I was determined to get him close. When the caribou bedded down, a rarity with caribou, we sneaked into a gully and followed it, out of sight of the bedded 'bous. The wind was with us, blowing away from them, and into our faces.

We came out of the gully, into rocks and lichens. Now, we had to belly crawl, which is not nearly as easy as they make it seem in the movies. I kept Mike behind me, carrying his rifle, as I am ever alert to the dangers of the excitement factor. We crawled two hundred yards. I only lifted my head enough to see the caribou and make sure they hadn't gotten up. I didn't let Mike peer up over the rocks at all. He could not see his unsuspecting victim, but they could not see him, either.

After about thirty yards, I coaxed Mike into position for the shot, and surrendered his rifle to him. I slithered out of my backpack, and he used it as a rest. He popped his head up. This was the first time he had a visual during the entire stalk. The three caribou were bedded together. I pointed at the biggest one.

Mike made the shot with ease. The caribou staggered to its feet, ran several steps, and stumbled to his death. He was stone dead; it was a perfect lung shot.

Mike turned to me, grinning. "That was awesome. I can't believe you were able to get me so close."

"Hey, you're the one who said you were a lousy shot. So I took you seriously and got you close."

He was ecstatic over the stalk, the shot, and the size of the animal. We would later learn the caribou green scored 417 inches gross, which easily made the record books.

After picture taking, I hiked back up and untied the horses and led them down to Mike and his caribou. Once butchering and caping were complete, we loaded the caribou on the packhorses and prepared for our trip back over the small plateau toward Bannock Lake.

Mike's caribou packed up and ready to go.

As we entered the thick-forested area around the lake, we had a mishap. I had allowed the packhorse carrying the huge antlers to run loose behind us. The packhorse decided to pick his own route through the trees and managed to get himself stuck, the huge rack jammed fast between two trees. Mike looked back and saw the dilemma before I did.

"Hey, Rob, the horse seems to be stuck."

I turned to see the antlers groaning between the two trees. The horse pushed forward with a look of determination on his face that clearly said I'm going forward with or without these antlers.

"Do you think those antlers will break?"

The antlers already looked bent beyond hope. They had curved up so badly the top points were almost touching each other, but I

Yukon Guide, Part III: No Bull Moose Hunting

had already developed a seasoned guide's rather cagey way of dealing with clients. It was a variation of never let them see you sweat, that was more like never let them know how bad it is.

As if I were an expert on the bending properties of caribou antlers, I reassured Mike, "Oh, no, they'll be just fine. They can bend a lot without breaking. This is nothing compared to what they do to them when they fight."

Fate was on my side that day. The horse gave one last mighty heave and pulled himself through the narrow gap between the two trees. The antlers sprang back to their original shape. I fetched the loose packhorse and led him the rest of the way back to base camp, and I never again have let a pack animal carrying valuable cargo run around choosing his own route.

We arrived at camp first. Jimmy arrived much later, after dark. To my relief, his hunter, Jeff, had also been successful. They had found the magic valley, and Jeff had harvested a good moose, which meant both our hunters would be going home with more than a bannock recipe. After cleaning and quartering the fallen moose, they had left it in the bush because the light had died.

The next day we headed out early with all the horses to retrieve Jeff's moose, preferably before a grizzly beat us to him. This was a very real danger, for if a bear shows up and claims a kill, there will be trouble. Aware of this peril, we approached from the upper side so we got a good visual of the moose and the surrounding area.

Jimmy had tied plastic grain sacks to the tops of the willow bushes around the carcass. It was the first time I had seen that, and Jimmy told me if the grain sacks were moving, or had been pulled down, there was a pretty good chance that there was a bear on the carcass. This old Indian had bush savvy like no one I had ever met before or since.

Determining that there was no bear on the moose, we approached. Considering how small my hopes had been of even finding a moose, I was thrilled with its size. At that time it was the biggest moose I

Left to right: Rob, Mike, and Jeff taking a break.

had ever seen. It was 56 inches wide, had 26 points, with 5 points on each brow palm. It would later score over 200 inches.

Jeff and Mike pitched in cheerfully and with the four of us working, it only took about three hours to have the entire moose loaded and ready to head back to camp. It took all four packhorses to carry the eight-hundred-plus pounds of meat.

That night we feasted on moose meat and bannock. Later Jimmy called Chris on the radio-phone and made arrangements for him to fly the mountain of meat back out to Goz Lake base camp. We hunted one more day over the plateau where Mike had shot the caribou, but we were unable to find another large bull moose. At least we were seeing moose.

The next morning, we packed up again and headed back to Porter Puddle. Jimmy said he knew of a lick there that usually held

Yukon Guide, Part III: No Bull Moose Hunting

moose. We spent that night laughing at Mike's jokes and enjoying the camaraderie amongst the hunters. They made hunting fun and didn't take anything too seriously, which made my job easy.

The next day after a relaxing breakfast of bacon, eggs, and Jimmy's bannock, we rode down a river valley to where the moose lick was located. Again, we seemed to have luck on our side. It wasn't long before we were looking at moose. Considering how few of them I'd seen for the rest of the season, it seemed like something of a miracle to be looking at eight of them.

There were four bulls and four cows. One of the bulls was a shooter. Jimmy and Jeff waited and watched while Mike and I executed the stalk. Once in position in the timber on the edge of the natural salt lick, everything looked different. We could see moose legs moving about in the trees, but could not tell which moose was which.

Mike exclaimed, "There he is." The moose heard him and began to exit, stage right.

I said, "You better shoot quickly because he's moving fast."

KABOOM went Mike's .300 Winchester Magnum rifle.

At this point I still hadn't had a good look at the moose, but could tell he was a bull. As we approached the fallen moose, my heart fell. He wasn't the big one. I felt sick as I knew that things had gotten out of hand and as a guide I had lost control. I thought that Mike would be angry at me for not taking a better look at the moose before telling him to shoot.

I turned to Mike and said, "That is the wrong moose." I braced myself for the tongue lashing that I was sure would follow.

But Mike was a true sportsman and a good man. He said, "I don't care how big he is. I'm happy with him. It's been an awesome hunt."

That was refreshing to hear. Most guys, myself included, would have sulked for the rest of the trip. The moose still ended up measuring 52 inches, which would have been good for a moose from southern British Columbia.

The hunters back at base camp. Mike's moose is second from left.

The rest of the day was spent getting all the meat back to Porter Puddle with Jimmy and Jeff's help. That evening, Jimmy called Chris and arranged for him to fly the meat back to Goz Lake.

We hunted several more days trying to find a good caribou for Jeff, but time was not on our side. We saw several small ones, but neither Jimmy Johnny nor I felt they were good enough.

In a change of plan, Chris flew into Porter Puddle to pick up Mike and Jeff. The next hunters were also delivered to Porter Puddle. And that's where the trouble began.

CHAPTER 15

Yukon Guide, Part IV: Trouble at Porter Puddle

A meat hunt takes on a whole new meaning to two bushed guides deep in the Yukon.

Chris Widrig flew into Porter Puddle to pick up my hunter, Mike. He was flying a SuperCub, so could only take one passenger out at a time. As he took Mike out, he dropped a new hunter off. For some reason, Chris had decided it was easier to do it this way, and it was. At least it was easier for him and for the hunters.

But when I had packed my skimpy bag—my one change of socks, and my one change of underwear—for this trip, I hadn't been counting on the fact I would not see the base camp again. Chris made a spontaneous decision to leave Jimmy Johnny and me at different spike camps, beside different lakes, for over a month, right up until the end of the season.

I had mistakenly believed I was roughing it before. I spent my last-month-plus as a guide without any creature comforts at all, and the weather was now changing drastically. By mid-September that hiccup of a fall was gone, and it felt like the dead of winter. I cannot tell you how I missed hot showers and food out of an oven instead of cooked in a frying pan. We lived out of a small tent, and I missed having a bed, and walls, and a heater. A good part of every day was now spent gathering and chopping firewood.

It got so cold that I could not even wash my meager supply of clothing. Any contact with water, and my clothes would freeze solid. Personal hygiene had long since stopped being a priority. My hands were completely black from cooking fires. I didn't have a razor and now sported a full beard. In photos taken during that time, I bear a striking resemblance to Jeremiah Johnson. I froze my toes, and the battle against the cold was constant. And so the last few hunts, rather than a pleasure for either guide or clients, became an endurance test.

The next hunters to be flown in found a pair of savages as their guides. We stank. We had long hair and beards. Our clothes were in tatters. Our gear was filthy. My feet were black where they had frozen. We were hardened and bad-tempered. We were developing a certain bitter attitude that comes from too long away from creature comforts. We hadn't had a shower for weeks. And campfire food is good for the short term. Long hauls on it make a man crabby.

Into this atmosphere, Chris dropped off my next hunter, a German whom I'll call Franz. As in some of the previous stories I have changed the names to protect the guilty. This was his second hunt with Chris. His target species were caribou and grizzly. He had harvested a moose on his previous trip.

Franz was dressed in army green clothing, which I thought looked ridiculously like a uniform from the Second World War. His pants had creases that would make a knife's edge envious, and he looked disdainfully at what remained of my wardrobe. Although Franz spoke English, I found him very difficult to understand.

Within seconds of introductions being made, Franz wanted to show me his rifle. It was European made, a .338 caliber, but I can't remember the brand. He was quite proud of it, especially sitting next to my rusty 7mm that was as beat up as I was. My rifle looked like it was worth about ten dollars.

"Rob," Franz said, stroking his rifle affectionately, "Only ten thousand U.S. dollars. You must get vun."

Since Germans are notoriously bad tippers, I knew I wouldn't be getting one on his dime. Besides, I liked my five-hundred-dollar rifle and was pretty sure I had taken more animals with it than Franz would see in his lifetime, let alone kill.

An hour later, Chris flew back in to take out Jeff, and bring in Jimmy's new hunter. He and Franz were friends. I'll call him Dieter. Added to his pressed green army outfit were high black combat boots. With his ice blue eyes and blond hair, Dieter looked like a poster boy

Yukon Guide, Part IV: Trouble at Porter Puddle

for the *SchutzStaffel (SS)*. Whether the look was intentional or not, I don't know.

Dieter's target species was anything with a heartbeat. He had a tag for every animal available in the northern Yukon: moose, caribou, sheep, grizzly. From the start, Dieter radiated a sense of his own superiority and a teeth-grinding arrogance.

I turned to Jimmy and muttered, "I think you have your work cut out for you this time."

Jimmy nodded. His face was creased into a look of dread that said it all.

That evening, above our camp, I spotted a small group of caribou bulls on a ridge. One of them was a shooter. Ironically, they had wandered in just that day. We had hunted in this same area with Jeff for several days and had come up empty. It is amazing the difference a day can make. After seeing the small herd, we made plans to pursue it. Franz and I would go after the caribou early the next morning. Jimmy would take Dieter to some meadows south of camp in pursuit of moose.

The next day I glassed the mountain where I had found the caribou the day before. They hadn't moved at all. I saddled up two riding horses and a packhorse and rode out of camp with Franz, who was flicking horsehairs off his slacks, in tow. We were able to ride most of the way up the mountain. The stalk was only about two hundred yards before we were in a position to shoot. I set up my backpack for a rest, and told Franz to use it.

"I don't need that," Franz exclaimed scornfully.

I shrugged. I could already tell he was the kind of guy you couldn't tell anything to. Besides, he might be right. The shot was about 110 yards, so it should have been easy.

He decided to shoot offhand at the caribou. He brought the rifle to his shoulder. I watched the barrel of Franz's rifle making large circles, like a Ferris wheel. I downgraded my assessment that he might be right. I couldn't see this going well.

Unquenchable Spirit

Porter Puddle.

Yukon Guide, Part IV: Trouble at Porter Puddle

Unquenchable Spirit

"Aim for the front shoulder," I told Franz.

KABOOM. The caribou's ass end dropped.

"I meant his other front shoulder."

The caribou then began milling around in circles, with a broken back. It seemed to be stating the obvious, but Franz was clearly waiting for direction, so I said, "Shoot him again."

Now Franz's rifle barrel was moving around even more wildly as his buck fever intensified. He fired three more shots, all clean misses. The wounded caribou continued to mill around not knowing where the shots were coming from. Now, in my frustration, I ordered Franz to use my rest. I just wanted to put the poor animal out of his misery. Franz complied and re-aimed, this time using my rest.

"Wait until he's broadside," I snapped.

Rob, living rough in the wilderness.

Yukon Guide, Part IV: Trouble at Porter Puddle

Finally, Franz fired and hit him in the boiler room, putting him down for good. I was relieved that fiasco was over, but I was already dreading going after a grizzly with this clown.

Once we arrived at the poor animal Franz had wounded to death, he turned to me and said, "Now vee must make photo."

He handed me his camera and after I had only taken two pictures, he said, "Good," and snatched his camera back out of my grubby hands, inspecting it for smudges. It was before the days of digital, and I didn't even care that he was only going to have two pictures to choose from.

As I prepared to cape the caribou out, he stopped me saying, "I only vant zee skull and horns." This was my first introduction to European trophies. It sure made my life easy, simply cut the head off and skin out the meat without any concern for keeping the hide intact. Consequently, it didn't take long to get the meat loaded up on the packhorse because there wasn't that much meat left after all the wild shooting. The antlers scored just over 370 inches.

We arrived back in camp for the evening about the same time as Jimmy and Dieter. Jimmy had seen a few moose, but nothing of size. As we suspected, Dieter was turning out to be high maintenance. Jimmy clearly did not look enthralled with the prospect of hunting with this man. As we prepared supper, I told Jimmy about my hunter's shooting abilities and that I was dreading going after a grizzly bear with him next.

Jimmy laughed. "It sounds like you have your work cut out for you."

That evening I decided I would take Franz to the valley where Sonny Milstead and I had had all the grizzly trouble. It would take two days to get there, so I would take a small tent with me as we would be spiking out. I would be gone for at least four days, possibly five. Jimmy was to stay behind with Dieter and focus on moose.

The next day, I saddled up four horses, two packhorses, and two riding horses. We had a long distance to cover, so we left camp

159

Unquenchable Spirit

early. As we entered the valley of the grizzlies, I spotted four bull caribou wandering toward us. They were migrating toward their winter range to the south.

Two of them were the biggest bulls I have ever seen, even to this day. We rode to within 100 yards of the curious beasts, and I was able to get a good long look at them. The biggest bull looked like he would go 450-inches-plus, the next biggest 430-inches-plus, and the two smaller bulls in the 370-inch range. I felt my heart sink, knowing that I was looking at a potential world record and my hunter was tagged out.

I turned to Franz as we watched them walk away. "Too bad you're already tagged out. That would be a nice one to go home with."

Franz studied them intently. "The one I shot," he announced definitively, "is the very same size."

OK. He couldn't shoot and he was blind, too. Or maybe he was blind, so he couldn't shoot. Whatever. It worked for me that Franz was clueless. A lot of hunters would have been trying to talk me into letting them shoot that bull. Then, when I refused to let them poach, they would probably sulk for the rest of the trip, and so long, tip. Not that Germans were known for giving lavish tips, anyway.

We camped that evening about five miles farther down the valley at a camp referred to as "Grizzly Camp." It is a name well deserved. Grizzly tracks pollute the area, and many trees along the trail had bear hair clinging to them from bears rubbing themselves in the spring after coming out of hibernation.

The next day, we saddled up and carried on down the river. By the end of the day, we were back at the same spot where Sonny had shot his grizzly. We set up camp. Although it had been less than a month, the carcass of Sonny's kill had been completely picked clean. All that remained were bones. I found old grizzly tracks in the mud around the carcass. It appeared that another grizzly had eaten this grizzly. As the sign was not very fresh, I didn't spend much time in this area.

Yukon Guide, Part IV: Trouble at Porter Puddle

We only hunted for one day there, and we did not see a single bear. As I had told Jimmy, we would only be gone for a maximum of five days. That meant we would have to start heading back the next day, which we did. After riding along the river, we arrived at Grizzly Camp in the early afternoon with plenty of daylight left.

After I set up the camp, we climbed a low hill above camp to do some glassing. It wasn't long before I spotted movement on the other side of the river just below the camp. Through my spotting scope I was able to determine that it was a large grizzly. It looked to be better than seven feet in length.

We quickly moved down the hill and got into a shooting position across the river from the bear. I ranged him to be at just two hundred yards. As I had very little confidence in Franz's shooting ability, I began breaking branches off a tree to make a rest for Franz to shoot from. Not taking the hint, he held his rifle freehand and started aiming, or rather pointing. I told him to use the rest.

"Ach. I don't need that."

Having heard it all before, I put my rifle on the rest and aimed because if Franz wounded that bear, I was going to finish him. The last thing I wanted was to track a wounded bear in thick willows. A wounded bear makes the most terrifying roaring sound you have ever heard. I knew Franz wouldn't go in after him, so I wasn't up for taking a chance. Just as I got the bear lined up in my scope, Franz took his shot.

The bear stood for a couple seconds before running into the willows. It was long enough for me to determine Franz had made a clear miss. He had shot right over him. Since he missed, I was relieved I didn't have to shoot. I did have to break it to Franz, who seemed to think he had hit the bear.

"You missed him."

Franz turned and gave me a look loaded with icy contempt for the colonial imbecile. "Zat eez imposseeble, sree, sree, aight does not meese."

"Well, your .338 just missed," I responded.

"I heet him," Franz insisted. "Vee must go get zee orses and cross zee river."

I sighed. "We'll go tomorrow and look. We are losing daylight."

I certainly was not going to go saddle up horses, cross a river, and beat bush to confirm what I already knew. No bear. Sulkily, Franz followed me back to camp.

I'm not sure how well Franz slept that night because in his mind he was convinced that there was a dead or injured bear somewhere on the other side of the river. I slept very well knowing I was not going to be looking for a wounded bear.

The next morning, I was in a hurry. We had a long way back to base camp, and now I had to squeeze finding a nonexistent dead bear into my schedule. I made oatmeal instead of bacon and eggs, which is what I had made Franz every other day. He took one bite and spit it out.

"*Uck,* these iss not food." He then dumped his bowl of oatmeal in the fire. "I vant bacon and eggs."

I'd had about enough of the noble hunter to peasant attitude and Franz was smart enough to see the look on my face. He looked crushed as he realized there was no way in hell he was getting bacon and eggs. Silently, I passed him a granola bar. He ate it like a sulky child.

"There's more where that came from, too," I told him pleasantly. His bacon and egg days were over. By now I had had enough of Franz.

I saddled up the two riding horses and we crossed the river. I found the bear's tracks in the sand where Franz had shot at him. There was not a single drop of blood or strand of hair on the ground. We walked in the brush where the bear had run in.

I walked well behind Franz. The image I had of him as he carried his rifle in the brush was that of Elmer Fudd hard on the trail of that "darn wabbit." There was no way I was going in front of that trigger-happy man. After about half an hour of crisscrossing

Yukon Guide, Part IV: Trouble at Porter Puddle

the area where the bear had run, we headed back to the sandy spot where he had missed him. I pointed at the ground and said, "Look. No blood. No hair. No bear." Franz' shoulders slumped under his uniform. He finally accepted the fact that he had missed the bear.

We crossed back over to our camp. Despite the time constraints, I was honor-bound to show him the truth. I set up a target at a hundred yards and was going to have Franz shoot at it.

"I'll load your gun." I loaded his magazine and pretended to jack a shell into the chamber and then handed it to him. I had him use a rest so he was steady. When he "pulled" the trigger, he jerked the rifle about a foot to his right. Click went the rifle. I turned to him.

"I see what your problem is. You have a flinch."

"Vot iss a flinch?" Franz asked.

"It means you are afraid of the recoil of your rifle."

"Here. You shoot it then, Rob." I think now he figured that the scope was out, anything but accepting the blame for his own pathetic shooting.

I dreaded firing his gun. By the bang that gun made, it was going to kick hard. So I aimed carefully as Franz watched the target through my spotting scope. I squeezed off. That gun kicked so hard it nearly took my head off. I thought back to our first meeting. *Only ten thousand U.S. dollars, the man had said?* This gun was a shoulder killer. I think it was nearly as dangerous for the shooter as it was for its victim. I could now see why Franz flinched so badly. My shot, despite the kick, was good. Bull's-eye. Now Franz knew that it wasn't the gun.

As time was now of the essence, we had to start heading back toward Porter Puddle. I packed up the remaining horses. It took us most of the day to ride back. Just before arriving in camp, I was met on the trail by Jimmy. His eyes were wide and bloodshot. Franz rode by him into camp to talk to Dieter, but Jimmy motioned for me to stay.

"Jesus Christ, Jimmy, you look like you've seen a ghost!

Jimmy with "Dieter's" moose.

He told what had happened while Franz and I had been gone. He had gotten a 59-inch moose for Dieter the same day Franz and I left camp. They had packed it back to camp and were in good spirits at the end of the day. Then Jimmy's eyes got huge and he dropped his voice to a whisper. "He pulled a condom out of his pocket, waved it in my face, and said 'vee must celebrate'."

At first I had a hard time not falling over with laughter, but Jimmy was clearly distraught about the incident. I tried to make light of the situation. "Jimmy, look at the bright side. At least he wanted to practice safe sex."

Jimmy didn't laugh. So I put on my best poker face and tried as hard as I could not to burst into laughter as he continued to vent.

"I got him a great moose," Jimmy said indignantly, "and then the %#@%&! wanted to use a condom on me?"

"So, what did you do?"

Yukon Guide, Part IV: Trouble at Porter Puddle

"What do you think? I jacked a shell in the chamber of my .30-30 and pointed it at the ground in front of him. I drew my line in the sand. If he crossed it, I was going to shoot him."

It occurred to me I could have ridden into a homicide because Jimmy was deadly serious, heavy on the deadly part. Jimmy was a man of few words, but at that moment he had plenty to say.

"I haven't slept much since you left. I would wait until the hunter would go to bed, and then lay by the fire watching the tent in case he came out. I stayed by the fire for four nights while you were gone. I was not going in the tent with him."

Jimmy helped me pitch my tent and then he crawled in and fell asleep in utter exhaustion. Franz and Dieter slept in the other tent. I'm not sure how that went, and, truthfully, I didn't want to know.

We moved camp the next day to another lake about twenty miles away. We spent the remainder of the hunt there, but I was unable to find any grizzlies there for Franz. During those last few days Jimmy did not leave my side the whole time. He kept a wide berth around Dieter, and I think mostly focused on not getting cornered. Dieter did not get any more animals on that hunt because Jimmy was spending most of his energy dodging being around him.

Jimmy and I basically set up another camp, separate from our hunters. He was mad at Dieter, and I wasn't cooking for Franz anymore. One memorable time, Chris air-dropped freshly baked cinnamon buns from the base camp, and Jimmy and I raced to the package and then slunk off by ourselves and ate every one of them. I'm sure we would have snarled like wolves on a carcass if Dieter and Franz had found us. We were the same way with our little tins of mandarin oranges: wolflike in our desire to have them only to ourselves. In other words, Jimmy Johnny and I were both completely bushed.

The day Dieter flew out, and Chris flew in his next group of hunters was probably one of the happiest days of Jimmy's life, despite the fact we were still stuck at Porter Puddle and he got no tip. I was

Jimmy cold, tired, and entirely disgruntled over his client's behavior.

happy to see Franz go as well. Franz had proudly presented me with a knife as a tip. I figure it was worth about five dollars. Although most hunters are great guys, it only takes one bad apple to sour a guide. And of course by then, I was pretty sour anyway.

The next hunters were a couple of elderly gentlemen from New York. As Jimmy looked on suspiciously, I asked them, "Are you guys normal?"

"What do you mean by that?"

I then told them what our previous hunters had been like. They broke into laughter, and the one I had asked responded, "Do you

Yukon Guide, Part IV: Trouble at Porter Puddle

mean he tried to play Pokemon with Jimmy here?" He pointed to poor Jimmy, who still wasn't laughing.

Though this hunt went better than it had with our German hunters, it was the last hunt of the season, and Jimmy and I were totally done. We had left Mayo in the summer, with temperatures hovering around thirty-degrees-plus Centigrade, with twenty-four hours of daylight. Now, temperatures could plummet to minus-twenty-degrees C during the night, and we were down to seven hours of light per day. When the Otter finally arrived to pull the guides and the last hunters out of there, it broke ice off the lake with its pontoons. Only two men remained to get the horses out; one was Jimmy Johnny.

Seventy-eight days after I had left civilization, it was my turn to go out. I looked out the window of the Otter, watching Jimmy as he got the horses ready for the long trail out. Jimmy had always known it would fall on him to get the horses out. My admiration for Jimmy and his skill in that land of such harsh extremes is absolutely boundless.

And I can say the same for all the men with whom I shared that summer in the Yukon. We parted more than friends, we had become part of a brotherhood of tough men, survivors, united by a never-say-die warrior spirit. I knew we would always be in touch, but at this precise moment, I was ready to go.

My thirst for adventure had been slaked. For now.

CHAPTER 16

Dream Dall

Magic unfolds in the land of the midnight sun.

The old mining road in the southern Yukon was rough, potholed, and washboarded. There were several creek crossings where all that remained of the bridges were splinters. The bogs and mud holes were deep, treacherous, and frequent. In other words, there was not a better place in the world to be trying out my brand-new Polaris quad.

As a sheep hunting fanatic of off-the-scale proportions, I had rearranged my whole life to be here in the Yukon. My thirst for adventure might have been temporarily slaked by guiding the previous year, but my thirst for the hunt had not. I was now a permanent resident in the land of permafrost.

And like most residents of the Yukon, my leisure budget went to outdoor toys. I needed a quad. I had just dumped thousands of dollars for this machine that would give me greater access to the backcountry to scout Dall sheep. Here I was twenty-five miles back, and I hadn't even broken a sweat yet. *Ah,* this was the life.

My fourteen-year-old daughter, Cassidy, visiting from British Columbia, fanatical-hunter-in-training, was behind me on the quad. (I am teaching her to ignore silly signs on quads that say things like "absolutely never ride double on this machine.") She, too, seemed to like riding a whole lot better than the manual method of arriving at those remote and rugged places where sheep hang out. I have hiked that kid to hell and back looking for big game.

However, I must have messed up slightly on the toughness training because when I encountered a log across the trail and found a way to get over it, my daughter wanted off the quad. When I showed no sign of slowing, despite frantic pounding on my back, she bailed! Girls!

Dream Dall

Whoa! I must have given the machine just a touch too much gas because, like a horse rearing, the quad went back on its hind wheels, hesitated, and then crashed over backward. That would be six hundred pounds of quad on top of me. In the distance I could hear a terrible shriek. It sounded like *"Daaaaad."*

I was pinned underneath the machine, against a rock. I lay there for a moment, with the breath squeezed out of me, trying to get my bearings. Obviously, this had the potential to wreck the trip for the kid (not to mention me) if I didn't do something. In my other life I am a carpenter, so I have a few muscles in the right places. A desperate heave, and I opened up a space just big enough to wiggle out from underneath the now broken-in wonder machine.

Cass came running over, regarded me solemnly, and told me for a minute she had concluded that I must be dead because I hadn't indulged in my normal burst of profanity. (We don't tell her mother about that part of hunter training.) Bravely, I reassured her that my injuries were minor . . . nothing more than a broken back.

But with the possibility of having wrecked my new piece of equipment (bye-bye thousands of dollars, not to mention a very long hike home), I quickly turned my attention to the machine.

Having realized brains are as essential as other body parts, I invited Cass back onto the team, and together we flipped the quad back on its wheels. I turned it back on. Hey, these things are tougher than they look, and they look real tough. I checked my gear for damage. My rifle had taken quite a bang right on the scope; in fact, it had a dent in the side of it where it had been pinned against the rock. I figured it would be OK as it had taken quite a bit of abuse on other trips. Only later would I realize how costly this assumption would be.

Once we were mobile again, we bounced our way to the end of the old road. My broken back (well, badly bruised) was killing me. I felt as if I had been run over by a quad. However, my desire to find sheep was stronger than my instinct to look after myself. (Why do I have the occasional fleeting feeling that someday I will pay for the abuse my body has taken in the name of sport?)

Almost immediately, we spotted rams. There were five rams in one group and twenty-plus ewes and lambs in another group close-by. One ram looked very old and had a heavily broomed horn on one side that was still well above his nose. I realized that I had found a good ram that probably went 38-inches-plus, and the bases of the horns had some weight to them. His horns were very dark, which meant either he was a really old ram or he had been rolling in black mud just like me.

There was one terrible problem with this ram. It was still four days until opening day! The kind of man who flips his quad on himself the first day he has it, generally is not good at practicing patience, but I marked that ram as mine in my mind, and we headed back to Whitehorse.

I felt 31 July came slowly, but I nursed my broken back, and dreamed about that ram. The day finally arrived, and we packed up our gear and raced back to our secret place only to discover that it wasn't such a secret place. The trail was littered with overturned quads. Well, not exactly, but we did meet several parties of people on the way in. Stealthy and cunning questioning revealed to me that none knew about my old ram.

When we arrived at the end of the road and set up our base camp, we could not find the rams, who also have a tendency to be stealthy and cunning. All we could find were the ewes and lambs on the face of the mountain. I decided to go for a hike around the backside of the mountain to see if I could locate him. Luck, the last of it that I would see for a long while, was with me. I found him about six hundred yards from where the ewes were lying down, just around the backside of the mountain. Reassured, I left him alone, undisturbed, and headed back to camp.

Dream Dall

I also found it reassuring that all the other hunting parties must have had their own secret places to hunt, for we had this spot all to ourselves. Anticipation made this one of the longest nights of my life. Finally at 3:30 AM (daylight this far north), fanatical-hunter-in-training's watch alarm went off, and she eagerly rousted me from bed. We ate sheep hunter stew—that would be mutilated granola bars and trail mix—and headed for the backside of the mountain. Ever the optimist, I figured I'd have my ram by 8 AM opening morning. As we were transcending the low pass that would take us to within shooting distance, I spotted the ram on the skyline ahead.

Unfortunately, he also spotted us. We sat down and waited him out as he headed toward the ewes and lambs. He came to within one hundred yards of them and bedded down below them. This could be a big problem if twenty sets of eyes—every single set with that eight power vision—focused on me and Cass, but for now, my luck held. The ewes did not see us.

We carefully planned our stalk to come up the backside of the mountain and to approach level to the ram, but slightly below the ewes and lambs. After several grueling hours of climbing, we were just coming into position when a huge fogbank came rolling over the top of the mountain. I thought this might be a blessing, as now I could get into shooting position under cover. I'd wait for the fog to lift then—*KABOOM*—all over.

Don't count your chickens before they hatch, and don't put your ram on the wall of your trophy room before you pull the trigger. Like most plans, this one was monumentally clever and virtually foolproof. That is, in theory.

I was getting into position when shadowy figures emerged from the fog. Fifty yards in front of me, the band of ewes and lambs were moving down the mountainside. They caught our scent on the wind, and all hell broke loose. They took off running, back up the mountain, magnum. I watched, horrified, as the bullet ricocheted off a rock four feet in front of the ram. The rams ran across the side hill below me, but stopped when they were about two hundred yards away. This time I held right on the ram's hindquarter, hoping to compensate. Again the bullet hit a rock about four feet in front of him. The rams took off, and this time they did not stop to see what all the noise was about.

Sick at heart, I remembered my casual assumption that, though banged, my rifle had survived the quad flip. Moping, I made my way back to the camp and bore sighted my rifle. It was out one foot to the right at twenty-five yards. At a hundred yards, it would be out by four feet!

I was sitting as close to sheep hunting heaven as I was ever going to get, and my rifle was useless to me now. Thankfully, I had another rifle back at our base camp, my trusty .257 Roberts with a 3-9 Leopold scope on it. The next day I hiked back and got it. It was afternoon before I returned.

Cassidy had stayed at our camp to keep an eye on those sheep, and when I got back she told me that one of the groups of rams had come off the top of the mountain and crossed the ravine below the tent. They had walked right past her. When they saw her, they spooked and took off back down the ravine.

There were still a few rams on the mountain, so we decided to have a closer look. We stalked two different rams that were full curl, but I passed on them as they weren't as big as the old one, the one I had shot at, or the other two exceptional animals that I had seen on the first day.

It was 11 PM before we dragged our exhausted bodies back up the mountain to our tent. Our third day of hunting had drawn to a close. Most of the rams were gone and now some ugly storm clouds were moving in from the south. It rained all night, and my spirits were as damp as the weather. Sometime in the night our tent sprang a leak. My legs were soaked, knees to toes.

Dream Dall

Rob with the caped-out trophy.

Unquenchable Spirit

Dreams do come true.

One look outside and Cassidy resigned the "fanatical" from her hunter-in-training title, pulled her sleeping bag over her head, and refused to budge. I forced myself out of bed. Our little cook stove was soaked and wouldn't light, so I ate a wet granola bar for breakfast.

I marched off toward the peak of the mountain. The wind was blowing, it was foggy, and there was a slight, cold drizzle. The fog thickened, and I zeroed in on a ridge where I would sit down and wait until the fog lifted. With the wind at my back, I moved through the thick gray mist, thinking to myself how foolish it was to be walking with my scent blowing ahead of me.

A swirl in the fog showed a dark outline and the hint of a curl. I stopped and squinted. Fifty yards from me was the ram of my dreams. His huge horns flared out dramatically. Lying down, he was peering haughtily down the mountain in the direction of our tent.

I knew that he would smell me at any moment. I dropped to one knee, slithered out of my pack, and brought the rifle up. I aimed

Dream Dall

behind the front shoulder. I squeezed off a shot. The ram jumped to his feet and looked right at me. Frantically, I ejected the spent shell and chambered another round.

I fired again and the ram leaped over the ridge and out of sight. I raced after him and on the other side of the ridge my ram lay dead. I canceled my sheep tag. I realized that he was even bigger than I had first figured. My tape confirmed he was 40¼ inches on the left side and 39 inches on the right.

This was the finest trophy I had ever harvested. He was perfect in every way. He flared out both sides, came down to the jaw line, and had heavy bases. He was ten years old and in the prime of his life. Ironically, this ram was less than seven hundred yards from where we were camped.

Sheep hunting is the most demanding of all hunts. And I have noticed this: on every successful and unsuccessful hunt, the sheep demand a toll. This time it was a damaged riflescope, a hurt back, wet sleeping bags, wrong turns, long days, sleepless nights, miserable weather, missed shots, and failed stalk after failed stalk.

And yet in the end, there is nothing so exhilarating as being on the side of a windswept mountain, triumphant over one of the most intelligent, resilient, and magnificent animals ever created. It's an experience I want for my daughter, too. We'll be back.

CHAPTER 17

Full Moon at Tombstone

A double-header caribou hunt on the Dempster.

The Yukon is an outdoorsman's paradise. Most of the population embraces hunting, fishing, trapping, snowmobiling, and snowshoeing. Very few residents of the Yukon do not have a rifle or at least know how to use one. This is a place with a rugged past. The poet Robert Service acknowledged the harshness of the land by saying it was a good land for men and dogs, but that it killed women and horses.

Most people who live in this land love the extremes of it, the true wild they are surrounded with, the daily challenges, the opportunity to honor a way of life and harvest sustenance in ways that are ancient. The people of the Yukon are infused with a warrior spirit. After two-and-a-half years in Whitehorse, I felt as if I was fitting right in with that group of people.

But in the summer, a separate population swells. Tourists pour in, and a huge percentage of these seem to be of the Earth Muffin variety. They are easily identified because these free spirits adhere to a strict dress code of dreadlocks, beads, baggy pants, and guru-inspired tunics. They usually have a dog or two, and the smell of a certain healing herb clings to their clothes and hair. Earth Muffins hate hunters and are, unfortunately, willing to air their views at the drop of a hat, especially if that hat happens to have a camo pattern on it.

In the summer of 2002, Cassidy and I had decided to take a trip up the Dempster in a quest for moose and caribou. Now fifteen, my daughter loved to hunt, maybe even lived to hunt, just like I did. We arrived, after a seven-hour drive from Whitehorse, at a campground with the very appropriate name of Tombstone—appropriate because the town of Tombstone was historically a place of showdowns, and this campground was very clearly being run by an eco-freak.

Full Moon at Tombstone

Our government campground "hostess" was an aging hippie with a tangle of long gray hair, no make-up, pants that looked hand-woven out of hemp, and a tie-dye shirt. Suspicion was written in her gaze as she looked over my truck, and the quad and trailer I was pulling. Obviously, I wasn't part of the motor home gang, the ones that travel pulling a full-size motel behind them. She reluctantly assigned us a camp spot.

Cassidy, exploring the campground soon after our arrival, discovered our most gracious hostess had set up a spotting scope. It was aimed at a mountain behind the camp. Cassidy put her eye to it, but had barely begun her inspection of the mountain when she was interrupted by a dismayed shriek from Ms. Granola.

"You guys aren't hunters, are you?" Hunters was spit out in a tone that should be reserved for ax murderers and people who cruelly torture small animals for fun.

"Us?" Cassidy asked, reading the tone, and reluctantly pulling her eye away from the spotting scope. She shoved her hands in her camo pants. "What would make you say that?"

"Why are you wearing commando clothes?" Ms. Granola demanded.

"Commando clothes?" Cassidy looked down at herself, as if surprised to find herself in camo. "It's just the latest style."

Apparently she wasn't very convincing.

"Get away from my spotting scope. I don't want you looking at those caribou."

Caribou? Cassidy thought with secret delight.

"What kind of savage would kill a defenseless animal? That's sick. Unevolved. Barbaric. There is no excuse for hunting when you can buy whatever you need at the store."

Cassidy, while pretending to be giving these arguments some careful thought, was actually thinking, *I didn't know there were caribou up on that mountain.*

Cassidy with her caribou.

Rob's massive caribou scored over four hundred inches.

    I was very aware that I probably had an audience from the campground below. If I didn't before, I'm sure that I did after the report of my rifle. I approached the great trophy and realized that this bull would measure well over four hundred inches.

    This animal was considerably larger in body than Cassidy's had been. It took several hours to debone and get all the meat in game bags. I took the cape also as this animal was big enough to mount. I arrived back at the truck about 10 PM, with antlers, cape, and one hindquarter. Exhausted, I went to bed without eating that night.

    The next day, Cassidy and I donned our packs and headed up the mountain to retrieve the rest of the meat. I had left a few pieces of clothing in the hopes that they would deter marauding grizzlies from taking my kill. This method works about 50 percent of the time, though I have had bears completely ignore all human signs around a kill in order to steal the meat.

Unquenchable Spirit

We arrived at the kill without incident and quickly loaded the bags of meat into our packs. But before we put the packs on our backs, I caught the glint of sun on glass. The spotting scope in the campground was trained right on us. I told Cassidy what was happening, and we looked at each other.

You know, I don't mind people having different viewpoints from me. I don't even mind them voicing them. What I do mind is people trying to impose their idea of how to live on me. There are several ways warriors show contempt. One, used by archers, shows the enemy they still have their middle finger. The other was used by Braveheart.

We chose the Braveheart method. Our laughter rang off the mountains as we made our way with our heavily laden packs down the steep incline. It wasn't exactly the showdown at the OK Corral, but there was a full moon at Tombstone, and that was good enough for us.

California Dreamin'

    She shares her love of her sport through her work as a staff writer on the *Woman Hunter* magazine, where she writes a regular feature. She remains what I like to call the real deal. There is no camera crew following her, her budget is limited, she works a real job, and makes true sacrifices to follow her heart. I think she may be the greatest woman hunter of her time, and no one would scorn me more for saying this than she.

    As this aging cripple continues to follow his passion, there is a feeling of intense pride and satisfaction in having passed the torch on to my daughter. I'm very proud of the woman Cassidy has grown up to be.

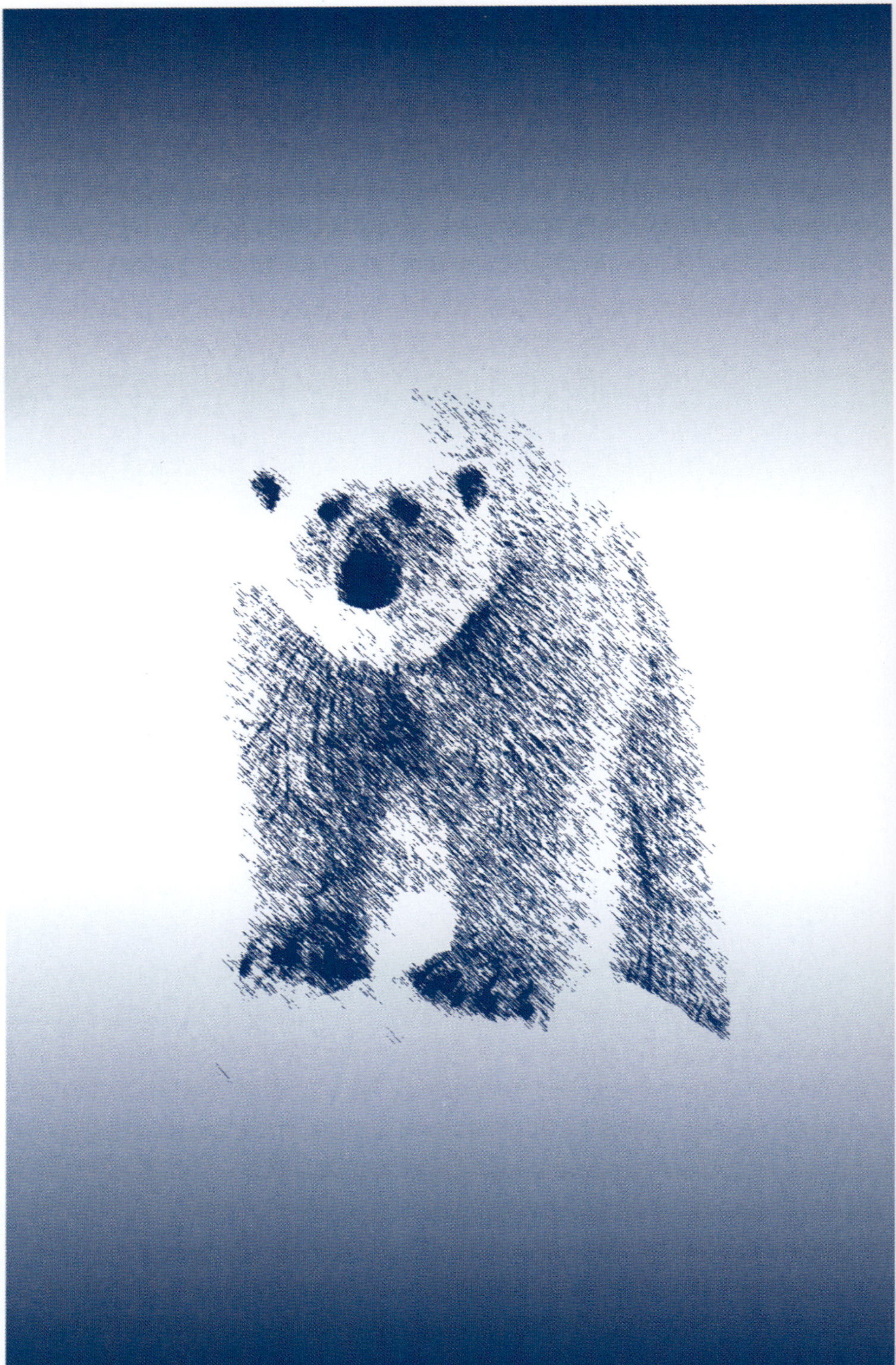

An Introduction to Quest for Nanook

by Fred Webb, April 2012

It was late spring, around 2004, and my partner Martin and I were at our base in Kugluktuk in the central Arctic. We were just finishing up a busy three-month hunting season for muskox, barren-ground grizzlies, and polar bears. In addition to our own polar bear hunts, we supplied marketing and training to half-a-dozen communities where their hunter and trapper associations (HTA) had access to tags but lacked the experience to run a sports hunt.

At this point, all our hunts had been successful, and only one hunter—Rob Shatzko—was still out hunting. We had not heard from Rob, but everything had gone so well that spring that we expected to enjoy a bit of a holiday down south before starting to get the logistics in place for our summer-autumn expeditions.

When the phone rang, I assumed Rob was checking in to tell us that he had been lucky, killed a big bear, and now wanted to leave for home early. Instead, I heard Martin exclaim loudly, "Didn't Fred send you to Gjoa Haven? What are you doing in Taloyoak? It's a hundred miles away!" He handed me the phone and said, "It's Rob, and I don't think he got a bear. He's irate."

Right on all counts. I would settle all the details later, but as the tag Rob held was good only for the one area and the season ended in less than a week, the only sensible thing to do was to book a return bout for the next year. This would spoil our record of 100 percent success on polar bears, but part of learning how to survive in the Arctic is knowing when to quit.

Without giving away the story, you know when Rob finds a hunting crew too dangerous to be out with, you can take it for granted they are not the guides we trained, but some dummy relatives of a local politician. I will leave Rob to tell you his story.

CHAPTER 19

Quest for Nanook, Part I

A polar bear hunt nearly exacts the ultimate price.

"Mayday. Mayday." If there was ever a word no hunter wants to hear spoken, it is that one. Mayday is the internationally recognized distress call. And there was not a doubt in my mind we were in distress that day in the high Arctic. My life and the lives of my Inuit guides were in absolute peril.

It had started as a polar bear hunt, a quest for Nanook, the huge, pure-white bear that is synonymous with the North. But at that moment, listening to the panicked guide screaming Mayday over the radio, it seemed like a very real possibility this quest was going to end in death.

The hunt had begun, as do most trips into the Canadian Arctic, with our ghastly, abysmal national hostage-taker, Air Canada. I left Calgary, Alberta, on Air Canada, and after a short flight to Edmonton I switched, gratefully, to the Inuit owned airline, First Air. First Air services the Northwest Territories and the then fledgling new territory of Nunavut. From Edmonton I flew to Yellowknife, and there I switched planes to another smaller First Air turbo-prop and flew to Gjoa (pronounced joe) Haven, Nunavut, where my trip was to begin.

My old friend, Fred Webb, had organized the trip. Fred was my go-to guy when it came to hunting in the Arctic. His T-shirt, No Bull S--- Hunting, said it all. He guaranteed nothing, in terms of success, but he ran safe, well-organized hunts in a part of the country where mistakes could turn lethal in a heartbeat. And despite the fact Fred does not guarantee success, all my hunts with him, to date, had resulted in the harvest of world-class animals.

Fred had been invited to partner with the Gjoa Haven chapter of the Hunters and Trappers Association (HTA) of Nunavut. They

Quest for Nanook

had a quota of polar bears, and the American market had dried up. While Americans were allowed to hunt polar bears, they were no longer allowed to bring their trophies home with them. That put an understandable damper on their enthusiasm for the hunt.

American hunters are probably the largest group of hunters in the world who can afford pricey, guided hunts. So many northern communities had relied heavily on guided hunts as a source of income, and with Americans no longer coming, these communities needed someone who could bring in Canadian and European hunters. Who better than Fred Webb? Fred had been conducting polar-bear hunts out of Arctic Bay on Baffin Island for many years.

Now, he was asked to expand his operation to Gjoa Haven, but, unfortunately, the invitation came late in the season and while Fred was busy with his own clients in Kugluktuk. Though it went against his grain to organize a hunt that was so hands-off for him, Fred agreed because he was promised safe, well-organized, completely professional polar bear hunts for his clients. He would later tell me, in typical Fred fashion, "Those bast@#%s promised me the services of two excellent guides who had worked with me in the past, and instead stuck me with two townies who couldn't find the airport unless they took a taxi."

But neither Fred nor I was aware of that when I was met at Gjoa Haven Airport, by Ted, head of the Gjoa Haven HTA. The Gjoa airport is typical for the northern areas, consisting of a cluster of prefabricated trailers welded together. Ted informed me that my guides weren't ready yet, and so I was delivered, by snowmobile, to the local hotel.

The local hotel, which was the only hotel, cost four hundred dollars a night. It was a large step down from a total dive. There were stains on the bathroom floor that looked like somebody had been murdered in there. The food was awful and expensive. There was no choice of a menu. Breakfast was thirty dollars, lunch was forty dollars, and supper was fifty dollars. These meals consisted of whatever lunacy the cook dreamed up for the day, which seemed to be a minuscule amount of identifiable food mixed into a large amount of grease.

Every day, for three days, a different guy would show up and let me know my guides weren't ready yet. According to these different representatives, they were preparing snowmobiles, a dog team, and other gear. In hindsight, I suspect they had to sober up the three guys who would be acting as my guides long enough so they could make the hunt.

The expedition was finally ready to depart Gjoa Haven. I was forced to part with twelve hundred dollars plus tax at the hotel. (I wouldn't be surprised if that hotel was partners with Air Canada!)

There were two guides, both in their early twenties. I'm tempted to call them Dumb and Dumber, but I'll call them Frankie and Henry, names invented to protect the guilty. I saw we were taking three snowmobiles, which I found strange, because as far as I knew in Canada we are only allowed to hunt polar bears with dog teams.

There was also an old man who was the dog handler and could not speak any English. As I arrived at our mustering point, the old guy was thumping each of his dogs on his head with a stick that looked like a policeman's baton. This dog team apparently was coming along to satisfy the letter of the law, because the dogs, after their thumping, were loaded into a box that was pulled by one of the snowmobiles. I rode in a very similar box, strapped to a sleigh (komatik) that was pulled behind one of the snowmobiles. The third snowmobile pulled a sleigh full of gear, including a tent, food, and empty gas cans.

Since it was May, the weather was far more hospitable than it had been on my other Arctic hunts. It was a relatively balmy minus five Celsius as we set out. We drove across the frozen sea ice from Gjoa Haven to Taloyoak, another Inuit community on the route to the polar bear area. We spent that night at one of

Quest for Nanook

Henry's friends' houses in Taloyoak. It was pretty plain, but better than the four-hundred-dollar-a-night hotel, and I did enjoy seeing authentic seal spears on the walls.

The next day we were supposed to get gas for the empty gas cans and carry on our journey, but it was Sunday, and the gas guy would not turn on the pumps on Sunday. So, another day of the hunt was spent in the very frustrating position of waiting.

During that boring wait, I was able to learn a lot about my guides, none of it very reassuring. First of all, they were all related to Ted, the guy who had organized the hunt. Second, the two young guides had never hunted polar bears before. Frankie had never seen a polar bear. The old man, the dog man, had hunted polar bears before, but he had never been to the place we were heading, and neither had the other two.

Warning bells were starting to go off. I was beginning to wonder what screw-up I could expect next. A smarter man might have tossed in the towel right there, but I had a lot of money invested in this hunt, and that was before airfare and the exorbitant hotel fee. And I trusted Fred. In hindsight, I should have given Fred a call before going a step farther. But most of all, I am a hunter, and sometimes the lust to hunt overcomes common sense.

The next day there was no early start. Henry had gotten drunk and was nursing a hangover, the other two seemed more interested in visiting with their friends than leaving in a timely manner. Finally, at ten o'clock that morning, after the dogs got their little ritualistic thump on the head with the stick and were loaded in their box, we were finally mobile and traveling across the Boothia Peninsula toward the Gulf of Boothia, a strait between the mainland and Baffin Island.

We traveled all day, first overland and then into a large open bay on the frozen sea ice. At the end of the day, we rounded a small

Unquenchable Spirit

island and headed toward the open Gulf of Boothia. This was where I first saw broken sea ice known as rough ice. We drove on, weaving our way through jagged pressure ridges, created by ice breaking and refreezing as the result of high and low tides. The tides can vary from twenty-five to thirty feet in elevation. At that time I was unaware of the dangers involved in these fluctuations of ice and water.

We set up camp on the other side of a large pressure ridge. We were on the frozen ocean. From my vantage point, I could see a rocky hump of island about a mile away from us. But mostly it was icy peaks all around us. Some of these pressure ridges were as high as three-story buildings. At the time, I never put two and two together; neither did my guides.

All I was thinking was, finally, next stop Baffin Island.

We had supper. They cooked up some Mr. Noodle for me, and they all carved strips off a haunch of frozen caribou, and ate it frozen. They also ate frozen fish, raw and intact. The guts had not been removed. I had assumed both the fish and caribou were being brought for the dogs.

Henry complained to me about the high cost of dope in Gjoa Haven. He told me he was paying twenty dollars for a joint. He wondered if maybe I could use the Canadian postal service and send him some. The warning bells weren't just tinkling, anymore. They were clanging. I knew I was in real trouble.

By morning, though, I was redefining trouble. That night the wind raged around the tent. In the morning, with the last wisps of the windstorm dying, Frankie got out of the tent first. "You guys need to come see this."

There was certain urgency in his voice that had all of us scrambling out of the tent. At first, I didn't comprehend what I was seeing. The hump of land that had been a mile away last night looked as if it was more like ten miles away this morning. We all walked out toward what used to be the pressure ridge.

Quest for Nanook

We were looking at open water. The ice, eight feet thick, had broken cleanly away.

We stood on a sheer ice cliff, staring at the raging Arctic water eight feet below. Our camp had broken away and had become a makeshift boat. It was being smashed with all the ocean's considerable fury. Below us certain death waited patiently to claim its next victim. Although our piece of floating ice seemed small, Frankie got on a snowmobile and did a tour. He came back and reported our floe was about ten square miles in size.

Once again, I was waiting. There was absolutely nothing to do except watch the old man, who also seemed to be waiting, and he seemed to be waiting for death. He stared off into the distance, his gaze faraway, not acknowledging any of us who shared this predicament with him. He was chanting in a low voice, his native tongue. There was no doubt in my mind he was preparing to meet his Maker.

Later that day, our ice floated right back to its original position and bumped into the pack ice off the edge of the island. I think the guides were hoping it would stick, but it didn't. Frankie once again fired up the snowmobile and drove out. The report he brought back was not encouraging: A number of chunks had broken off and now our icy lifeboat was dwindling in size.

As the tide moved in and out, our ice floe would actually slide under other pieces of existing ice and then break off as the tide rose. My sense of impending doom and grave danger became acute. By the end of the day, our piece of ice was less than one square mile in size.

By evening, I was sick of the lack of a plan, the lack of motivation, the lack of any sense of survival smarts. Frankie, who kept driving his snowmobile around our ever shrinking island, was obviously hoping for our chunk of ice to hit the main body hard enough to stick and form a bridge that we could get across. I had a feeling that saving face was a huge part of the equation for the Inuit guides. They had

The next morning we hiked up the little hill and spotted a polar bear with a cub moving slowly on the rough sea ice. I felt my heart rise at the first sighting of nanook. On my previous hunt, we had not even seen a bear. It is amazing how hard it is to see a white bear moving against a white backdrop.

We continued glassing, looking for a male, and it was several hours before we saw one. Amazingly, it was I who caught the first glimpse of the magnificent white bear moving majestically through the sea ice. He was moving in the same direction as the sow and cub.

Although the bear was a long way out on the ice, Joe said, "I think he is worth a closer look."

The guide with the snowmobile was left at camp as Joe had total respect for the law that says a polar bear cannot be harvested with the aid of a motorized vehicle. Joe harnessed his dog team, and I sat on the sled, while he rode the back runners and mushed the dogs. The ride was surprisingly smooth, the dogs lunging against their harnesses in their eagerness. This was exciting in itself; the fact that we were on a quest for nanook made it even more so.

It didn't take long to find the bear's tracks. They were huge. I could fit both my feet together in one of his tracks. There was no question; this was a shooter.

The dogs were frenzied now that they had caught scent from the track. We followed the tracks and kept a watchful eye on the horizon ahead for the bear. It still took nearly two hours to catch up with the polar bear. Once a visual was made, the dogs started barking, a baying sound very similar to the sound a cougar hound makes when it is getting ready to tree.

Joe threw an anchor out the back of the sled. It was like a grappling hook and it grabbed onto the ice and stopped the dogs who were straining against the harnesses wanting to get at the bear. He then turned two dogs loose on the bear.

Joe driving his dog team.

    While I retrieved and loaded my rifle, the bear swatted at the dogs with his massive paws, but they darted out of his reach, circling him, barking at him, hounding him. Meanwhile, Joe removed the anchor and drove about seventy-five yards from the bear and then hooked the anchor on the ice again, again freezing the forward motion of the frenzied dogs. I can just imagine what a mess it would be if the entire dog team, complete with harnesses, and sled, were allowed to surround the bear. No doubt the dogs would be killed and the sled ruined.
    The bear, to this point, had been totally distracted by the irritation of the dogs. Now he saw us, and made a few fearless steps toward us. He was now totally ignoring the dogs leaping around him. His size, this close to him, was absolutely formidable. He hissed with such menace that the hair on the back of my neck rose.

Unquenchable Spirit

"Shoot him, he is going to charge!"

I got down on one knee, aimed, and squeezed off a shot just as he lunged. He flipped over backward, and the two loose dogs attacked him from both ends. The bear had taken a frontal shot right into his lungs and was dead by the time we got to him.

"Glad you made the shot," Joe said with a grin. "I forgot my rifle back at camp."

It was decided we would load the bear on the *komatik* and pull him back to our base camp, by the little island, and skin him there.

Rob's polar bear—note the size of head and paws.

Quest for Nanook

That bear felt like he weighed a thousand pounds as the two of us rolled him onto the sled. Joe and I both sat on the bear and rode back to camp. The dogs pulled the load effortlessly.

Back at camp, the other guide was genuinely excited. The Inuit love polar bear meat (cooked, not raw), so nothing went to waste. We skinned the bear, and that night we feasted on fresh polar bear. I tried it and found it to taste exactly like pork.

Although this was to be a twenty-day hunt, we were done on the second day. The third day we packed up and headed back to Taloyoak. The hunt had been a total and complete contrast to the one the previous year.

My quest for nanook was over. The bear was ten feet long, nose to tail, and was 10 feet, 6 inches across from paw tip to paw tip. In other words, he was a mighty big bear. The hunt would rate as perfect, except for one footnote, thanks to my favorite airline, Air Canada.

When I arrived in Calgary, two days later, my bear hide did not arrive with me, despite the fact I had paid a cargo fee of three hundred dollars to have the hide checked straight through to Calgary. I went to the Air Canada lost luggage counter.

After making a phone call, the clerk informed me with that utter arrogance that is Air Canada that my duffel bag that contained the bear was at the First Air cargo depot and that they were not bringing it to Calgary. There was no apology and no explanation.

I asked to use the company's phone to check on the well-being of my bear—this was before the days of cell phones—and the clerk refused my request. The famous Shatzko temper kicked in about then. I took the luggage that had arrived and found my truck. I drove from the Calgary airport to Edmonton airport. It is a 235-kilometer trip, airport to airport. It usually takes two-and-a-half hours. I am pretty sure I made the trip in just over an hour.

I arrived at the depot and was greeted by a sympathetic First Air baggage handler. He told me that when the clerk from Air Canada

Rob with Joe's family.

found out it was a polar bear, he flatly refused to take it. Even though it had been prepaid and wrapped so well that there was no possibility of leakage or smells, Air Canada had refused to take an "endangered polar bear" on their plane.

    I couldn't believe it, but why wouldn't I? This is Air Canada, our great national airline. I made some phone inquiries from his office to Air Canada and got nowhere. I was never compensated for my troubles or the baggage fees I had paid. I did tell them I knew of two guys, named Frankie and Henry, whom I thought would do really well working for them.

The Forty-Four Ram

rams running all around us as the rut was in its peak (California bighorns rut from about the last week in October until the second week of November).

If the rams were aware of us, which is doubtful, they did not seem to be afraid of our presence. Rather, they were focused on chasing ewes. They stopped long enough to beat each other up, and then resumed the chase moments later.

Within minutes of Abe and Barry's arrival, we spotted the big ram chasing several ewes down a hill toward us. They stopped when they were about one hundred twenty yards away. The ram was slightly quartering, away from us. In that moment where opportunity meets destiny, calm descended. I set up my shooting sticks, aimed, and squeezed off. In disbelief I watched as the ram started trotting up the hill, apparently unscathed, certainly undeterred in his pursuit of the ewes.

I had clearly missed the shot of a lifetime. But then, he stopped broadside at one hundred fifty yards and sent a look back at me. Not quite as calm as before, I took a deep breath, gathering myself, aimed right behind the front shoulder, and fired again. The ram folded immediately, as though he'd been shot in the neck or head. I thought that was odd. With most lung shots an animal will usually run fifty or more yards before stopping.

We walked up to the fallen giant to discover that my second shot had gone right through the neck, nowhere near where I had aimed. After the heady high fives had concluded, I took some well-deserved ribbing for my poor shooting and the truth is I deserved everything I got.

I later discovered the rifle to be "out" by three inches to the left and one inch high at twenty-five yards. This could easily have resulted in a catastrophe. After a lifetime of pursuing sheep across mountaintops a million miles from civilization, it seemed "wrong" to be able to drive my truck to within one hundred yards of him. Even given the near catastrophe, this was undoubtedly the easiest sheep I have ever

Unquenchable Spirit

Left to right: Barry Bennett, Rob, Abe Dougan.

harvested. We loaded him whole, transported him back to Kamloops, and skinned him in Abe's garage for a life-size mount.

My ram was just shy of 40 inches on one side by 39 inches on the other. After 60 days drying time, I had him officially scored. He grossed 185⅛ inches and netted 184⅘ inches Boone and Crockett points. I was elated, even though I've always maintained that nets are for fishermen.

The Forty-Four Ram

I've started calling him the Forty-Four Ram because I was forty-four years old when I took him, and I am the forty-fourth life member of the Wild Sheep Society of British Columbia. At this writing, the Forty-Four Ram looks as if he will be the number five taken for British Columbia, and number six for the world. He is a ram worthy of the once-in-a-lifetime opportunity I was given, and he is also a ram that commemorates a lifetime devoted to hunting the monarchs of the mountains.

Footnote: I would like to thank Abe Dougan for helping me in the harvest of this tremendous ram. It was an honor and a privilege to share this great hunt with someone as capable, as knowledgeable, and as dedicated to the sport as Abe.

CHAPTER 21

Sheepish: A Horse-Hunting Adventure

Anyone who has a horse knows they have an absolute penchant for getting into trouble. Of course, the same could be said for sheep hunting with dear old Dad.

A good story rarely comes from a quiet, uneventful hunt, so if you're looking for a good story, stick with me. I have always pushed the envelope, done and tried things that other people (more sensible, some would say) would back away from.

Horse hunting opened a whole new world of adventure for me, and not just because horses can get you into remote areas that would be impossible to access otherwise. If you're going to hunt with horses, it's necessary to understand a fundamental fact: Horses have personalities. They don't always want to do what you have in mind. And anyone who has a horse knows horses have an absolute penchant for getting in trouble. This is particularly true of young horses.

For most horse people, just driving for two days (twenty-plus hours) with seven horses can be quite an adventure. But for me, the real adventure is the trail in and out of the hunting area. The actual killing part of the hunt can be great, but the true adventure happens on the way there. Or on the way out. To paraphrase my old friend, Fred Webb: If there is no danger and if there is no moment when your life hangs in the balance, you haven't really got a story, and you haven't really had an adventure.

My kids know that about me. That when you go hunting with dear old dad, there is going to be some adventure. If you asked them, they might say things have a tendency to go sideways. For some unknown reason, they hunt with me anyway. I like to think I am passing on the baton. I suspect they think, Watch how Dad does it, and don't do it that way.

In the particular year when this adventure occurred, my daughter, Cassidy, was hunting with me. I was also pleased that my son, Richard,

Sheepish: A Horse-Hunting Adventure

Rob's favorite mountain horse, Chance, gearing up for the great adventure.

was joining us on this trip. Richard is not fanatical about hunting, and his work and school schedule often came first. (Imagine that.) But that year our stars had lined up, and Cass and I both wanted Richard to experience the thrill of hunting sheep.

    As both Cassidy and I had harvested sheep in the past, we would give Richard the first opportunity. I would only shoot one, after him, and if it was a monster. Cassidy had harvested two Stones, a 37-incher and a 39.5-incher, and she had basically come for the ride and to help her brother get his first sheep.

We traveled north with seven horses, stopping every four to five hours to let them out to stretch their legs, drink, and eat. This is typical of travel with horses. It takes an hour at each stop, so for that journey, it added about five extra hours of travel time. On the first day we drove thirteen hours and the second one eight, reaching the trailhead at the end of the second day. The next day, we packed up the horses and headed up the trail.

I had a young Fjord named Cody, and this was his first trip. My method of packing is to let the packhorses string loose between the riding horses. I first used this method while guiding in the Yukon, and it is still my favorite routine. But it does invite "incidents."

The first mishap occurred when Cody took it into his head not to follow the rest of the horses. They followed a well-worn trail to the left of a tree; Cody went right. He went off the trail and fell in a deep hole. Upside down. We all bailed off our horses and watched helplessly as Cody flailed around, tangling himself in the dense undergrowth and managing to get himself pinned across his belly by a small tree.

I had to wait until he quit kicking to get a closer look. All three of us got down in the hole with him, and we tried in vain to flip him over and get him upright. It is not that easy to move a thousand pounds of horseflesh, and by that point Cody was wedged in pretty tight. Attempt number one was a complete failure.

Next, I took a rope and wrapped it around Cody's rump and secured the other end around Weiner's, my horse, saddle horn. This was Weiner's debut as my lead horse, and he performed this first challenge like a trooper. But Weiner's straining forward only made Cody more frantic. His four legs, pointing skyward, kicked wildly. Rescue attempt two also ended in failure.

At this point, I realized I would have to remove his packsaddle while Cody was still upside down. Luckily, I was able to get at the girth without cutting it. And luckily, I was able to get the saddle loosened without getting my head kicked in. Once Cody realized he no longer had the weight on his back and was not wedged in so

Sheepish: A Horse-Hunting Adventure

tightly, he calmed down a bit, even though he flailed around some more. However, there was a small broken tree pinning him across his underbelly, and several more tangled his hind legs. Rescue attempt number three: failed.

Now I had to get creative. I realized I would have to remove this tree to free him, so I took my chainsaw from one of the other packhorses and started it up. I revved it beside Cody to see if he would kick, but he was all tired out from his previous escape attempts. Cassidy and Richard were exchanging glances, but they had to know the chainsaw was a more viable option than trying to swing an ax that close to the trapped horse.

I cut only inches from his belly. My kids watched in horror as the blade edged close to everything important to life. After cutting a few more branches from around his back legs, he was now free to roll over, but he didn't. He just lay there looking gloomy and helpless.

Once again, I hooked the rope around his rump. I had Cass put a lead rope on his halter. And then I pulled. Cody grunted. And then rolled. And then, with a mighty leap, he found his feet and jumped out of the hole. He shook himself off and stood quietly. Cody has a facial expression that is all his own—a kind of blank look that says "what?" I retrieved the packsaddle, blankets, and gear and proceeded to tie all the gear back on him.

The whole incident probably took half an hour, but it seemed like forever. As I got back on my horse, I couldn't help but notice Richard staring off into the distance. Just like Cody's look said "what?", Richard's said, "What on earth have I let myself in for?" Luckily, the rest of the day was uneventful, with Cody performing his duties cheerfully as if nothing had happened.

The next day we passed through an outfitter's camp. A guide invited us in for coffee, which we gladly accepted. Once inside the cabin, he quizzed us as to where we were heading. I told him I was passing right through his territory and into the next one. That seemed to make him

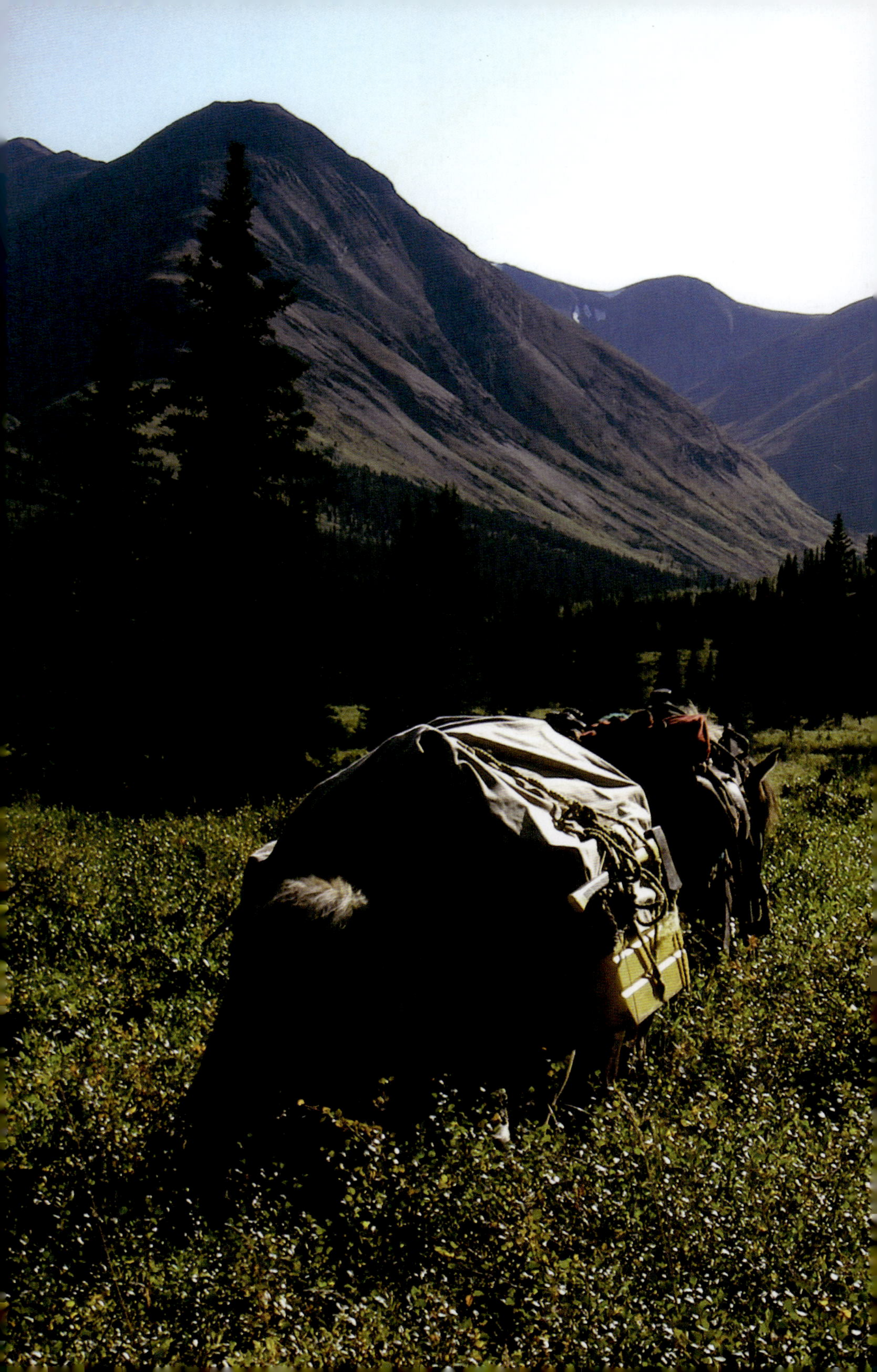

Rob leads the charge.

happy because that meant we weren't going to be competing with him or his clients for sheep.

Back on the trail we traveled for about five more hours before finding a camp spot that was already occupied by an elderly gentleman. He was a horse packer. With him was a client from southern British Columbia, who was also hunting Stone sheep. That evening he told me about a shortcut that would cut hours off my trip.

The next morning we set out on the trail. I found the place I thought he had described the evening before. Part of me had a bad feeling about this, but it was going to save me a lot of time.... At first the trail looked great, but eventually it became so crisscrossed with elk trails that I lost it. Soon we were lost in the thick poplars as we meandered down the ridge. The going got worse and worse. We either had to go back the way we came or find a different route.

I decided to try to cut straight down the mountain and join up with the trail we had left. The forest closed in on us as we moved down a nearly straight up and down grade to a lower in elevation. It was so steep that I suggested we get off and walk to avoid the saddles slipping right up over the horses' heads. The going was extremely rough. I kept tying up my horse, and going ahead trying to scout a different route. I must have walked ten miles up and down that mountain trying to find a way through the trees.

Then my packhorses started getting stuck between the small poplar trees. One of the rear horses knocked a tree over, and it landed on his pack boxes. It looked exactly like a javelin on a war horse. He leaped forward, crashing into the trees. I was in front of him.

Since I was about to get run over, or possibly impaled by the tree on his back, I leaped forward in an effort to get out of the way. That action further complicated the already dicey situation. My effort to get out of his way got my horse, Weiner, stuck between two trees. The horse behind us continued his wild course toward us. Just when I was pretty sure things could not get any worse, they did. Something stung my head. And then something else.

Sheepish: A Horse-Hunting Adventure

Bees started stinging me and Weiner, and Weiner went berserk. All the packhorses jammed up against me, and they were all getting stung as well. What a mess! I was yelling profanities as I fought to get away from my stinging assailants. The horses began bucking and running in different directions as I tried to get things under control. By now Cassidy and Richard were also getting stung.

I yelled, "Get out of here." I pointed to the tree we had upset that contained the angry bees.

The horses scattered, but they were getting tangled in the thick brush. One of the other horses managed to buck his saddle and the gear off, which scattered all over the hill. I managed to catch and tie up all the horses except one. Poor Cody was stuck between two trees and the bees just went crazy on him. I went to rescue him, pushing him backward out of the trees, both of us getting stung the whole time.

Finally, he was free, and I got him away from the bees. He was trembling profusely, which I was sure was a reaction to the bee stings. Although I managed to get him out of harm's way, he would not move. He just stood there trembling. I unpacked him and saw bees had even gotten up under the blankets to sting him. I tried to lead him empty, but now that the attack was over, he was completely paralyzed. He would not come. His whole face was already swollen from bee stings. I thought he was going to die.

By now we had been on this treacherous "shortcut" all day. I estimated we had only an hour or so of light left. We needed to get off the mountain soon. I tied Cody to a tree and left him and his pack there while we headed down. Cassidy set a point on her GPS so that we could find the horse later, if he would even still be alive.

We beat our way straight down the mountain and stumbled blindly onto the original horse trail. I was overjoyed to see it. We limped our sad-looking packtrain down the trail for another hour before we found a creek with a semilevel spot to camp at. We set up camp in the last of the light and had a quick bite to eat.

Unquenchable Spirit

Leaving Richard to look after the horses at camp, Cassidy and I fought off exhaustion and resaddled our riding horses. Then we put a packsaddle on my best packhorse, Chance, and led him back up the trail. Armed with flashlights, we headed for our lost horse. With the GPS we found him easily, other than the bushwhacking back up the steep incline. He was still alive and had stopped shaking.

I was glad to see his condition, for I had been preparing myself for the worst, a dead horse or a horse that I would have to put down. I put all Cody's gear, including his packsaddle, on Chance. I tied him behind Chance, and, probably frightened of being left alone again, Cody didn't need much persuasion to head back down the mountain.

It was about two o'clock in the morning when we arrived back at camp. Neither of the kids said a word to me about the shortcut. Believe me, they didn't have to. I like to think I've learned my lesson. Stick to the trail.

We slept late the next day and had a large breakfast of bacon and eggs. We left camp late and about four hours later came to another

A much-deserved rest for both man and beast.

Sheepish: A Horse-Hunting Adventure

outfitter's camp. After a short visit with the outfitter, we headed down the trail. That evening, we camped beside a large river.

Cassidy managed to find an adventure all on her own that evening. She went for a walk and was charged by a grizzly. She tells about that encounter in a story called "Fifteen Seconds," which I have included with her permission. The story first appeared in her segment of the *Woman Hunter* magazine, a section aptly named "The Adventure" with Cassidy Caron. She takes after dear old dad more than she wants to admit!

The next day we were going to have to cross the river, and I was dreading the worst, swimming. I crossed first and left all the horses tied behind as I was trying to ford the murky water without swimming. I wasn't afraid of swimming; I just didn't want my kids to get soaked to the eyeballs if I could help it. I think their faith in my leadership had been damaged enough by our previous adventures. I was lucky on the first attempt to find a way across that did not involve swimming. Once safely across, we carried on up the other side of the valley. We rode one more day before we found any sign of sheep.

We rode into another large valley and found yet another outfitter's camp. He also invited us in for coffee. His lodge was by far the fanciest one I had seen yet, and definitely the most remote. He could not believe we had ridden so far. We had now traversed over a hundred miles on horseback. I told him we were hunting sheep but informed him that I would not get in the way of his guides or his clients.

We rode on up the valley and camped about two hours up the trail. The next day, we put in another long day on horseback, but found a nice place to camp away from the outfitter's guide camps. This entire valley was loaded with game. The mountains had sheep on them, but mostly ewes and lambs with some small rams. We were literally tripping over elk. We were also seeing lots of moose, mostly bulls.

The next day, in the heart of sheep country, we began our sheep hunt. The mountain south of camp looked the most promising. We put empty

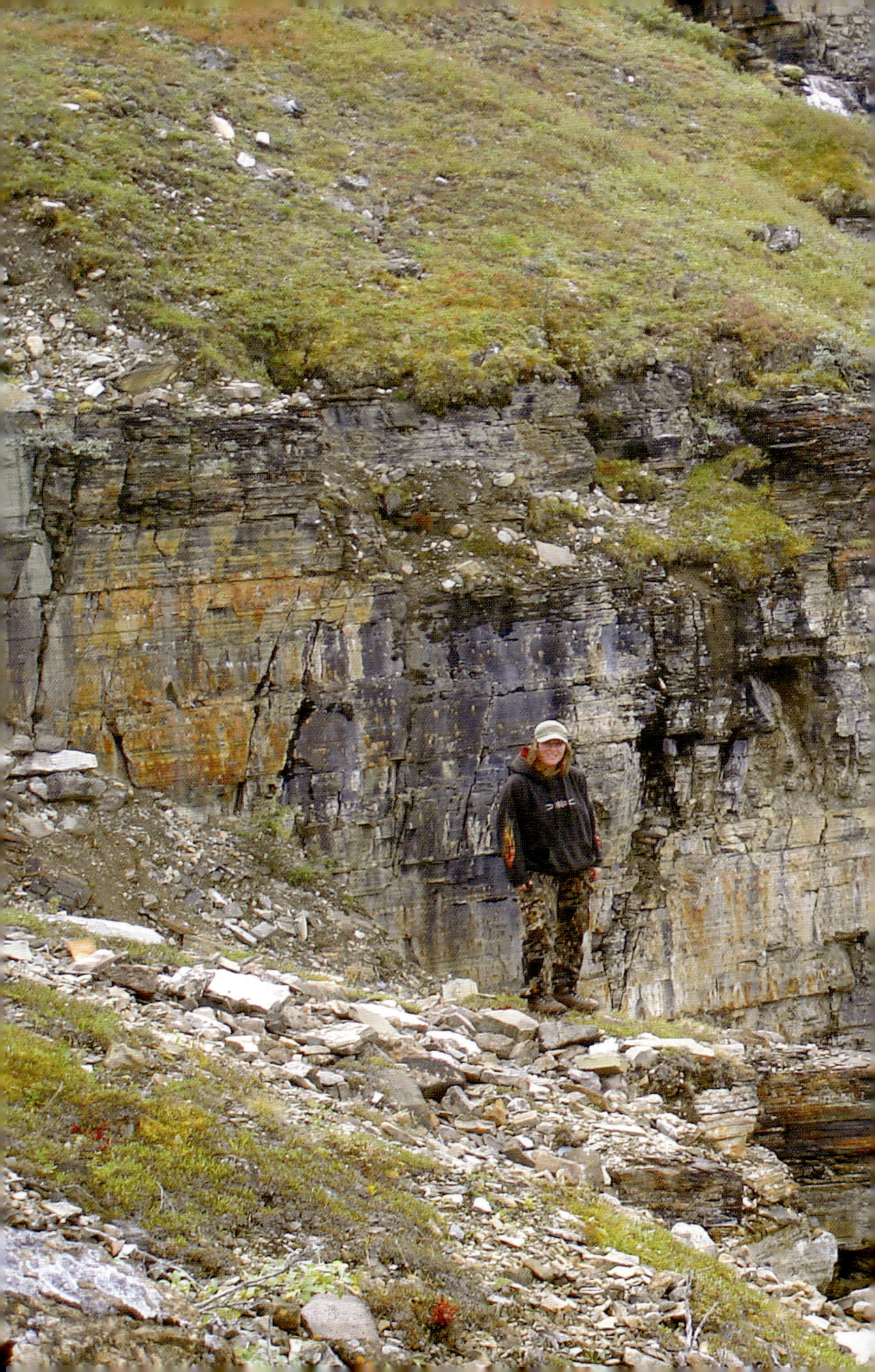

Cassidy, always at home in the high country.

packs on the horses and headed up. Once on top, I spotted some rams directly to the north of us on the other side of the river, only about ten miles away. There were no sheep on the mountain we had climbed, but we needed to stretch our legs anyway after six days in the saddle.

That evening a lovesick bull moose came out from behind our camp and became enamored with my horses. Even though they were hobbled, they wanted no part of him, and fled across the river. This was around 10 PM, and the light was now fading. I had just crawled into my sleeping bag when Cassidy yelled, "Dad, I just watched a moose chase the horses across the river."

I was not happy with the prospect of crossing the frigid water up to my chest in the dark, but it had to be done. With our boots left on for better traction and armed with headlamps, halters, and two bridles, Cassidy and I marched in. In the beam of my headlamp, I saw the stunned moose was close to the horses, still grunting. He was wild eyed and crazy.

I yelled some profanity at him, and he just stared at me shaking his head from side to side. He finally walked away, but he certainly was not showing much fear of us. His attitude did not bode well for our comfort. Cassidy and I caught two horses each, riding one bareback, and leading the other with the halter shank. The others followed. We crossed the river, and this time we tied them all to trees.

I crawled back into my sleeping bag soaking wet and shivering. Richard, exhausted from all our previous adventures or not yet accustomed to the constant drama, hadn't even woken up for this one.

All night long, I could hear that crazy moose grunting on the other side of the river. I thought of shooting him, but by that point in my hunting career I had learned not to shoot a moose on a sheep hunt. In the morning, luckily for him (and me) he was gone.

I was able to find the rams first thing in the morning. There were five total. Through the spotting scope, I determined that one of them was legal. I made a plan of attack, and the three of us began the long

Sheepish: A Horse-Hunting Adventure

Richard with his ram.

stalk in quest of a ram for Richard. Just before we were in a position to shoot and after four long hours of climbing, the wind changed. I crawled over the ridge to look at the spot where the sheep had been bedded. No sheep. I did see a herd running away.

I never found those sheep again. Dejected, we descended the mountain to our waiting horses. Once at the horses, I took a quick look to the west. There was a group of five more rams feeding on an open ridge. These were two mountains away, so I knew they couldn't possibly be the same rams we had seen earlier. Once I had the spotting scope set up, I confirmed that they were not the same rams. Two appeared to be legal.

We were so very tired that we decided to ride across the river to our camp. We would make a play on these rams the next day. That night we anxiously lay awake thinking whether this new group of rams would still be there in the morning. As luck would have it, they were. We saddled our riding horses and tied empty packs on and rode toward the rams.

This time I was extra cautious and was very careful about the direction of the wind; I also ensured that we were well hidden from their view. We rode about six miles up the valley before tying the horses up. It was a textbook stalk. We were able to get within two hundred yards without them detecting us. Richard made an excellent shot from his .300 Winchester Magnum, and the biggest ram dropped on impact.

Although there was another legal ram, I decided to pass on him, and Cass was not interested. We were all very happy with Richard's hard-won ram. That night we celebrated with Cassidy and Rich each drinking a beer they had been saving just for this occasion. We were all worn out by that point, so we decided the next day to head back to the truck.

The trip out was mostly uneventful, except we had one last wreck. Richard got bucked off his mostly bombproof horse. When asked what had set his horse off he said, "I don't know. He just started bucking when I went to put my rain jacket on."

"It's always a good idea to get off your horse when putting on a rain jacket. They don't like that wrinkling plastic sound."

Five, ten-hour days later, we finally loaded our horses in the truck and headed for home. There is something about a trip like that that makes home look pretty darn fine. Cody's expression even changed from his usual blank "What?" expression to one of nearly delirious joy, as in "Look! I survived!" Come to think of it, Cassidy and Richard had that very same expression on their faces!

As we unloaded the horses and our gear, including Richard's sheep, I was feeling pretty satisfied with life. After all, I had given my kids another unforgettable adventure with dear old Dad.

CHAPTER 22

Fifteen Seconds

Bear encounters of the worst kind.
by Cassidy Caron

The bear's beady black eyes—fiery, unblinking, glowing with bloodlust—bore into mine. With each leap forward, his powerful chest heaved, paws thumping onto the river rocks, claws clicking as they scraped for purchase. Ragged breath hissed out of his half-open jaw, white pointed fangs angled in anticipation of the attack. We were on a collision course with fate, and in a matter of a few precious seconds he would reach me. Waiting there, I was certain of one thing: One of us would die.

I swung out of the saddle, legs stiff from eight long hours of hard riding. The subalpine meadow glowed under the bright, northern British

Cassidy enjoying a scenic moment in sheep country.

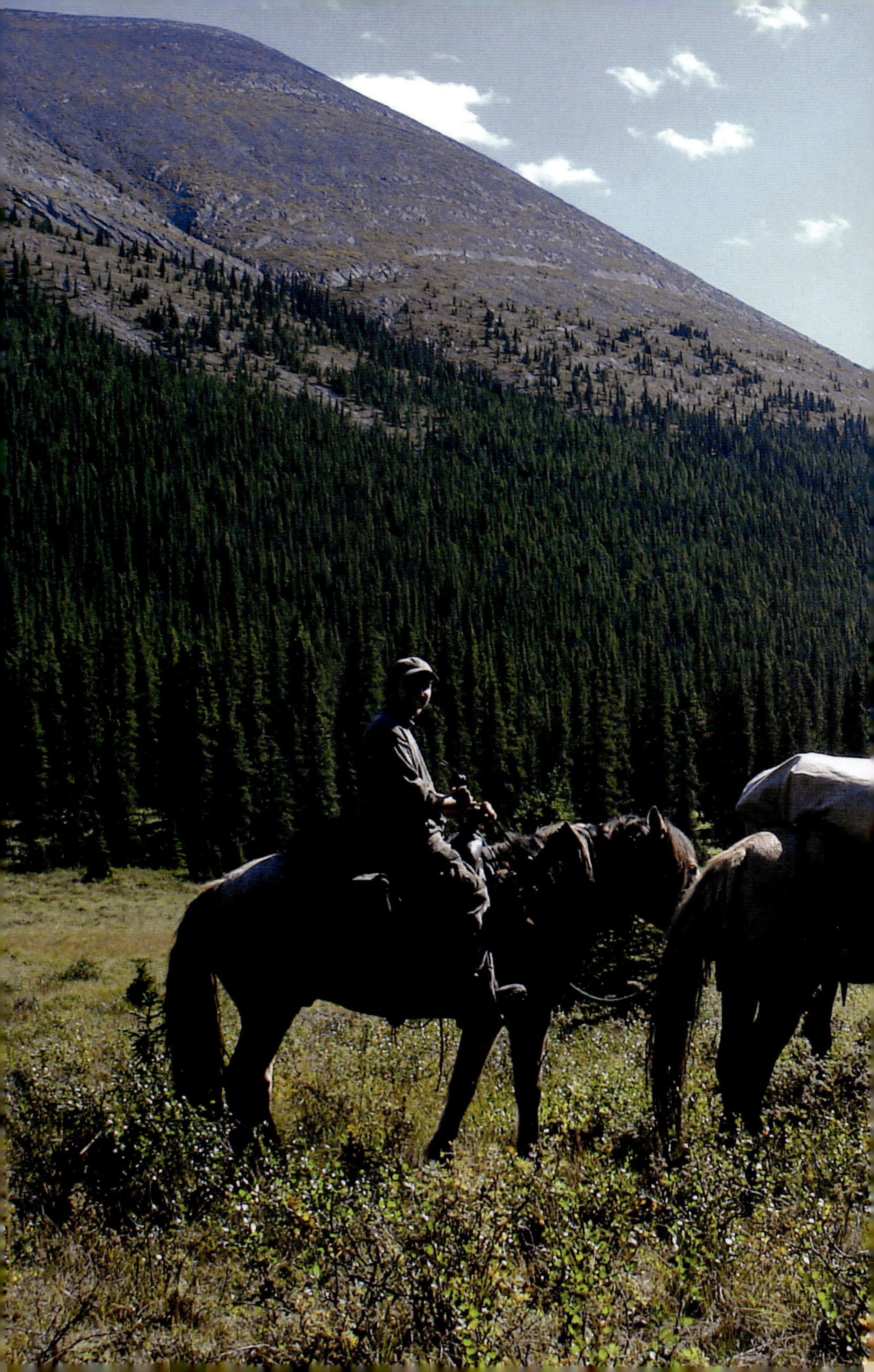

Cassidy's brother, Richard, and Rob moving the packtrain onward.

Cassidy on top of the world.

Fifteen Seconds

Columbian sun, and my horse snorted happily as I turned him loose upon the lush August grass. A cool light breeze whispered down from nearby peaks. I closed my eyes and took a deep breath, a feat that over the last few days could not have been accomplished without inhaling a mosquito or two.

For four days my dad, brother Richard, seven horses, and I, had been trailing toward the high country through endless muskeg and beaver-flooded valleys. We had battled every type of airborne bloodsucking bug, and we had tiptoed around myriad underground hornets' nests planted like landmines in the middle of the horse trails. Finally free of the lowlands, I gazed at the mountains. So close now, they were drawing me with magnetic intensity toward their slopes with the luring promise of Stone sheep.

Needing to stretch my legs, I grabbed my spotting scope and binoculars and, as afterthought, my rifle, and headed away from camp to do some scouting. The late afternoon sun was hot on my back as I hiked up a wide, barren creekbed. Pausing for a sip of water from the deceptively small channel responsible for the massive flood plain, I watched a handsome bull elk emerge from the timber.

I crouched low as he strode across the open ground and stopped on the opposite edge of the creek only thirty yards away. It was one of those moments that drives my passion for the hunt. It wasn't the chase, or the challenge, or the kill. It was that beautiful moment when you know you are one with nature.

After a long drink, he jerked his head up and stared, noticing me for the first time. Hesitantly, he lowered it again, eying me cautiously. After some moments of indecision, he turned and made his way slowly toward the tree line, looking back over his shoulder. "Good luck friend," I said, as he turned one last time to face me before disappearing into the timber.

As I walked on, the peaceful state of mind that the encounter with the elk had induced in me exploded. The serenity I had felt was chased away like the sun before an oncoming thunderstorm. It was like the perfect day of snorkeling until suddenly you see a gray fin circling and you realize that you are far from shore. Instead of a circling fin, my calm was shattered by a brown hump moving below the lip of the streambank.

I hastily set my spotting scope on the rocks at my feet and slung the rifle off my shoulder. Fifty yards away along the streambed was a medium-size boar grizzly. I could see the muscles in his neck tense as he spotted me. I didn't have to glance around to know that I was stuck out in the middle of the flood plain in a vulnerable position with nowhere to go. "Hey!" I shouted as I chambered a round.

The fact that I could talk did nothing to discourage his course. His pace increased to a hard, rapid stride in his effort to close the distance between us. His paws flicked aggressively with each brisk step, and I could feel his eyes lock on target. Cradling my rifle in one arm, I waved the other in the air as a last-ditch effort to display that I was not normal prey material. "Hey bear, hey bear," I yelled. But his mind was made up. In an instant, his aggressive gait shifted seamlessly into a dead run as he charged.

The will to live is an incredible phenomenon. In the fifteen seconds before I estimated he would reach me, my brain locked into survival mode. So many critical facts flashed through my mind: I only had three bullets and my scope was still on 9X, useless at such close range. If I missed, would I have time to reload? Probably not. Fear was an option that could only lead to death.

Nothing existed but the bear racing toward me. *Hoooof, hoooof, hooooffff*, his gasps were in rhythm with the rise and fall of his chest. I could see saliva dripping off his black lips. He was coming so fast now. How far? Not yet. Steady. Not yet. Steady. I could smell him now. Looking down the side of my barrel into the mass of raging grizzly bearing down on me, I pulled the trigger.

The bear disappeared from view. Like waking from a nightmare, I cycled the next round instinctively, my mind not yet registering the

The elk Cassidy was admiring moments before she saw the bear.

inert form sprawled seven yards in front of me. I kept the gun trained on the lifeless grizzly even as blood began to darken the river rocks. As the stain grew, creating a grotesque aureola of rose around his head, I was wrested at last from this deadly incubus.

I began to shake as the reality of what had just happened struck home. *What if I had missed? What if the gun misfired? What if I had spotted him too late?* As I walked in a state of disbelief back toward camp, I gazed up at the last of the sunset retiring behind the vast mountaintops and whispered my thanks to the winds of fate. This time, at least, they had sided with me.

CHAPTER 23

A Buck or Two

Why not dream big?.

"Today," my hunting buddy Jason Wall said jokingly as we saddled horses in the pitch black, "I'd like to harvest a muley that scores around 190 net, typical."

It was five o'clock in the morning, 14 November, the second to last day of the muley season in British Columbia, Canada. Jason and I had already driven two hours on snow and ice-covered mountain roads to our favorite muley area. The cold was numbing.

"Hey," I joked back, "Why not dream big? I'd like to harvest a 230 nontypical."

This was way too optimistic for the area. Jason had taken a 180 net typical here, and four years earlier my daughter had harvested a 196 gross. I'd never seen a nontypical over 180 in our "spot," a migration and rutting area for local mule deer. While it's a good area for finding mule deer, the area is not for the faint of heart as it can be accessed only on foot or by horseback.

Riding in the dark in snow that sometimes reaches the horse's bellies is also not for the faint of heart. Those die-hard mulies don't move down until they absolutely have to. Still, we were at some openings in the timber at first light, and I had a good feeling about today's hunt.

We spotted several groups of deer as dawn painted the sky around us, but there was nothing big. When the trail divided about two miles into the clearing, Jason and I decided to split up. I took the high trail and Jason elected to take the low trail.

I spent the next few hours on horseback plowing through deep virgin snow. By noon I was discouraged. I had crossed only one set of tracks, and they were heading down. I decided to head down myself to see if I could catch up with Jason. I found his tracks and followed them. Deer sign became more evident as I descended.

A Buck or Two

my now loaded packhorse. We figured I'd need a half hour head start to get in position for when the deer came running up the hill.

As I was riding around a twist in the trail, Jason intercepted me, way ahead of the schedule we had discussed. He was literally jumping up and down, waving his hands over his head. Every hunter knows this lingo: something big. Something really big.

Jason could barely talk he was so excited. He had seen a huge nontypical. He guessed it at 230 inches. I remembered our conversation from that morning when I'd told him I was going to dream big. Part of me thought he must be pulling my leg, but looking at him, I knew he was no Jeff Bridges and no one but an academy award winner could manufacture that kind of excitement. Knowing that he had seen something truly giant, I tied the horses and grabbed my rifle and backpack.

We inched down through the trees that concealed the trail and carefully poked into the open hillside. There were deer everywhere. But 550 yards away, straight down, and completely unaware of our presence was the deer. With my Leica 10X42, I could clearly see him: points popping out all over his head, amazing drop tines.

For a moment, when you see an animal like that, like nothing you have ever seen before, everything stands still, including your heart. But when it starts beating again, it is beating so hard and so fast it is almost impossible to be calm enough to get a good shot. Though I had found a rest, I could not get steady. I was in the throes of buck fever.

"We have to get closer," I whispered to Jason.

We picked a route through thick cover that would conceal us from the other deer and began the long, slow, careful crawl down the hill through the wet snow. When we emerged, the buck was still there, but there was no place left to hide. It was that do-or-die moment.

I ranged him at 280 yards. He suddenly sniffed the air, and his head swiveled toward me. I rested my .300 Winchester Magnum over a fallen log and aimed . . . but there was a bush sticking up just enough that I knew it would deflect the bullet.

The buck's muscles bunched up. He was ready to go. I made a slow slide to another log and was just resting my rifle when he decided to bolt. I fired and . . . missed. I led him almost to the heavy timber and fired again. This time he made a sharp ninety-degree turn and headed back into the opening.

"Did I hit him?" I yelled.

"Can't tell for sure, but it sounded good."

Now the monster buck was running through some scrub trees, so I held on a small opening in front of him and waited. His body appeared and I touched off my last shot at 330 yards. He disappeared from sight.

I yelled again, "Did I hit him?"

"I can't tell. I can't see him anymore."

We raced down to where I had taken my first shot; there was no blood in the snow. I could feel my heart sinking like a stone as we moved to where he'd been when I took that second shot. Still, no blood. We followed his tracks in the snow to where I had fired my final shot. This time I had connected, and there he was lying where he had fallen. One more shot, and he was done.

I've had exciting moments in my life: I've been charged by grizzlies, I've been in an aircraft that slid off a runway in icy conditions, and I've been in a Zodiac that flipped over in high seas. But I don't think I've ever felt the adrenaline rush and pure excitement I felt at that moment when I gazed down at the tangled rack of this incredible animal.

Jason and I celebrated, admired the buck, and took a few field shots. Then reality kicked in. Dark was coming fast, and it was getting colder. It was starting to snow. I retrieved the horses, we skinned out the deer, and then we loaded the horse to go.

We had come up in the dark, and by the time we were finished, it was dark again. This time we were soaking wet. The teeth-rattling

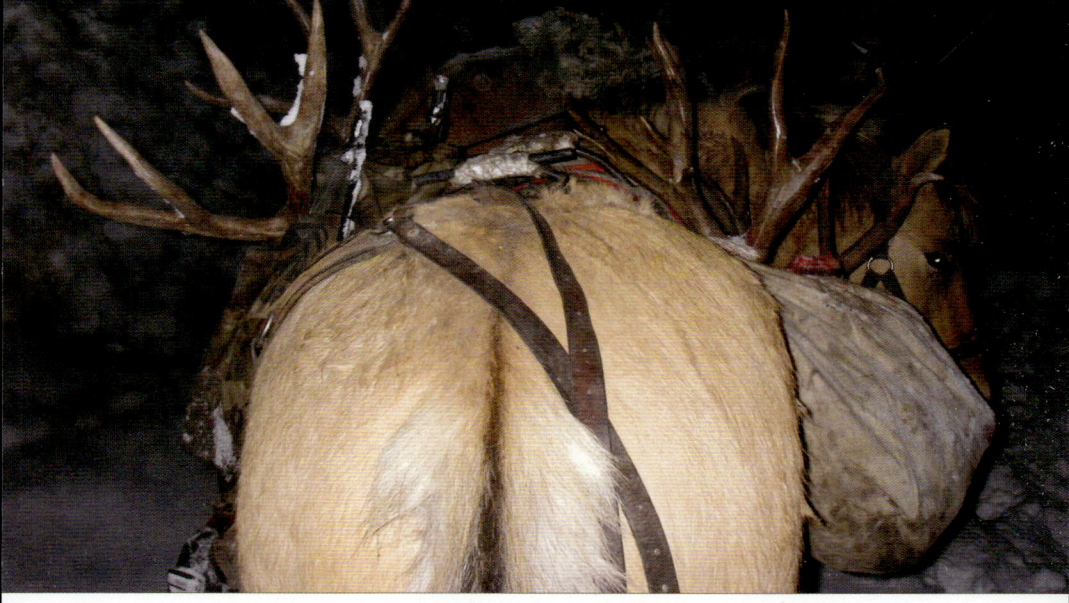

Chance, the wonder horse, packs out the two deer through a snowstorm.

discomfort was a small trade for the most magnificent trophy of my life. It is a trophy I am well aware I would not have if it were not for the generosity, hunting skills, integrity, and high ethical standards of Jason.

After 60 days drying time, the muley buck was officially scored 229 4/8 net according to the Boone and Crockett scoring system. He grosses 235 and change. When I entered him in the British Columbia record book, I made sure that Jason Wall's name appeared with mine.

CHAPTER 24

Sheep against a Wall

How do you repay the friend who helped you get a record book muley? When I realized Jason Wall had never been on a sheep hunt, I had my answer.

"How far is he?" Jason whispered.
"Seventy-five yards," I whispered back.
KABOOM.

This hunt actually began a year before on 14 November 2009, to be exact. Jason Wall had helped me harvest the biggest mule deer of my hunting career. It scored 235 inches gross, nontypical.

How do you repay a favor like that? Jason had never been on a sheep hunt. He had hunted elk, deer, and one goat. I feel a lot of trepidation about asking people to hunt with me, especially sheep. Though, I worry about them keeping their mouths shut about my favorite places, my biggest concern is always, do they have what it takes? Because I hunt hard. Really hard. Anyone who hunts sheep knows the level of difficulty is higher than when hunting other species, and I often take it one level beyond that.

Still, I was aware of owing Jason big time, and after hunting mulies with him that 2009 season, I thought he was tough enough. I've been wrong before, however. I've also asked people to hunt with me, and they've jammed out at the last minute. Still, I decided to take a chance because I wanted to repay a debt. I asked him if he would like to come on a horseback sheep hunt next year.

He responded, "I'd love to."

As we drove up the Alaska Highway, with six horses in tow, Jason had already passed the first test. He'd showed up. After two days driving from our hometown in the Kootenays, we arrived at the trailhead. There was several other horse trailers parked there, and that just proved to me that there were others equally or more obsessed with sheep hunting than I. This was 26 July and opening day was

Sheep against a Wall

not until 1 August. The obsession to hunt sheep is not unlike that of the early prospectors chasing the dream of gold. I have certainly been chasing those curly horns with the same kind of addiction as the men chasing gold did in the last two centuries.

The trip began like most of my other pack trips with the exception I had a real greenhorn under my wing. Jason had never been on a horse-pack trip. In fact, he had never saddled a horse before, let alone packed one. Most people who haven't been around horses much have one burning question they need to ask, and Jason was no different.

"Does this horse buck?"

"Of course not. Do you really think I would put you on a horse that bucked?" This was the absolute truth. I've seen old wranglers who think it is funny to put a greenhorn on a bad horse, but I don't see the humor in that at all. An injury several days in from medical attention is not a laughing matter.

Jason was on my horse, Schnitzel, a big Fjord cross who was really coming into himself. He had several years of packing behind him, and we'd ridden him quite a bit. He'd unloaded my son, Richard, the year before, but with provocation.

"Just don't try to put on a rain slicker while you're riding him."

I gave Jason a crash course in what his job description was to be. "Just chase the loose packhorses and keep them moving along the trail. They will try to stop to eat if you don't push them."

About two hours into the trail, I heard a commotion and turned to see Jason flying over the top of his horse's head. He landed with an unglamorous splash right in a mud hole. My horse who was definitely not a bucker unless provoked was bucking so hard his hind feet were straight up in the air. He continued to kick his heels up and down for about two minutes after he'd unloaded Jason.

I caught Schnitzel and tied him and several of the horses to some trees. The whole packstring was all wired up, full of vim and vinegar. They get like that when they have been cooped up for several days in

Rob and Chance setting out on one more adventure.

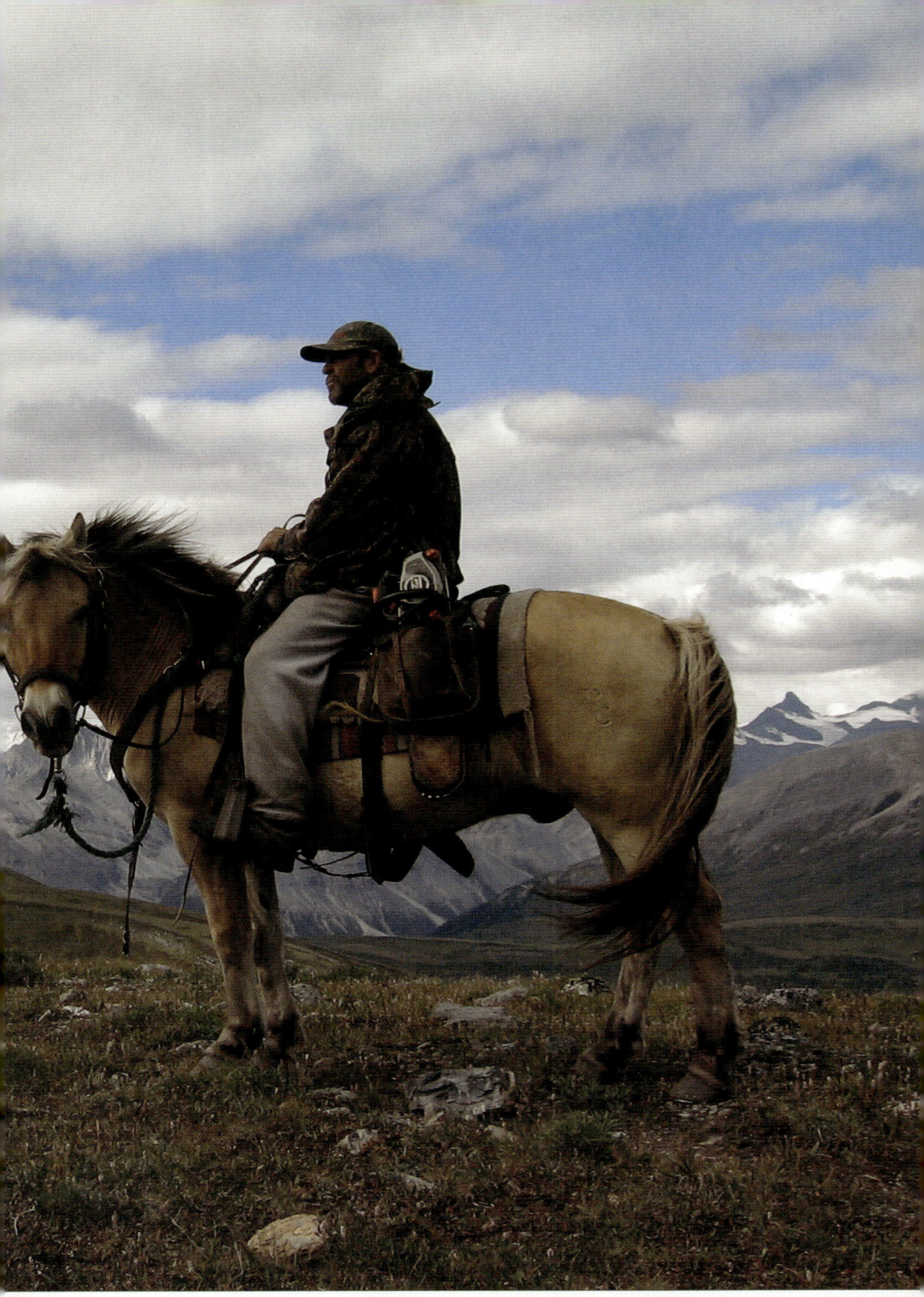

a horse trailer. Jason came limping up the trail covered with mud. The only thing hurt, thank God, was his pride.

"I thought you said this horse didn't buck?"

I guess with some horses, you just don't know what's going to provoke them!

"You must have said something to set him off, "I kidded Jason, and then gave him the bad news. "Well, you can't let him win. You have to get right back on him."

Nervously, Jason climbed back on. I gave him a few tips. "This time hold the reins a little tighter so that he can't get his head down. Oh, and don't get too relaxed." The danger of Jason relaxing was minimal at that point!

We rode hard for about six more hours before finding a spot to camp. It took that long for my fired-up horses to settle down. That night we slept to the sound of mosquitoes buzzing in our ears. I knew what to expect on these trips as this was about my twentieth northern pack trip. For Jason it was probably one of those baptism-by-fire deals.

The horses were more relaxed the next day. I believe the grim fact of where they were settled in on them and they realized that they were going to have to work hard for the next few weeks. This wasn't their first rodeo, either. They were probably thinking, *We'd better save our energy as this numbnut isn't going to feed us much.* Still, Jason switched to my dead-broke Appaloosa, Dessie.

On the evening of the fourth day, after crossing a plateau, several swollen rivers, numerous bogs, and passing through two different outfitters' territories, we finally arrived in sheep country. We had now logged close to forty hard hours in the saddle. I estimated we had traveled one hundred and fifty miles.

By now, Jason had really proven himself. He could saddle his own horse, throw the saddles on the packhorses, and tie the diamond, something that some people spend a lifetime trying to learn and never

Sheep against a Wall

quite conquer. He was a quick study, tough as nails, and didn't have one whisper of whine in him. He was never still. When we arrived at a camp spot, he went to work. He never stood around waiting for direction; he just did what needed to be done. I think he was a natural born sheep hunter.

Anyway, arriving in sheep country, I spied the perfect camp spot, which was on the other side of a rather treacherous-looking body of swift running water.

"Let's camp over there," I said.

"What's wrong with here?" he wanted to know.

"I think it will be better on the other side. Besides, once we're on the other side, the horses won't cross back over by themselves."

This was something I had discovered through a lot of trial and error. If there was no barrier, like water, the horses, even hobbled, would graze back the way they came. They can easily meander ten miles in a night. Because of this, I try to find a way to contain them; moreover, I always keep one tied up so that I have a backup to find the others with in the morning. But I understand why Jason would be hesitating on this crossing. The water was a dirty gray from the glacier melt. It was cold. We could not see bottom.

I nudged my well-behaved horse into the murky abyss and immediately was swimming. One of the other packhorses followed, but the remainder had other ideas. This was our first true swim of the trip. I yelled, "Come on Jason, push the others in and let's go."

It was the only time on that trip that Jason balked. "No way!" he shouted.

I knew, by then, that all he could see was my head and my horse's head sticking out of the water. Once on the other side, I walked onto a gravel bar and called encouragement to Jason. Without any guidance from him, however, the other packhorses meandered about fifty yards down the other side of the river and entered the water. They crossed without even getting their waists wet. None of these horses

255

Unquenchable Spirit

Jason Wall in front of a natural hot spring after switching to the more mild-mannered Dessie.

Sheep against a Wall

had ever been in this place before, so I really don't understand how they intuitively knew where to cross.

This scene seemed familiar; only this time I was playing the part of Yukon hunting guide, Chris Widrig, who had an absolute gift for ferreting out the wrong place to cross a river. Now it was Jason's turn to laugh at me, soaked to the eyeballs, as I had laughed at Chris when he was bucked off. Karma's a b#@&#!

I was glad to get out of my wet clothes that evening. After the long trail in, we only had one day to do some scouting for sheep before opening day, and we still hadn't seen a single sheep. The next day we set out from our camp on our quest. Although we rode all day and glassed a lot of country, by that evening we were still sheep-less.

I lay in my sleeping bag that night worried that we would not be able to find any rams on opening day. Failing to find even a token member of the species reduces the hunter's chances of harvesting a sheep greatly. Most good sheep hunters are usually camped on a ram at least one or two days in advance. There were other hunters in the area and sometimes competition can be stiff, even this far north. As darkness was falling, I took one last look at a sheepish-looking mountain.

And that's when I saw them! There they were! Three rams were feeding on the skyline. I set up my spotting scope and zoomed it to 60-power. There were no full-curl rams in this group, but at least I now had a starting point in the morning.

The next day, Jason and I rode our horses toward the mountain where I had seen the sheep and turned up a valley to the right of it. By midmorning, I found two rams, and I was ecstatic to see both of them were full curl, well over the nose.

Through the spotting scope I could see one was deep and only over the nose by about half an inch. He had a dark gray neck. The other had a tighter curl and was about two inches over the nose with wide flaring horns; this one had a white neck. Of the two, the deep curl

Riding the endless Kyrgyz plains toward the mountains.

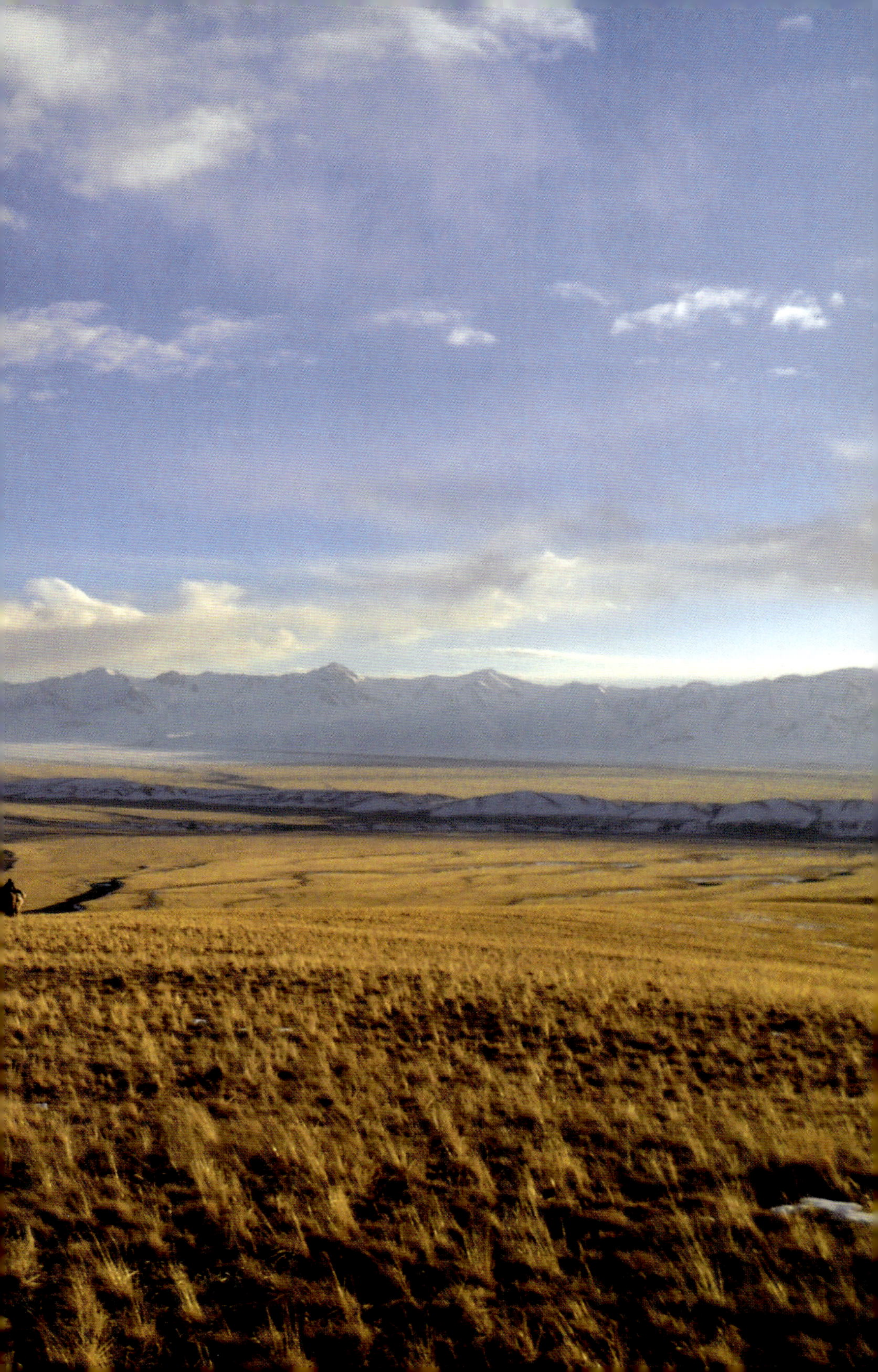

Unquenchable Spirit

a last-day shot, followed by a desperate push back toward base camp in the darkness.

For those two weeks, we had scoured extreme peaks, exceeding 13,000 feet in elevation, braved minus 20-degree Celsius temperatures, been buffeted by ferocious winds, hiked thousands of vertical feet, and dragged the poor horses through miles of brutal mountainous country.

The local cuisine provided little sustenance for the extreme demands of the hunt. For the past week I had existed mainly on chai (tea) and what I had dubbed "hubcap bread." Pie-shaped, this bread resembled something baked over a fire in a car hubcap, which probably wasn't much of a stretch. As far as culinary progress goes, I suspect that it hadn't evolved far from the hardtack served on the *Mayflower*.

Cassidy on a small but sturdy Kyrgyz mountain pony.

Other than the hubcap bread, the only item of food that we had an abundance of was canned Russian fish. These cans contained black minnows, packed in pungent slime. Each fish sported glazed eyes, agape jaws, and sharp white teeth. As a culinary treat, they were about as appealing as playing strip poker at an old folks' home.

I had come to admire the toughness of my guides and their mistreated mounts, but the language and cultural barriers were difficult to overcome. I was less than thrilled one evening, as the sun began to dip and the night chill set in, to discover that my sleeping bag and tent had been left behind at the last camp to lighten the load.

"Sleep, sleep," said the guides as they pointed at the frost-covered ground and the sweaty horse blankets. The thought I may not survive this expedition entered my mind for the first time, but not the last.

That was a long night, with sleep coming in short intervals before violent shivering forced me awake. My feet were so close to the fire my socks were in danger of melting to my soles, I had my metal saddle for a pillow, and the only covering I had consisted of damp horse blankets. Ice coated my hood and my hair was frozen to the edges of my face. Yet, as I sprawled on the cold earth looking up at stars spilling across the cold November sky and despite the discomfort, I felt oddly exhilarated.

We had hunted hard and seen hundreds of ibex, but, so far, a trophy-class billy had eluded us. Many times the ibex were simply too far away, the shooting distance unrealistic. On the last possible day of hunting before the long trek back to base camp, we spotted a large herd in a difficult-to-access valley across from us. The guides were nervous about going after this group, given that I was due to be on a plane soon, but I was determined not to go home empty-handed.

We crested a ridge after three hours of climbing, slogging through deep snow and crawling across sharp rocks. My heart hammered from the climb and the excitement. I could see the group of billies four hundred yards away. It was my last chance at an ibex.

I settled my rifle on a flat rock and took aim at a magnificent billy with wide flaring horns jutting from his head. One shot dropped him, and the weariness of two hard, frustrating weeks faded into elation. But there was no time for celebration. The clock was ticking relentlessly.

So, here I was on my final push to base camp. How much farther did we have to go? Ten miles? Five? A harsh wind whipped unchecked across the barren landscape. My tired eyes searched the darkness until I picked out the shape of the horse bearing my ibex horns. I ran a hand through my wind-tangled dreadlocks, and as I did, I caught a whiff of burned yak dung. When had I last had a shower? Canada? Bishkek? Twenty days ago? Did it really matter? I had my prize. I had my ibex.

It barely mattered that we still had a long night's march to base camp, or that the drive to Bishkek tomorrow—on roads better suited to donkey caravans than motor vehicles—would take twelve hours, or that my flight was less than thirty-six hours away, or that I hadn't heard from my father who was hunting Marco Polo in some other province for over a week. I had my ibex. That was all that counted. Little did I know that my adventure was far from over.

Finally, we stumbled into base camp, cold and exhausted. The few precious hours of sleep in an actual bed ended too soon. Although it was just sunrise, the base camp was in chaos as everyone packed up in preparation to leave for the winter. I found my ibex head and set to work caping it, despite the protests of the guides who were convinced my female brain was not up to the task.

Finished with the cape, I had time to notice some of the camp members cutting up what seemed to be an unusually large pile of ibex meat. Just by the way they were cutting it and stuffing it all into a large barrel made me suspicious. I was pretty sure that no one in the camp was supposed to be shooting anything but me.

We broke camp before noon. A dozen people, bags of gear, Stalin-era rifles (carefully hidden beneath seats) and the barrel of suspicious meat were all crammed into every available space in an old Russian van and a more reliable Subaru Forester. We looked like some sort of traveling circus.

Driving over the barely viable track across the desolate tundra was comparable to being an ice cube inside a cocktail shaker. The four other people inside the Subaru chain-smoked brutally harsh Russian cigarettes with the windows rolled up. As if the cigarette smoke was not bad enough, noxious blue fumes escaped from the Soviet van trundling along ahead of us. If there was ever a recipe for carsickness. . . .

Finally, we hit the highway from China, Kyrgyzstan's main thoroughfare. It was not much of an improvement from the tundra track, and it wasn't long until we came to a roadblock. Two military-looking men were trying to get inside the van while the eight passengers inside kept pushing them out.

In the ruckus, the lid was pried from the suspicious meat barrel. To my horror, the woman who ran the hunting camp sprang out of the back of the Subaru, which is no small feat as she was rather large, and began wildly waving the permit for my ibex about, jabbering and pointing at me. It took only a glance at the permit and the barrel. Six hoofs protruded from the top of it. Great. Six hoofs do not add up to one ibex.

In a sudden flurry of activity, the rusted door of the van was slammed shut from inside, and it rumbled away at its top speed of fifty kilometers an hour. With an angry shout, the military guys ran for their Jeep, but with an impressive burst of speed the fat woman made it back to our car first. The back springs sagged as she leapt through the door all the while screaming hysterically.

Tires spun on loose gravel as we shot back onto the road. Instead of gaining speed, we began to creep along the dead center of the highway behind the van. By now, I had a pretty good idea an extra ibex had been poached, even though I could not confirm my hypothesis since no one spoke English.

Thinking we were probably going to be shot at any second, I tried to maneuver myself so that the fat woman behind me would serve as

Cassidy and her ibex.

a shield. Every time the pursuing Jeep tried to pass us and catch up to the fleeing van, our driver veered in front of it. The first hour was tense. I felt rage, anxiety, and confusion. But as it became apparent that we were going to cross the entire country like this, all emotion settled into a kind of seething disbelief.

Darkness fell and still we drove, pursued by the Jeep. We were threading the needle between Chinese semis that were crisscrossing the empty straight stretches. By now we had lost sight of the poacher van completely. The people in the Subaru with me seemed to forget we were in a high-speed chase. They were dozing, smoking, laughing.

It seemed unreal that a roadblock hadn't intercepted us. No sooner had that thought crossed my mind when our situation changed. We started to descend a steep mountain pass into the first town since the chase had started four hours previously. As we careered around the last blind switchback on the wrong side of the road, narrowly missing a transport creeping up the hill, there was the roadblock.

Actually, it was a line of unarmed policemen holding hands across the road. I groaned as our driver gunned the engine and sped right at them. Swinging nightsticks at the windows as we broke their line, they jumped aside. The Subaru accelerated into an unlit residential area going over eighty kilometers an hour on an uneven dirt street. The Jeep remained close behind. We fishtailed around a ninety-degree corner and crashed through a sawhorse that marked where the street had been dug up.

The driver veered left and nailed the frozen dirt pile. If you're a "glass-is-half-full" person, that outcome was slightly better than the gaping hole to the right. In slow motion, the Subaru rode up the pile and began to tip over.

I grabbed for dear life to the "I-think-I'm-going-to-die handle" with both hands, braced for impact, and closed my eyes. The car began to rock and voices shouted outside. The Subaru slammed back onto all four wheels. Opening my eyes, I realized that three guys had jumped out of the Jeep and had righted us.

The doors were yanked open, and they tore our driver out by his hair and started working him over. I couldn't really blame them, after four hours I was ready to deck the guy, too. Suddenly he managed to break free and jumped back into the car. Door wide open, he began driving down the road even as the police were trying to pull him back out of the car.

We made it another three blocks before we were completely boxed in by six cars. Over twenty men surrounded us. As if the situation wasn't bad enough, Mrs. Fat jumped out and demanded to speak with the person in charge. When he stepped forward, she went nuts and started screaming and slapping him in the face.

I thought the police couldn't get angrier, but they did. They opened the hatch and threw my duffel bags into the street. So far, I had stayed totally neutral, hoping to demonstrate that I had nothing to do with what was going on, but, when they tore open my bags and started picking through my gear, I had had enough.

I stormed over to Mrs. Fat, who was still making a scene with the boss, and wrestled her away from him. She tried to shake me off, but my blood was boiling. With a few choice words in the universal language, I steered her toward the car and shoved her into the backseat. She protested loudly and tried to get back out, but I slammed the door on her. Twice.

I turned my back to the door, leaning against it so she couldn't open it again, panting heavily. That's when I noticed twenty shocked, young Kyrgyz policemen frozen on the spot, staring at me. The two going through my bag zipped it shut and hurriedly put it back in the trunk.

A few phone calls were placed, a corrupt politician was reached, and two hours later, the police let us go. I made it to the airport forty minutes before my flight departed. As the plane banked sharply over the snowcapped peaks, I smiled to myself. My epic ibex adventure had been anything but orthodox.

CHAPTER 26

Into Asia

Defeat is not an option: returning to Kyrgyzstan for an ibex and Marco Polo ram.

Why would anyone leave the balmy, tropical breezes and beauty of Hawaii for the harsh, barren mountains of Central Asia? Any hunter can give you the answer: the opportunity to harvest a truly great animal. For me that was a Marco Polo ram. I, along with many sheep hunters, consider the Kyrgyz variety of the Hume argali the Holy Grail of sheep hunting. I also hoped to get a mid-Asian ibex.

So, in early February of 2011 I cut a Hawaiian vacation short to head back to Kyrgyzstan. I had been there late in 2010 on a quest for a Marco Polo that had failed. The outfitter, Bryan Martin, was as anxious to get me one of those sheep as I was to take one, and so I was back for round two.

I landed in Bishkek, a city of over a million people. It is dominated by the uninspired cement-square-box architecture of the Soviets, whose occupation of the country ended in 1990. I was greeted by my interpreter Cairat, who ushered me to the VIP line where I immediately got a visa and rifle permit. The VIP service allows a traveler to bypass the process of waiting in line to clear Customs, which is an exceedingly long process. It can add two hours to a journey that already had taken thirty hours.

I was not happy to see Cairat. I had encountered him on my first trip to Kyrgyzstan months earlier with my daughter, Cassidy. Between us, we called him Weasel-Rat, instead of Cairat, a name he earned. He was dishonest and sly. We had figured out his character even before we discovered he had pocketed the tips that we had left for our other guides.

Corruption is a way of life in Kyrgyzstan and is culturally entrenched. Bryan was up against a whole lot of challenges trying to run his

Riding on a frozen river in a quest for Marco Polo.

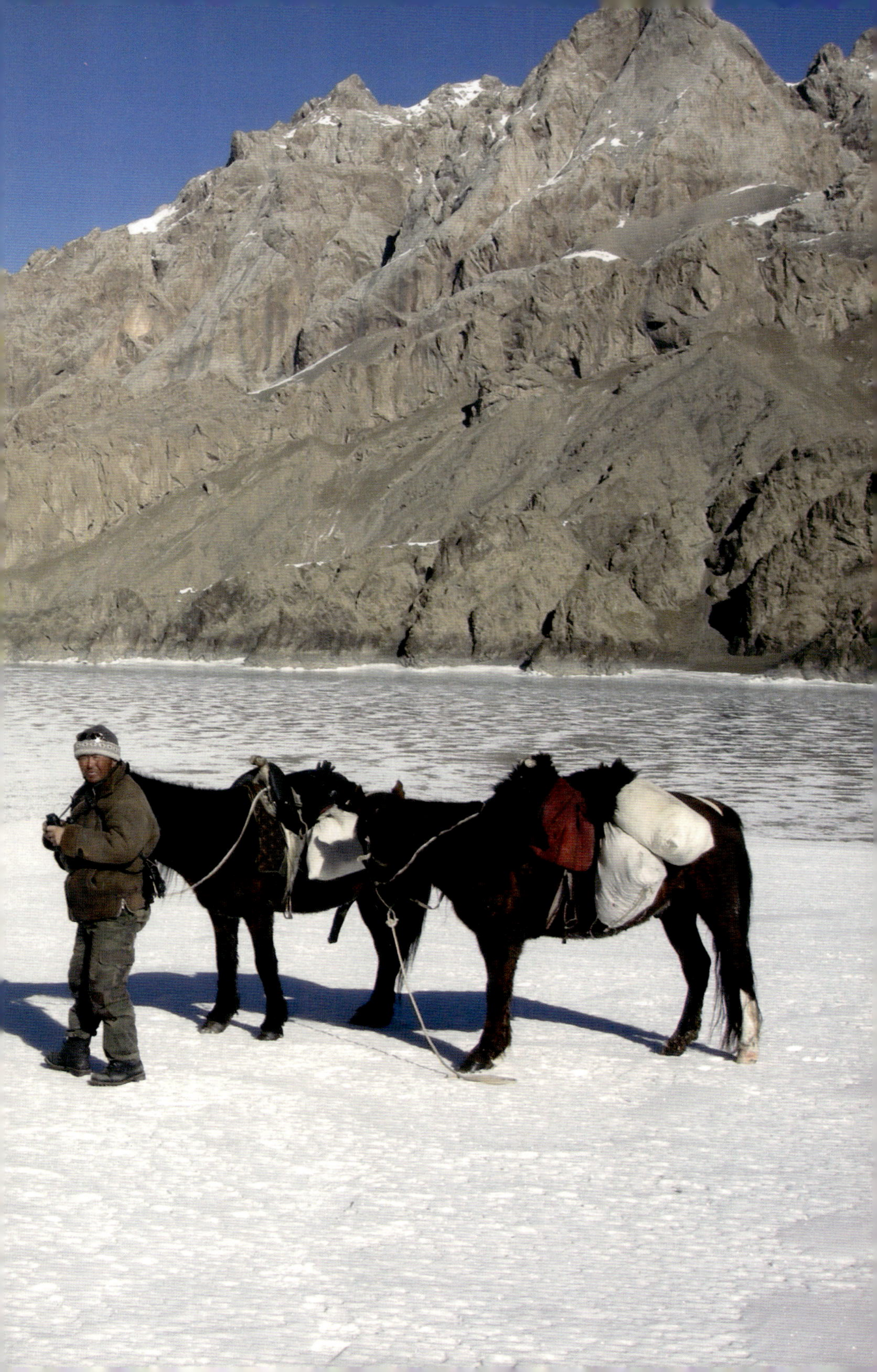

company, Asian Mountain Outfitters, in a country that institutionalizes dishonesty; it certainly has totally different cultural and ethical values from our own. I was glad Bryan was to accompany me on this trip so that I wouldn't totally be at the mercy of Cairat.

After a day's rest in Bishkek, the three of us were en route to the hunting area. The roads were passable, by Western standards, but rapidly deteriorated the farther we drove from Bishkek. The highway was full of potholes and patched sections. There were even washed out bridges that we had to negotiate by fording the creeks along rough goat trails made of gravel. The deplorable road conditions were the result of the post-Soviet regime's lack of spending on infrastructure; obviously, it was not a priority. In addition, we passed through military checkpoints, which proved to be a cultural lesson for me. Police armed with AK-47s strapped over their shoulders demanded a bribe to let us through.

Cairat, the weasel, would stop at the checkpoint and count the number of personnel. Then he would line up the correct number of shot glasses and fill them up with vodka, give one to each soldier, and one for himself. They'd shoot them back and have another, then Cairat would give each soldier a pack of Russian cigarettes, as foul as burning filthy socks when they were lit. Finally, the guard would lift the gate and happily wave us through. We went through this procedure five times before we arrived at the house of our Kyrgyz outfitter, Bolot (pronounced Bullet) late that night. Bryan must subcontract to a local in order to be allowed to hunt in these areas.

A ten-foot-high stone fence surrounded Bolot's house, and the iron gate was locked. His house was fancy by Kyrgyz standards. There was a table, which is unusual because most people eat on the floor, and there were carpets on both the floors and walls. He drove a Lexus, so I was beginning to smell corruption here, also. Still, for all the show of prosperity, there was no plumbing in the house. An outhouse, with no seat, just a hole in the ground, was located in the yard.

By the time we arrived, Cairat, our interpreter and driver, was fairly inebriated. More vodka was passed around before supper, which was served by servants. The meal consisted of boiled mutton with a few potatoes. I took a peek in the cooking pot and saw about 30 percent of it was fat globules. We finally went to bed, on the floor, after midnight.

The next morning, we awoke early, packed our gear back in the car, and headed up the road toward the Chinese border. There were no more military checkpoints, which was a good thing as Cairat had left us and gone back to Bishkek. Bolot drove. Bryan and I were now the only people who spoke English. About an hour later we met our guides at the end of the road. It had been getting steadily colder as we headed into the mountains.

We were to hunt with horses, and they were all saddled up and ready to go when we arrived. Kyrgyz horses are tiny—about the size of a pony—but extraordinarily tough. Kyrgyz people do not name their dogs or horses, and seem to have relatively little attachment to them. I heard they were great horseman, but as a horseman myself, I found their treatment of their animals very hard to accept.

I cannot remember the guide's names so I will refer to them as No. 1 and No. 2. After introductions, they tied our gear on the horses behind our riding saddles. It was to be Bolot, Bryan, No. 1, No. 2, and myself. There was only one packhorse for all five of us, which I would say is abusive. When I pack at home, there is one packhorse per one rider. This poor, tiny horse carried all our gear, plus several sacks of grain.

The riding was difficult. The snow was up to the horses' bellies in places. In spite of the snow depth, we made camp by nightfall. We were deep in mountains, jagged peaks rising steeply on all sides. We had seen lots and lots of ibex on the ride to base camp.

The camp consisted of three Russian-built semitrailer units. It is almost impossible to fathom how these structures were brought into the middle of nowhere. Still, I was glad they were there because it was minus twenty degrees Celsius that night; I had been dreading the thought of sleeping outside. The trailers came complete with beds and a stove, which No. 2 guide quickly got going. In no time, I was down to my T-shirt as it got quite cozy inside.

The next day all of us saddled up and rode farther up the valley toward sheep country. That day we again saw many ibex, but no sheep. Some of the ibex were quite big, and I was feeling excited about the prospect of harvesting a good ibex. The going continued to be extremely tough because the snow was deep. It was clear but very cold. We rode back to base camp that evening and made plans to travel farther the next day. The only way to do that was to make a spike camp with tents. Travel back and forth to the base camp was eating up too much time.

And speaking of eating, the food in this Kyrgyz camp was horrible. It consisted of frozen sausage, frozen cheese, and frozen bread. They ate these at all three meals. For drinks, they had tea (chai) and vodka (two cases). Because I had been here before (and had lost twenty pounds on my twenty-day hunt), I had brought my own freeze-dried, prepackaged food this time. Mountain House has never tasted so good!

In the morning, we set out again, and this time we ventured farther down the valley. The snow depths got progressively deeper as we went. We traveled until the horses were exhausted. By late afternoon we set up camp.

There was a windswept hill above camp and after the horses were each given a handful of grain—about enough to sustain a rabbit—they were hobbled and turned loose to feed on the little clumps of grass they dug out of the snow. Some of the horses already had sores. As I said, I felt really sorry for these poor animals.

From camp, Bryan spotted some Marco Polo rams about five miles down the valley. All day we had been seeing ibex on both sides of the valley. Although it was cold, minus twenty Celsius, we were comfortable in Bryan's Hilberg tent.

The next day was sunny, but cold. After our delicious freeze-dried breakfast, we caught the horses. (You could actually see them losing

Exhausted, Rob has a rest at camp.

weight.) We rode out. The rams were still in the same spot as the day before. It took us nearly four hours to cover four miles in the deep snow. We rode through a frozen river canyon that had open water in several places. To say it was dangerous would be an understatement.

Once we had gotten as close as we dared, without detection by the rams, Bryan set up his spotting scope. He said that the biggest ram would probably go about forty-four inches in length. Our plan all along had been to shoot nothing under forty-eight inches in length. When I looked at the ram through the scope, I agreed that he wasn't quite what I was looking for, even though I had never shot Marco Polo before. To me, he looked like a good Stone sheep, but not an animal you would travel halfway around the world for.

By midafternoon, we found more rams farther down the valley but were unable to find anything big. Plowing through the deepening snow was proving a limiting factor for any further travel, so we decided to turn around and head back to our spike camp.

Having not seen any large sheep, we decided to shift our focus to ibex. That evening, we spotted a good ibex from camp that was back in the same direction we had come that afternoon.

The next day found us once again slugging through the snow toward the ibex we had seen. We reached a vantage point by midday, and Bryan set up his spotting scope. At that time No. 1 took a quick look back the way we had come and spotted a giant ibex. It was directly above our spike camp. The guide was very excited, so we turned the spotting scope in the direction he was pointing.

The ibex was huge. Bryan said he was about the biggest one he had ever seen in all the years he had been outfitting in Kyrgyzstan. The ibex looked magnificent through the scope. His horns curled back, nearly touching his rump. He was definitely the one I wanted, but we were a long way from making that dream a reality.

We had traversed five miles of very tough ground for nothing, and now we had to go back the way we had come. Thankfully, the trail was already broken, so the return trip was easier. Back at spike camp, we planned a stalk where we would attempt to not be seen. This was difficult as the area was completely treeless. With a plan in place, after much sign language and confusion, we set out past our camp and began to execute our stalk from the other side of where our tents were pitched.

Bolot and No. 2 were to break camp and load all the gear on the horses and move them toward base camp. Bryan, No. 1, and I would hike up and make a move on the ibex from the next mountain over, and then meet them. To make sure everyone had a clear idea of what they were supposed to be doing, Bryan made a call on his satellite phone, and had a translator in Bishkek relay the instructions to Bolot and No. 2.

With the plans in place, we were ready. Getting to the next mountain was not easy because of the deep snow and the high elevation. Progress was painfully slow; consequently, the climb took much longer than expected. When I finally reached the spot where I was to shoot from, it was nearly dark. There was probably only a few minutes of shooting light left.

Bryan confirmed it was the same ibex, and he estimated the range to be 420 yards. This is an incredibly long shot, but I knew it might be the only chance I had. e used Bryan's pack as a rest. The ibex was bedded down, unaware of our presence. As time was of the essence, I got right down to business. I had to shoot quickly before the light had completely faded.

Even through my new Huskemaw scope, I could barely make him out. I breathed out and gently squeezed the trigger. At the report of my 7mm, I heard a distinct *wump*, the sound of a bullet hitting home. With the recoil, I lost sight of the big billy, but Bryan confirmed that he had been hit and hit hard.

I lowered the rifle and watched as the ibex stumbled down the hill. I was preparing for a finishing shot when he collapsed and rolled down the mountain on a steep snowslide. We were ecstatic—high fiving and jumping around in our excitement. Celebration is a universal language.

As darkness fell, reality set in shortly thereafter. We donned our headlamps. Luckily, I had an extra headlamp I could lend to No. 1, who was ill prepared. We started the arduous task of scaling the open avalanche chute in front of us. We slipped and slid over the extremely steep and treacherous mountainside. It took nearly half an hour to reach my fallen trophy, and by then it was completely dark.

We rolled him down the mountain for several hundred yards before we found a flat spot suitable to take pictures without falling off the mountain. Then, in complete darkness, with the aid of the headlamps, Bryan and I began to cape the animal out right there.

The guide waved his hands, insisting that we should drag the heavy animal all the way to the bottom of the mountain. It was difficult communicating because of the language barrier; really, none of us could understand what the other wanted. Because Bryan and I had backpacks, No. 1, who had no pack, volunteered to drag this animal down the mountain. (At least that's what I thought he said!)

Reluctantly we agreed, though dragging and sliding a four-hundred-pound animal down that kind of incline is extremely difficult, especially when the slope leveled out or when the snow deepened. Two of us had to break a trail while the other pulled the ibex, guts and all in the snow. We switched around, but as the going became more difficult, Bryan ended up doing the lion's share of the work. I was simply worn out at this point.

We were all sweating and soaked from the snow. The temperature was dropping fast. Near the bottom, when we emerged from the avalanche chute, we were relieved to see our rendezvous had worked out. We could see the headlights of Bolot and No. 2. After another two hundred yards of pulling and sweating, we reached the horses.

Rob with his trophy ibex.

We rested briefly while No. 1, No. 2, and Bolot pounded back a few rounds of vodka. After catching our breath, Bryan and I taped the ibex. It measured 51.5 inches on the long side and 49 inches on the short side. We pulled out our caping knives and went to work. At this moment No. 1 and No. 2 pulled out their dull, rusty butcher knives.

Bryan put his hands up, saying, *"Nyet, nyet,"* which means *no* in Russian. He explained to me, "We can't let them touch the cape. We just cannot risk having its nose or ears cut off, not to mention having various other important parts go missing."

When they finally figured out we didn't want their help, they sat down and continued to drink more vodka. As soon as we had the cape removed, they attacked the carcass with fervor. I could now see why Bryan did not want them doing any fine work with a knife. Very little

Once again riding the dangerous frozen rivers.

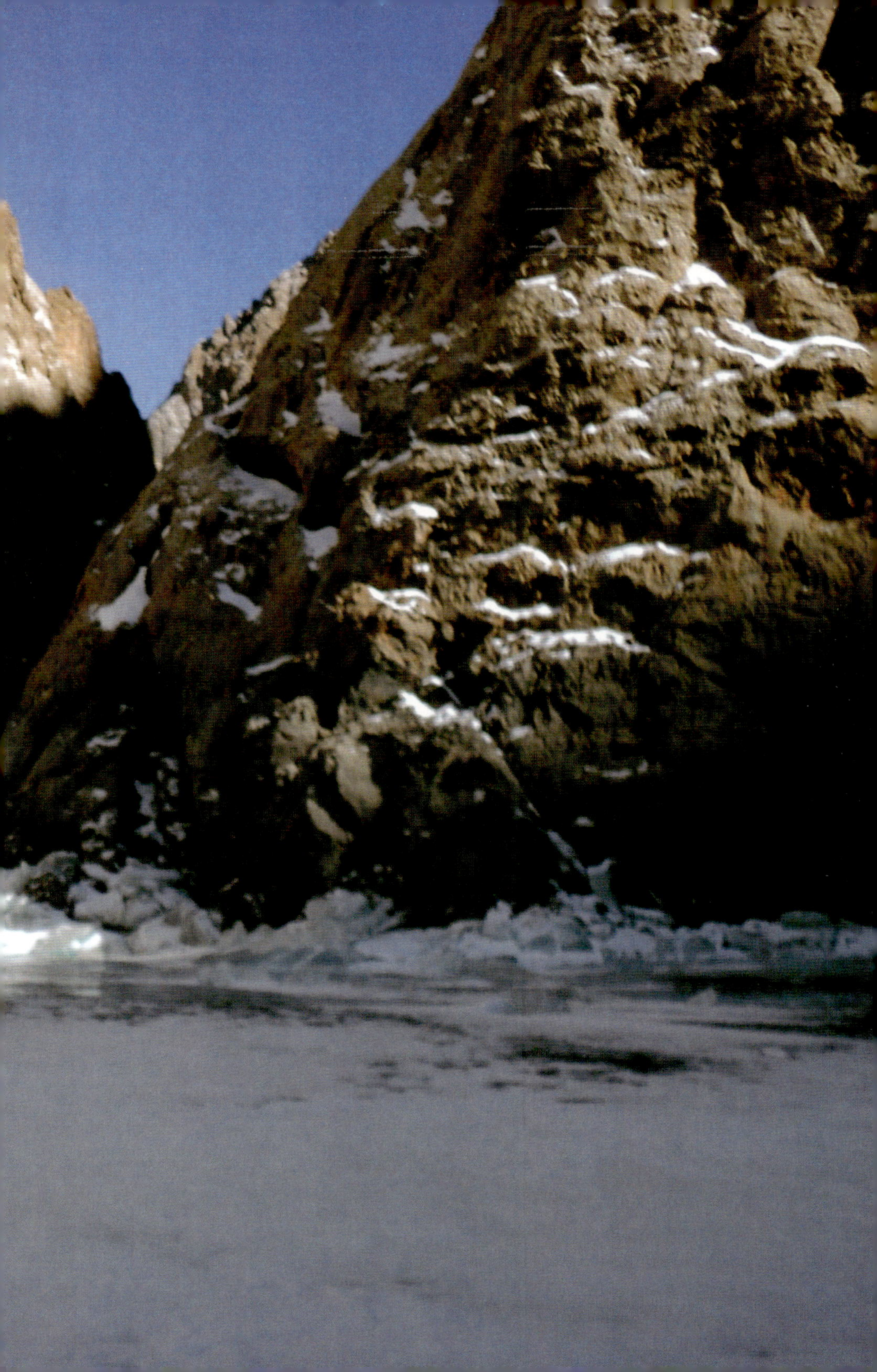

went to waste. They stuffed the meat, bones, and whatever was left into grain sacks; they had the entire carcass loaded in a matter of minutes.

I watched in horror as they came dangerously close to each other with those dull butcher knives. No. 2 broke his knife on a bone and looked on sadly as the others continued their attack. In sympathy, I loaned him my hunting knife, which he grabbed enthusiastically. Within minutes he broke that too. Now it was my turn to be sad. It had been a pretty good-quality buck knife. He then handed it back to me, but I insisted, "No you keep it. I don't need it anymore." Of course, he didn't understand a word I said, but kept the knife anyway.

Once mobile, we climbed on our now very overloaded horses. It began to snow as we rode. The wind came up and it was extremely cold. Since I was wet from coming down the mountain in deep snow and since I was sweating, it was difficult to stay warm. I would jump off my horse and try walking in the deep snow in order to stay warm. Walking was so difficult, however, that after a short while I would mount my horse once again. I would ride until I was again very cold. This routine happened numerous times. The temperature was well below minus twenty degrees Celsius with the snow blowing and the wind howling.

It was two o'clock in the morning by the time we reached the semitrailer camp. Bryan and I, both in wet, now frozen clothes, were on the verge of hypothermia. In the trailer, we put on dry clothes while No. 1 got a fire going in the stove. Soon we were toasty. Bryan and I fell asleep while the guides and Bolot drank more vodka well into the night. The next day we began to head back toward the road.

Bryan had to leave for the United States, so Bolot would escort him back. I was to continue hunting for Marco Polo sheep with No. 1 and No. 2. About five miles from the vehicle, we split up and Bryan and I said our good-byes; that meant I was the only English-speaking person in our entourage. By now, the poor horses were skeletons, and most had sores.

The three of us set off up another valley toward the Chinese border. The snow was not quite as deep as the area where I had harvested my ibex. We hunted hard for the next four days, exploring several different valleys.

We did a lot of riding on ice on the creeks, and the guides' horses fell through several times. I followed and tried to avoid the holes they had made. In an effort to get around one of their holes, my horse went through the ice. His hindquarters were underwater, but with his front legs still out, he was scrambling to find solid ground, and I was not wet.

I could clearly see there was a huge air pocket between the ice and the water below it, so it was almost like we had been traveling across the water on an ice bridge. I yelled, and the guides jumped off their horses and ran back for me.

Above me on the ice, they reached down their hands, calling to me in their own language. I managed to get hold of a hand and was yanked off the horse. Free of my weight, the horse launched himself out, and nearly landed on top of me.

I caught my breath, aware I had escaped death once again. I've lost track of how many times now I've cheated death, but certainly I've used more than my allotted nine and certainly most were related to my obsession to hunt.

We carried on up the valley. Around the next corner we walked right into two Marco Polo rams. Without even looking closely, both guides began to shriek the one English word they knew. "Shoot! Shoot!"

I was exhausted, and that exhaustion made me very susceptible to the urgency of their shouts. But by the time I had the rifle ready and was aiming, the rams were more than three hundred yards up the mountain and covering ground fast. I squeezed off at the front ram. I missed. My next shot was at five hundred yards, another miss. Knowing that any more shots would be hopeless, I pulled out my spotting scope and set it up on the running rams.

Unquenchable Spirit

As the snow became deeper, their progress slowed and I was able to get a better look at them. The lead ram would have barely broken the forty-inch mark. The other ram wasn't even over the bridge of the nose. It's was a darn good thing I missed.

I have never liked shooting at animals before I have been able to determine for myself how big they are or whether or not they are even legal. Still, you can usually trust the guide. I realized, in this circumstance, that these guides did not share my expectations. Whether these guys were not competent at judging trophy size or whether they had a different agenda from mine, I didn't know. I did know, however, that from now on I would have to make sure of what I was shooting at myself.

We saw a dozen more rams that day with the largest one maybe forty-five inches in length. The guides wanted to go after them, but I didn't consider them worthy trophies.

Farewell to Kyrgyzstan.

Into Asia

With time running out, we decided to throw in the towel and head out. Back at our tent camp, I made a phone call to Bryan's main interpreter, Asyl, and handed the phone to No. 1. Through her interpretation, she made arrangements for a car to meet us at the end of the road. We arrived at the waiting car in another blinding snowstorm in the dark. I left the guides and those poor overworked horses. They would have miles to go still in the storm before they were home.

I stayed at Bolot's again that night, and he appeared relieved that we had made it out in such a bad storm. Despite his limited English, he made it clear money was still owed to him. Because Bryan had left, he expected me to pay, which I did. Of course, I would find out later, there was no such money owing, but that's why Bolot had a Lexus when everyone else in his country had a donkey.

After a grueling drive out, I was once again in Bishkek. My dream of Marco Polo had been thwarted for the second time. But that's hunting. I have come to know if you get what you want every single time, it's not hunting anymore. It's shopping.

So, I was leaving Asia once again, and not only was I still alive, I had a magnificent ibex to show for it.

Footnote: Bryan Martin has since rectified the problems I previously encountered on my Kyrgyzstan hunt, up to and including providing a Western guide. His operation, Asian Mountain Outfitters, remains among the best in navigating the many hurdles of international hunting.

CHAPTER 27

The Holy Grail

Reaching the pinnacle after twenty-five years of hunting.

The tips of the Pamir Mountains are ragged. The mountains are desolate. Their beauty is savage. After seventeen grueling hours, we had at last arrived on the edge of them.

The road to the mountains was paved in places, and then washed out. The pace was fast, slow, fast, slow. Mostly slow. In between passing through half-a-dozen or so military checkpoints, the driver, Shavkat, had to get out and roll boulders off the road so that our Toyota Land Cruiser could get through. We had to work our way, with much blasting of the beloved car horn, through herds of sheep driven by swarthy men in baggy stained clothes, their heads covered in turbans or fezzes.

I am a carpenter. A guy from British Columbia, a town so small that it barely makes a map. How does a guy like me end up in Tajikistan, following a road through the Panj River Gorge where jagged cliffs rise on both sides? On the other side of the river is Afghanistan. Occasionally, on the Afghan side, I catch glimpses of people who look nomadic, always walking, leading heavily laden donkeys. How did I end up here?

At every place where we emerge from the canyon, if the ground is remotely flat, a village squats. Huts made out of rocks are a testament to the fact we are in an earthquake zone. The houses mostly stand, the roofs, constructed of wood dragged from who knows where, are caved in or partially caved in. Smoke comes from chimneys that protrude from the parts of the roofs that are still intact. No one seems to be making any effort at repair.

The village men, craggy-faced and stoic, show no interest in the vehicle. That is until they see me—blue-eyes, blond, and skin with that distinctive Canadian winter pallor. Then they stare, not hostile, curious. Women, some veiled but not as high a percentage as I had expected, scurry about carrying water, baskets, babies.

Rob on a footbridge north of Khorog.

    I am astonished to see how many people in these villages have cell phones—bustling inhabitants with their phones glued to their ears. It is the Stone Age meeting the Space Age. I begin to notice many of the huts, with no evidence of a power line, have satellite dishes, the old variety, like capsized spaceships, in the yards. The children are in school. We pass schoolyards with rock and dirt soccer fields. Shavkat tells me education is important here, especially learning to speak English.

    Again, I ask myself that question. How did I, least likely of world travelers, end up here, a world away from all that is familiar? When I shot my first Stone sheep, I was twenty-six years old. I could not have imagined it would lead me here. At twenty-six, that first sheep felt like the end of a quest. Instead, it was the beginning, the jumping off place that would lead me, twenty years later, around the world to the Holy Grail for all sheep hunters, the Marco Polo.

Every sheep hunter understands the mystique of hunting sheep. It is not just a hunt. It is the most extreme of challenges. Every hunt is a push against your own limitations. Every hunt calls you to dangerous places of steep drop-offs and ledges, adverse weather, discomfort, hardship. You are sleeping under a piece of plastic, clinging to the edge of a cliff. This is not for those who crave a five-star hotel experience.

And yet the adventure calls to me. The adrenaline of one hunt has barely settled when the next hunt begins to take shape in my mind. I have found a place where I feel fully alive. Fulfilled. Whole. Not so surprising that I would want to journey there again and again.

Over that twenty-year period leading to the Marco Polo, I had the privilege of experiencing successful sheep hunts six times. All but one was self-guided. I had a Stone, three Dalls, a Rocky Mountain big horn, and a California bighorn. I had worked one season as a Dall sheep guide in the Yukon. I had experienced the great pleasure of introducing sheep hunting to other people, including my daughter, Cassidy, who embraced the quest, the calling, as surely as I had.

I had, of course, seen pictures of Marco Polo rams. Drooled over them, experienced that stab of envy, the resignation it would never be me. The price was prohibitive for one thing. But for another, despite adventures in my homeland—including five trips to the Arctic—I had never traveled out of North America.

Then I met Bryan Martin, of Asian Mountain Outfitters, at a Wild Sheep Society fundraiser in Kamloops, British Columbia. The talk turned to sheep, and somehow to Asian sheep. Bryan had hunts in Kyrgyzstan at that time. The seed of possibility was planted.

I overcame the "North American" barrier with a hunt to Africa. And then the seed planted by my meeting with Bryan came to fruition in 2010, when I found myself in Kyrgyzstan. Skunked. A month later,

Rob pausing to catch his breath at 14,000 feet.

in 2011, I was back in Kyrgyzstan. I had harvested a huge ibex, but still no Marco Polo. I saw many, but THE one that I wanted eluded me.

For me, failure triggers obsession. At home, I did something that comes unnaturally to me, homework. I soon found out Tajikistan has more sheep and they are genetically larger. I had really enjoyed working with Bryan Martin, so when I found out about his hunts in Tajikistan, I approached him. Bryan had been as disappointed as I by my lack of success in Kyrgyzstan. We struck a deal that may or may not have involved my soul. And so, in November of 2011, less than a year since my trip to Kyrgyzstan, I once again found myself making the thirty-hour journey from Calgary to a territory of the former Soviet Union.

Unquenchable Spirit

Left to right: Shakar, Rob, Shirinbek.

 I arrived in Dushanbe, the capital of Tajikistan. I managed to get myself lost going through Customs by going in the wrong line. I was met by a Customs official who handed me a form to fill out that was written in Cyrillic. He addressed me in Russian. I could understand the occasional word, as my grandmother, many, many years ago had

The Holy Grail

spoken smatterings of it at home. Unfortunately, I understood only enough to confuse me more. I was ushered to a line of equally confused-looking people.

"Mr. Shatzko," I heard in a very strong Russian accent. "Marcel is my name. The VIP service was supposed to pick you up at the plane and escort you through Customs and past the main entrance but they forgot you."

I felt shades of Kyrgyzstan creeping up behind me. In third world countries, nothing seems to run smoothly. Marcel took care of the visa and helped me through Customs and then to the baggage carousel where I had my first meeting with Shavkat.

Shavkat is Bryan Martin's partner in Tajikistan; he would also act as my interpreter. He spoke good English, had a firm handshake, and a steady gaze. He soon revealed himself to be a bit of a worrywart, concerned about every detail of my journey, and I appreciated that quality was as much as any of his other characteristics. Throughout my journey in Tajikistan, Shavkat's concern for my safety, comfort, and satisfaction was genuine.

After another hour of paperwork, we were loaded into Shavkat's Toyota Land Cruiser, and that is how I, a carpenter from British Columbia, least likely of world travelers, ended up headed for the Pamirs, a name that translates to "rooftop of the world."

After seventeen hours on the road, we arrived at Khorog, (pronounced *Horog*) Shavkat's home town and the access point to the hunting area. After traversing that primitive landscape, I found Khorog to be, if not exactly a mecca of civilization, not prehistoric either. With a population of 25,000 inhabitants, Khorog benefited from Russian occupation with the building of dozens of schools and colleges. One of Tajikistan's main universities is located there; there are several major hydroelectric dam projects as well. Stone is still the main material used in buildings, but now the structures are three or four stories high. Still, the buildings are plain and square. Again, the

Unquenchable Spirit

Downtime after the hunt, visiting a sheepherder's home.

about every 300 yards; soon I couldn't make it more than 50 yards without stopping. It took over five hours to move 2,500 vertical feet. When we were above 15,000 feet in elevation, my lungs were burning with the sensation of someone slowly sliding a ragged-edged blade in and out of them.

The Holy Grail

When we finally reached the top of the mountain, we found the rams bedded about eight hundred yards away from us. Shirinbek decided we needed to sneak down a little closer and cut the distance. Even though Shirinbek was a man of very few English words, his ability to overcome the language barrier through sign language was some of the best I've ever seen.

We crawled to the spot where I would shoot. Cleverly, Shirinbek arranged four rocks in the same pattern the rams were lying in and then pointed to the one that was the biggest. This took all the guesswork out; in fact, he couldn't be clearer. This allowed me to focus on shooting. As I estimated the range at 172 yards—which was better than I could have imagined—I thought, *This is really going to happen.* I was about to realize every sheep hunter's dream of the Holy Grail.

I squeezed the trigger on the bedded ram and heard the *wump* sound of a well-placed shot right behind the front shoulder. At the sound of the shot, the rams exploded into flight. Amazingly, my ram got up and started running after the others. He required two more shots to put him down for good. I have never seen sheep as tough as these. They are more like mountain goats in their ability to take lead.

A universal celebration ensued; high fives and bear hugs were exchanged. Everyone knew I had just harvested the trophy of a lifetime. As I walked up to my prize, there was no ground shrinkage. In fact, quite the opposite happened. The ram started to grow and grow. I looked at him and thought, *If that is what a 57-inch ram looks like, then I've underestimated the true size of these animals.* I stood in awe for about ten minutes before even touching him. I knew I had harvested a truly great animal.

We spent the next half-hour taking pictures and talking about the stalk, the trophy, and the entire experience. Finally I couldn't take it any more; I had to put a tape on this ram. He measured more than 60 inches on the long side and 59⅝ inches on the short side.

Unquenchable Spirit

My tape only went to 60 inches. I love it when a guide's mistake on estimating length works out in my favor; however, I would have been just as happy if the ram had measured 55 inches. He was everything I ever dreamed of in a Marco Polo ram, and more.

Now the really hard work began. We had approximately four hundred pounds of ram to process. Backpacks are a rarity in this part of the world. We had the one I brought with me. I envisioned the horns, cape, and one quarter would all go in the pack. I was wrong. These people had survived a long time without my backpack.

Shavkat informed me they would "carefully" drag the ram across the hill to the nearest snow patch where they would "toboggan" it down the 2,500-foot elevation drop. To say I was a little reluctant about this idea would be an understatement. At first I checked the ram often for hair slippage, but their tried-and-true method worked amazingly well. By the end of the day, we had loaded the sheep, still entirely whole, guts and all, in the Jeep and headed for camp.

We caped him out for a life-size mount, which I felt only fitting for such a magnificent trophy. A shoulder mount wouldn't do him justice. Nothing went to waste. They even scooped out the contents of his stomach. I was scared to ask what they did with it, but lunches for the next couple of days were soup, and they were quite good, spiced to perfection. I would rather not know what I was eating, so I didn't ask.

Since I had harvested the ram on the second day of a ten-day hunt, we spent the next three days hunting for ibex, but I saw nothing bigger than what I had harvested in Kyrgyzstan the year before. Shooting anything after my great ram would have seemed anticlimactic.

The elation of taking such a magnificent Marco Polo ram put me in a great frame of mind. I thoroughly enjoyed the camp, the food, the hiking, exploring the countryside, and watching Afghani people across the river loading their camels. When it was time to go, I felt I was saying good-bye to old friends as I bade Shirinbek, Shakar and Shavkat farewell.

The Holy Grail

Rob with his Marco Polo ram, the pinnacle of achievement from twenty-five years of seeking adventure.

Unquenchable Spirit

It took seven hours through a blinding blizzard and fighting four-foot snowdrifts to make the journey to Khorog. Finally, I was on the long trek back to Dushanbe. The trip only took a speedy thirteen hours, in part because the non-English-speaking driver kept his wallet above the steering wheel and liberally greased the palms of the officials at every military checkpoint, expediting our quick clearance. I met up with Bryan Martin the next day, who had just arrived from Kyrgyzstan after seven successful hunts there. He was elated to see my beautiful 60-inch-plus ram and to hear the story of my hunt.

The hunt had gone so smoothly, that now, once again in the traveling phase and at the mercy of airport officials and airlines with their seemingly constantly changing regulations, I waited for the snag. Lost luggage I could have lived with, but my trophy? Everything went without a glitch; in fact, the return trip was so effortless that I am still in a state of shock.

And every time I look at those magnificently curled horns in my living room in a town so small it barely makes the map, I feel the thrill anew. How did a guy like me end up attaining the Holy Grail?